Additional Exercises for

Successful
College
Writing

Additional Exercises for

Successful College Writing

Fourth Edition

SKILLS · STRATEGIES · LEARNING STYLES

Carolyn Lengel

HUNTER COLLEGE

Jess Carroll

MONTANA STATE UNIVERSITY IN BOZEMAN

BEDFORD / ST. MARTIN'S
Boston ◆ **New York**

Manufactured in the United States of America.

4 3 2 1 0 9
f e d c b a

For information, write: Bedford/St. Martin's, 75 Arlington Street, Boston, MA 02116   (617-399-4000)

ISBN-10: 0-312-53283-0

ISBN-13: 978-0-312-53283-3

Preface

These additional exercises for *Successful College Writing* are meant to be a student's self-tutorial. Each exercise set includes clear instructions, and all sentence exercises include a hand-corrected example. The exercises are double-spaced to make revision easier. Answers and suggested responses are included in the answer key in the back of the booklet, making it easy for you to check your own work. Also included is a writing assessment, Appendix A, which will help you and your instructor determine aspects of your writing that you need to improve.

The exercises cover topics from Chapter 6, "Drafting an Essay" (Exercises P.1, P.2, and so on), Chapter 9, "Editing Sentences and Words" (Exercises E.1, E.2, and so on), and Part 7, "Handbook: Writing Problems and How to Correct Them" (the exercise numbers correspond to chapters in the handbook). They provide opportunities for you to practice crafting paragraphs, editing for sentence style and word choice, identifying parts of speech, and editing sentences for problems with grammar, punctuation, and mechanics. Also included is a section on ESL troublespots.

Interactive versions of these exercises and additional practices are also available online. Visit http://www.bedfordstmartins.com/exercisecentral to access Exercise Central—Bedford/St. Martin's extensive electronic exercise bank.

Contents

PARAGRAPHS

Name _____ Date _____ Section _____

Exercise P.1 Topic Sentences

For help with this exercise, see Chapter 5 in *Successful College Writing*.

Read the following sentences and determine which make effective topic sentences and which make poor or unfocused topic sentences. If the topic sentence is effective, write effective. If the topic sentence is poor or unfocused, rewrite the sentence so that it is an effective topic sentence for a paragraph.

EXAMPLE:

➤ Many Americans spend more than they earn.

The widespread availability of credit cards allows many Americans to spend more

than they earn and accumulate a lot of high-interest debt.

1. Americans often wonder why the French don't get fat.

   _____

   _____

2. Every Thursday, I take my dog Buster to the children's hospital to visit the patients.

   _____

   _____

3. The Boston Marathon is a very tough race that requires a lot of training.

   _____

   _____

4. People who choose high-stress jobs they do not enjoy in order to make a lot of money often find themselves unhappy and unsatisfied later in life.

   _____

   _____

5. Online dating is a dangerous way to meet people.

   _____

   _____

6. In the interest of closing the digital divide, several companies are currently developing inexpensive laptops to distribute to underprivileged school-children around the world.

_____

_____

7. Celebrities are given far too much attention in our culture.

_____

_____

8. Many Hollywood movies stereotype minorities and perpetuate limited, biased views of them.

_____

_____

9. I can no longer afford to visit national parks on my summer vacations because it's too expensive.

_____

_____

10. Because many drugs that children now take for depression and other mental illnesses have not been tested on children, we have no way of knowing whether their benefits outweigh their possible side effects.

_____

_____

Exercise P.2 Topic Sentences

Each of the following paragraphs contains only supporting sentences. The paragraph may also contain a transitional sentence. Write an appropriate topic sentence in the space provided within each paragraph. (The thesis of the essay from which the paragraph is taken is provided for you.)

For help with this exercise, see Chapter 5 in *Successful College Writing*.

1. **Thesis:** A balanced-budget amendment to the U.S. Constitution is unnecessary and inappropriate.

    Proponents like to argue that a balanced-budget amendment would force the government to be more frugal, like ordinary citizens. _____

    _____

    If everyone who bought a house had to come up with the full price in cash, very few Americans would be homeowners. The same is true of cars, which are often financed through banks or automobile companies. Most people can't come up with $40,000 for a new sport-utility vehicle, so to get one, they borrow. In addition, keeping up with the Joneses is a time-honored tradition in this country. If our neighbors have a pool, we want a pool, too — and how do we pay for it? We use loans, credit cards, or other buy-now-pay-later financing.

2. **Thesis:** The lifestyle that many Americans enjoy contributes to poor health.

    Medical science has proved that people need exercise if they are to look and feel their best. _____

    _____

    Many people's parents and grandparents earned a living through physical labor. Today, most workers in this country don't have to exert themselves. In the past, people had to leave the house for entertainment. Now everyone has a television and a remote control, so no one has to get off the couch. When modern Americans do go out, they almost always drive to their destinations. Then, when they arrive, convenient parking and the increasing availability of elevators ensure that people walk no more than a few steps unless they choose to exert themselves.

3. **Thesis:** Parents should give their children the best possible start in life.

A child is capable of hearing sounds even before it is born. By the time a fetus is a few months old, it can respond to noises it hears. At birth, babies know the sound of their mothers' voices. But voices are not the only sounds infants can distinguish. Many parents also tell anecdotes about their children recognizing music that the parents played frequently before the children were born. While scientists do not yet know much about the way human brains learn before birth, they do know that when schoolchildren listen to music, especially classical music, their mathematical abilities often improve. Some neurologists speculate that exposure to music might affect the developing brain of a fetus as well. _____

_____

_____

Name _____ Date _____ Section _____

Exercise P.3 Relevant Details

For help with this exercise, see Chapter 5 in *Successful College Writing*.

In each of the following paragraphs, underline any sentences containing details that do not support the topic sentence.

1.   (1) The long and interesting history of pinball spans a period from ancient times to the present. (2) The first game on record that can be considered an ancestor of modern pinball was an ancient Greek sport in which players rolled balls down a hill, trying to drop them in holes. (3) During the Renaissance, a tabletop version of the game, then called *bagatelle,* was invented. (4) A stick propelled the bagatelle balls up a tilted board filled with holes. (5) Interestingly, the word *bagatelle* can also refer to a short poem or piece of music. (6) In 1930, David Gottlieb designed a bagatelle board with a plunger, and modern pinball was born. (7) Later improvements included the "tilt" alarm, in 1933, and bumpers, in 1936. (8) Pinball was outlawed in some places during World War II because authorities likened it to gambling. (9) When the flipper was added to the game in 1947, pinball became more decidedly a game of skill, and eventually it became a legal, if not always reputable, sport across the country. (10) However, video games are probably more popular than pinball today.

2.   (1) Although big-budget disaster movies have depicted this scenario, the possibility that a meteor will strike the earth and cause significant damage and loss of human life is very remote. (2) Most meteors are relatively small, some (known as *micrometeors*) only the size of a grain of rice. (3) These meteors burn up as soon as they enter the earth's atmosphere. (4) According to folklore, when observers see one of these "shooting stars," they should make a wish. (5) Vaporized matter from burned-out meteors adds about ten tons to the mass of the earth every day. (6) About 150 meteors per year actually do survive the trip to earth and strike it. (7) Most of these do no damage even if they hit a spot where people live. (8) Since most of the earth is covered with water, however, meteors are much more likely to land in the ocean.

(9) Scientists estimate that a deadly meteor strike—one large enough to kill a hundred people and positioned to strike a populated area—would occur no more often than every 100,000 years, so the average person doesn't need to worry much about such an event.

3.   (1) Working on a custom cutting crew is a difficult way to make a living, and it's getting harder all the time. (2) First of all, custom cutters—traveling workers who supply the machinery and labor to harvest farmers' crops as they ripen—are able to work only seasonally. (3) Running a family farm has never been easy. (4) Grain crops in the South begin to ripen in the spring, and cutting crews follow the harvest north as the weather warms throughout the summer; when the harvest is finished in August, the work is over for the year. (5) Nor is custom cutting an easy task: The work is hot, dirty, and difficult, and the hours are long. (6) To make matters worse, the machines needed to harvest grain are very expensive, so start-up costs for a custom cutting crew are prohibitive. (7) The expense of new harvesting machines, called combines, and the need to get the harvest in as quickly as possible are major reasons farmers hire custom cutters rather than doing the work themselves. (8) In addition, the amount of work available, and the wages to be earned from it, depend on the success of the farmer's crop. (9) This success, in turn, is dependent on factors beyond human control, such as the weather. (10) Finally, as small farmers become an increasingly rare breed, there is less and less need for custom cutting.

Exercise P.4 Paragraph Unity

Read through the following paragraphs and decide whether the paragraph is unified or not unified. If the paragraph is unified, write *unified* on the line following the paragraph. If the paragraph is not unified, write *not unified* and then eliminate the sentences that are off-topic.

For help with this exercise, see Chapter 5 in *Successful College Writing.*

EXAMPLE:

➤ Most people believe that you can never drink too much water, but studies are now showing that drinking too much water can be very dangerous to your health. In fact, being overhydrated is much more dangerous than being dehydrated. ~~I try to drink eight glasses of water a day.~~ Overhydrating reduces the sodium levels in your blood and can cause confusion, seizures, and even death. ~~On very hot days, many people are in danger of becoming dehydrated. Dehydration is one of the factors that can contribute to heat stroke.~~ Athletes are actually better off waiting until they are thirsty and drinking only what their bodies can absorb.

_____*not unified*_____

1.   One alternative to drugs for treating depression is the controversial Eye Movement Desensitization and Reprocessing or EMDR. This treatment is particularly useful for people who are depressed as a result of a traumatic event. Prozac is also useful for treating depression. For those who don't respond to Prozac, doctors often recommend Zoloft. In an EMDR session, the therapist makes hand motions or flashes a light in front of the patient's face while he or she talks about an upsetting experience. People who have experienced trauma often need a lot of support. Many people have found this nontraditional therapy to be very helpful in processing their experiences, though no one knows for sure why EMDR works. _____

2.   The advertisements that now appear before the movie are not effective because they only make moviegoers irritable. Coke is one of the most frequently advertised products and one of the most recognized American brands. People often drink Coke or other soft drinks when they go to the

movies. Ads take away from the otherwise enjoyable experience of seeing a movie in the theater. These days, you have to sit through ten minutes of commercials before the previews start. Advertisers also use product placement as a way to increase their product's visibility. By the time the movie begins, you may already have been in your seat for half an hour. Because of this inconvenience, people may decide that it's worthwhile to wait for the DVD and skip the ads. Movie-theater owners would be wise to remember their paying audience and reconsider this partnership with advertisers. _____

3.   Contrary to what a person might expect, training to become a clown takes a lot of hard work and dedication. Many clowns-in-training spend significant amounts of time learning their art at one of the many clown schools around the world. These schools teach gesture, expression, and movement in addition to make-up technique and costume design. Some schools specialize in training certain types of clowns, like the "character" clown or the "white-face" clown, and require that students focus on one style of clowning. In addition to choosing a focus and going to school, clowns must be disciplined in order to remain playful, curious, and physically limber. Goofiness is not as easy as it looks. _____

4.   One of America's most well known and important court cases is the Scopes "Monkey Trial." Students should learn their country's history at an early age. Knowing the past can help us predict the future. In 1925, John Scopes, a high school biology teacher, was charged with violating state law by teaching the theory of evolution to his students. He believed he was teaching an important scientific theory, but others believed that evolution contradicted the story of creation told in the Bible. The trial became famous because so many people had such strong feelings on both sides. It has also remained relevant because we haven't come to a definitive conclusion about which ideas students should or should not learn in school. There are many

old conflicts that remain unresolved. For instance, people have been arguing for decades over whether or not abortion should be legal.

_____

5.   More animal shelters should adopt a "no kill" policy. Controlling the stray animal population by euthanizing is not the best solution. Killing unwanted pets solves the problem of overpopulation only temporarily, and it creates a bigger problem because it teaches people that animals are disposable. Many people don't consider snakes, iguanas, and other reptiles as pets. When I was seven, I adopted a snake from our local shelter, and he turned out to be a wonderful pet. We need to learn to be kinder and more responsible when it comes to animals. We need to have pets fixed and accept them even when they have special needs. We need to accept humans with special needs as well. Many of the animals in shelters are there because they were neglected or mistreated. If we change our own behavior, fewer animals will end up abused and unwanted. _____

6.   Buying a house is not always a good investment. People who sell their houses after owning them for only a couple of years often lose money. Spending money on a computer is not always a good investment either. Computers lose their value very quickly. Unless the buyer uses the computer for work, money spent on a computer is money lost. People who don't buy enough insurance for their homes can lose money if there is a fire, flood, or other disaster. Houses also require a lot of maintenance. When people sell their houses, often they find it difficult to make back the money they spent fixing up the house. Sometimes people are better off investing their money in something that does not cost so much. _____

7.   Keeping up with all the new developments in communications technology has become nearly impossible. Just knowing what is available takes many hours of research. A new cell phone with better reception and more features may be convenient in the long run, but finding out about it can be time-

consuming and inconvenient. It's important to draw a line somewhere to avoid becoming overwhelmed by all the new technology. When drawing the line, it's often best to let necessity be your guide. _____

8. Hilary Swank is a positive role model for young actresses. Jennifer Lopez is a good role model for future dancers and singers. Many girls look up to their mothers as well. Unlike many successful women in the movie industry, Swank is not afraid to challenge herself when choosing roles. In both *Boys Don't Cry* and *Million Dollar Baby,* Swank focuses not on looking pretty but on inhabiting her characters and their difficult lives. Her determination and willingness to take these risks may come in part from her background. She was not born into a rich or privileged family and, like some of the characters she plays, has had to work very hard to achieve her goals. Many famous people have rough starts. Jennifer Lopez did not come from a rich family. It's important for young girls to see a successful movie star who has dedication, integrity, and a real love of acting. _____

Name _____ Date _____ Section _____

Exercise P.5 Specific Details

Rewrite each of the following vague, general paragraphs to include concrete, specific details. You may add new information and new sentences.

For help with this exercise, see Chapter 5 in *Successful College Writing*.

1.   A family gathering is supposed to be a happy occasion, but it may not be. Getting together for a family event can produce negative emotions just as often as positive ones. Just because people are related to each other doesn't mean they understand or like each other especially well. People usually try to be on their best behavior, but the strain of trying to be nice can make them tense. At a big gathering, there are bound to be relatives present who don't get along. Finally, if one of them snaps and an argument ensues, everyone else has bad feelings about the conflict.

2.   A movie can't be good unless all of the pieces come together successfully. Sometimes I see a film and think that the concept is great, but the script is just awful. I've seen other films with good scripts but bad acting. Then there are times when the pace is all wrong, and I wonder what the director was thinking. The music, too, can make or break a film. With so many variables, it's a wonder that any good movies exist. They do, of course; I could name two or three recent ones that did almost everything right.

3.   Children should have a pet. Taking care of a pet is a good experience for any child. For one thing, having a pet teaches children to assume responsibility. Additionally, pet care can teach children about loving and protecting a crea-ture weaker than themselves. Both of these lessons are valuable for a child. Finally, a pet returns affection and can actually make a child's life happier. Most adults who had a pet in childhood believe that it was a positive experience.

For help with this exercise, see Chapter 5 in *Successful College Writing*.

Exercise P.6 Paragraph Development

Read the following paragraphs and decide whether they are well developed or underdeveloped. On the line after each paragraph write *well developed* if the paragraph is well developed and *underdeveloped* if it is underdeveloped. If you determine that the paragraph is underdeveloped, write three questions or suggestions that might help the writer develop his or her ideas more fully.

EXAMPLES:

➤   The number of children suffering from asthma has reached epidemic proportions over the last two decades. According to the Centers for Disease Control, over 9 million American children have been diagnosed with this chronic respiratory disease. Several factors have been blamed for this growing problem, though no clear cause is known. Air pollutants, such as ozone and sulfur dioxide, may play a role in the development of asthma. Indoor pollutants, such dust mites, molds, animal dander, and tobacco smoke, may play an even bigger role. Some experts believe that the increased incidence of asthma is the direct result of children spending more time indoors exposed to these allergens. Whatever the cause, it is clear that children's developing lungs are particularly at risk. Until we know how to stop the epidemic completely, the best we can do is try to minimize exposure to dangerous environments and treat the life-threatening symptoms aggressively.

_____ *well developed* _____

1. _____ *If the paragraph is well developed, leave these lines blank.* _____

2. _____

3. _____

➤   Many developing countries are finding it easier to join the developed world by way of technological leapfrogging. Leapfrogging helps developing countries improve their technologies. This entails skipping the intermediate steps of technological development and starting instead with the most current technologies. For instance, an area that has never had phone service might decide it's more efficient to build cell phone towers rather than old-fashioned phone lines. Other areas might decide to install a wi-fi Internet connection, rather than running telephone lines for dial-up service. There are problems with leapfrogging, too, of course. It isn't the right solution for every agricultural economy looking to get up to speed. Sometimes, the old tried-and-true technologies have advantages.

_____ *underdeveloped* _____

1. _Which countries are finding success with leapfrogging?_

2. _Identify several reasons why a country might choose to leapfrog._

3. _Describe a situation in which leapfrogging would not be advisable and explain why not._

1.   Children's museums are growing faster than any other kind of museum in the country. Parents like museums where their children are allowed to touch and interact with the exhibits. Other museums rely on seeing objects and reading information, which can become tiresome for children. Children's museums are usually educational as well. They introduce kids to many different things, as well as allowing them a fun, safe place to play. Museums are a great place for children to learn about anatomy, geology, and astronomy. Some of the best children's museums are in big cities like Boston and Cleveland. It's interesting that children's museums are growing faster than natural history museums or aquariums, places that also specialize in children's exhibits.

_____

1. _____

2. _____

3. _____

2.   Though the methods have improved somewhat over the last century, coal mining is still a very dangerous way to make a living. Coal miners are more likely to die on the job than workers in nearly any other occupation, the obvious exception being soldiers in the military. Even the well-organized coal miners' union cannot protect workers from some of the industry's unavoidable hazards. Some people wonder why anyone would do this kind of work. Many people work in coal mines because it's what their fathers and their fathers' fathers did. It's tradition. Some would even argue that the danger of the job is part of the coal miner's tradition. Tradition or not, the government should do more to protect workers from society's necessary but hazardous jobs.

_____

1. _____

2. _____

3. _____

3.   With her album _Little Sparrow,_ Dolly Parton broke away from modern country and successfully embraced "newgrass" music. In contrast with

country's slick and often electric sound, this unique style offers a contemporary spin on traditional bluegrass. Newgrass is old-time bluegrass, with its stringed instruments and tight harmonies, that has been influenced by the sounds of jazz, country, rock, and pop. Parton embraces this style on *Little Sparrow* by returning to some of the Appalachian songs of her childhood and giving them a slightly cleaner, more rehearsed, modern feel. In addition, she takes songs that are not in the least bluegrassy, like "I Get a Kick Out of You" and "Shine," and lends them the harmonies and twang of bluegrass. Parton was rewarded for her beautiful musical blending on *Little Sparrow* with a 2001 Grammy Award.

_____

1. _____

2. _____

3. _____

4.   Soap making is a fun and fascinating process. People have been making soap in one way or another for thousands of years. Because most people these days buy their soap at the store, very few of us know how soap is made. In fact, the process hasn't changed much over the years. The basic principles are the same. Most soaps are made by combining two or three things that are easy to get. By adding a few extra ingredients like eggs, you can even make a decent shampoo. It's strange to think that egg could be used to clean your hair. Unfortunately, soap making has gained a somewhat sinister reputation because of movies like *Fight Club*. This reputation is completely undeserved, as any investigation into the subject and the product would quickly reveal. Perhaps if more people took the time to learn the how to make soap, they would realize how enjoyable and useful it can be.

_____

1. _____

2. _____

3. _____

5.   It is unlikely that any baseball team will ever match the comeback that the Boston Red Sox achieved in the 2004 American League Championship Series. Behind three games to zero, the Red Sox came back to win four straight games and beat the seemingly unbeatable New York Yankees. No team in the history of baseball had ever come back from being three games behind to win a postseason series. The fact that the Red Sox achieved this while playing their archrivals only made the victory more memorable. What

most baseball fans will remember most, though, is how the Red Sox rode the wave of their playoff comeback. They went on to win the World Series for the first time in eighty-six years. That's a comeback story that will be hard to beat.

_____

1. _____

2. _____

3. _____

6.   Recently, political discourse has gotten so ugly that some Americans have taken to calling it the "inCivil War." YourDictionary.com even named "inCivility" the Word of the Year last year. The problem with incivility is that it usually sparks a chain reaction. The chain reaction leads to an escalation of the conflict, making mountains out of molehills. People have a difficult time responding politely to uncivil comments and thus spark more uncivil comments. As a result, public discourse has taken on a shrill, adversarial tone. This tone is not constructive and just results in more conflict. Unfortunately, we seem to pay more attention to those speakers who are confrontational and offensive.

_____

1. _____

2. _____

3. _____

7.   "The New Black" may be the most overused phrase in the fashion industry. Every color, at one point or another, has taken its turn being the new black. Even black has been the new black. The question that no one seems to be asking is, Why does black need to be replaced, anyway? Black is for more than just funerals. Urban working women, in particular, have found black to be very useful. They have discovered that wearing black is a good way to look formal and chic without a lot of effort. Also, owning a lot of black clothes reduces the amount of time a person has to spend worrying about whether or not her clothes match.

_____

1. _____

2. _____

3. _____

8.   Teenagers who ride their skateboards on city sidewalks create a hazard for everyone. Many passersby are injured every year by skateboarders who are riding in prohibited areas and/or riding too fast. I know several people who have collided or nearly collided with a skateboarder in a pedestrian zone. This can be very dangerous. Several of these incidents resulted in minor injuries to both the skateboarder and the pedestrian. Often, skateboarders are looking to practice their skills and are not simply trying to get from one point to another. They should find other places to practice so that the sidewalks are safe for the rest of us.

---

1. _____

2. _____

3. _____

Exercise P.7 Transitions and Repeated Words

Add transitions, repeat key words, or add synonyms as necessary to make the following paragraphs coherent and connected.

For help with this exercise, see Chapter 5 in *Successful College Writing*.

1.   The French may still have the international reputation of being the people most interested in gourmet food. Americans are quickly gaining an interest in gourmet food. "American food" meant fast foods like hamburgers and hot dogs. People around the world still associate these foods with American culture. U.S. food lovers may seek out the best burgers, fries, and barbecue foods. They also want to sample foods from ethnic cultures within the United States and other countries. People want the best of what American produce has to offer and will go far to find fresh, local ingredients that are expertly prepared.

2.   Modern conceptions of timekeeping owe a lot to the ancient Babylonians. The ancient Babylonians gave people today the twelve-month year, the twenty-four-hour day, the sixty-minute hour, and the sixty-second minute. The number *twelve* was significant to the ancient Babylonians. They noticed that there were usually twelve full moons in a year. The Babylonian calendar contained twelve months of thirty days each. Five days were left over each year; every six years they had to add an extra month to the year. They divided the day and night into twelve hours each. The number *sixty* was important to the Babylonians. The number *sixty* can be evenly divided by many integers —two, three, four, five, six, ten, twelve, fifteen, twenty, and thirty. They divided each hour into sixty minutes and each minute into sixty seconds. The Romans changed the length of some Babylonian months from thirty to thirty-one or twenty-eight days. The Babylonians' other time measurements survive to this day.

3.   The Restoration period in England, which began with the return of the monarchy in 1660, was marked by the kind of public behavior on the part of aristocrats and courtiers that would still provoke a shocked reaction today.

King Charles II served as the model of moral — or immoral — behavior for members of his court. There were no children by his wife. He had a large number of children by his several mistresses. Young male courtiers boasted of numerous love affairs. Court poets and dramatists composed bawdy, amoral literary works. Many contained words and suggestions that even modern newspapers would not print. The public loved to attend performances of plays. Simply being seen at a theater could give a person a questionable reputation. The clergy and other representatives of moral authority protested the literary, theatrical, and personal misbehavior of the aristocrats. Bawdiness became less fashionable. A much more conservative age followed the Restoration.

Exercise P.8 Outlining

For help with this exercise, see Chapter 5 in *Successful College Writing.*

Read through the partially completed outline below. Then read through the list of missing notes/phrases that follow. Identify which note or phrase goes in which blank in order to best complete the outline. There are ten phrases and ten blanks, so you will need to use all ten phrases in order to complete the outline.

Title	**More Than Just a Place to Sleep**
Introduction	*Thesis:* Though it requires some preparation and adaptability, staying at a traditional Japanese hotel, or *ryokan,* is an enjoyable and worthwhile way for a Western visitor to learn about Japanese culture.
Body Paragraph 1	Finding a *ryokan*

- _____

- determine your price range

- _____

- make advance reservations

Body Paragraph 2 Apparel etiquette in a *ryokan*

- take off your shoes when you enter the *ryokan* and put on slippers

- _____

- wear *geta* (wooden clogs) if you stroll around the *ryokan* grounds

- _____

- _____

- wear a *tanzen* (outer robe) over your *yukata* if you get cold

Body Paragraph 3 Japanese bath etiquette

- the Japanese often bathe before dinner

- in changing room, put *yukata* in basket provided

- _____

- do not drain the water from the tub when finished

- _____

Body Paragraph 4   Engaging with your host or hosts

- learn a few key phrases in Japanese
- ask about the building and garden
- _____

Body Paragraph 5   A day in the life of a different culture

- _____
- enjoy the serenity of life without television
- try meditating
- _____

Conclusion   While staying in a familiar Western-style hotel might feel easier, after a night or two in a *ryokan* you'll find yourself more mindful of Japanese culture and traditions, and remarkably refreshed.

1. be willing to try unusual breakfast foods, like cold squid and miso soup
2. decide how formal or informal a *ryokan* you'd like
3. take off the slippers when walking on the tatami mats
4. wear your *yukata* (robe provided by the *ryokan*) when in the *ryokan*
5. ask about the best sights to see in their town
6. locate Web sites that list *ryokans*
7. *yukatas* should be worn left side over right; right side over left is for funerals
8. dry yourself thoroughly before returning to the changing room
9. wash yourself in the bathing area using shower or basin before entering the public bath
10. adjust to the firmness of a futon mattress

EDITING SENTENCES AND WORDS

Name _____   Date _____   Section _____

Exercise E.1 Wordy Sentences

Revise the following sentences to make them as concise as possible.

For help with this exercise, see Chapter 7 in *Successful College Writing*.

EXAMPLE:

➤ ~~At some point in time~~ Ẽvery year, a list of the most popular names ~~for children~~ in the United States is published. *[children's inserted above]*

1. It seems likely that American parents choose really carefully when naming their children.

2. Making comparisons between popular names of today and the names that were popular in the past shows how much our ideas about naming children have changed.

3. The names chosen for girls have undergone the most changes.

4. Forty years ago, the majority of baby girls received names that sounded traditional rather than being considered unusual.

5. Some of the older names gradually became less popular over a period of time, and newer names, like Jennifer, now a perennial favorite year after year, took their place.

6. In these modern times, parents often give their daughters names that were once considered masculine, like Sidney or Taylor.

7. It is also true that some parents try to make their daughters' names seem quite unusual by spelling a traditional name in a way that is not considered traditional.

8. Boys' names, however, have really changed very little and not as noticeably.

9. For decades the most popular of the names parents have given to boys has been Michael.

10. It may perhaps be true, as the results of a recent poll suggest, that parents think having an unusual name is helpful to girls and having an unusual name is harmful to boys.

For help with this exercise, see Chapter 7 in *Successful College Writing*.

Exercise E.2 Combining Sentences

Combine each of the following pairs of sentences to create a compound or complex sentence.

EXAMPLE:

➤ Many people start smoking as teenagers, ~~They~~ think it makes them look mature.
(because they)

1. Nicotine is an ingredient in cigarettes. It is an addictive drug.

2. No smoker sets out to become addicted to cigarettes. Most people have difficulty stopping once they start smoking.

3. Movies can affect young people profoundly. Movies often portray smokers as glamorous and sexy.

4. Many thirty-year-old people do not smoke. They are unlikely to begin smoking.

5. The tobacco companies need new customers. They are more apt to find such customers among the younger generations.

6. Some teenagers take up smoking. They don't consider the possible consequences.

7. The Joe Camel cartoon advertisements were controversial. Cartoons often appeal to children.

8. The Joe Camel advertising campaign was withdrawn. New restrictions have been placed on tobacco ads.

9. Smoking can be unsightly and unhealthy. It is legal.

10. The number of lawsuits against tobacco companies has risen recently. Families have argued that tobacco companies are to blame for the deaths of their loved ones.

Name _____ Date _____ Section _____

Exercise E.3 Adding Modifiers

For help with this exercise, see Chapter 7 in *Successful College Writing*.

Revise each sentence by adding the modifiers in any appropriate place.

EXAMPLE:

➤ Scientists have studied criminal behavior.
[*Modifiers:* hoping to find ways to prevent crime; for many years]
Revised: For many years, scientists have studied criminal behavior, hoping to find ways to prevent crime.

1. Criminal tendencies were thought to be related to physical traits. [*Modifiers:* in the nineteenth century; mistakenly]

2. Phrenologists mapped the human head. [*Modifiers:* who studied bumps on the skull; for antisocial protrusions]

3. They hoped. [*Modifiers:* before crimes occurred; that they could identify potential criminals]

4. Other researchers measured the proportions of the human head. [*Modifiers:* followers of a pseudoscience called craniometry; carefully recording their findings]

5. Craniometrists inferred conclusions. [*Modifiers:* using measurements of skull circumference; about brain size and intelligence as well as criminality]

6. These scientists' studies were fatally flawed. [*Modifiers:* from the beginning; because they found what they expected to find]

7. Researchers have been focusing on psychology. [*Modifiers:* since these "sciences" fell out of favor in the mid-twentieth century; as a means of understanding criminal actions]

8. The debate continues. [*Modifiers:* over which influence is stronger, heredity or environment; among social scientists]

9. The issue may never be resolved. [*Modifiers:* one of the key controversies among scientists; to everyone's satisfaction]

10. Important questions generate useful research. [*Modifiers:* In scientific inquiry; as well as theories that are later discredited; however]

Exercise E.4 Parallelism

Correct any errors in parallelism in the following sentences.

For help with this exercise, see Chapter 7 in *Successful College Writing.*

EXAMPLE:

➤ Americans should investigate renewable energy sources, including solar heat and
~~power from the wind.~~ *wind power.*
  ^

1. The United States uses large amounts of energy, is depending heavily on oil, and imports much of that oil.

2. Burning oil for energy pollutes the air, destroys an irreplaceable commodity, and is wasting resources.

3. During the 1970s, an embargo made oil expensive and it was not easy to get.

4. The oil crisis led to a wider interest in alternative energy sources that would be renewable, environmentally sound, and would cost less than oil.

5. Some new homes used solar heating, although it was expensive to install and despite its being still relatively untested.

6. Many Americans expected electric cars to be perfected and that they would be widely available by the end of the twentieth century.

7. Instead, the embargo ended, the cost of oil dropped, and there were declining gasoline prices.

8. At the same time, money to invent alternative energy technologies, to develop new products, and for marketing the products dried up.

9. Scientists and those who study the environment hope that there will be plentiful renewable energy sources someday.

10. It would be better to have alternative energy possibilities soon than waiting for the world's oil reserves to run dry.

For help with this exercise, see Chapter 7 in *Successful College Writing*.

Exercise E.5 Strong, Active Verbs

Revise the following sentences by using strong, active verbs.

EXAMPLE:
➤ ~~There are major fashion shows~~ *Fashion designers parade their wares* every year in cities like Paris, Milan, and New York.

1. Big crowds are drawn to annual "Fashion Week" events in American and European cities.

2. Shows by new and established designers are attended by photographers, journalists, models, and celebrities.

3. Many people in the audience have model-thin bodies and photogenic faces.

4. Often, *haute couture* shows with their expensive, trend-setting fashions are the highlight of the event.

5. *Haute couture* garments are not expected to be worn by ordinary people.

6. *Haute couture* creations are frequently more like works of art than mere outfits.

7. Such clothing can be worn in public only by runway models.

8. Other people seem ridiculous in *haute couture* clothes.

9. Clothes can be draped more easily on models who have very thin bodies.

10. Some people are more impressed by the spectacle than by the clothes.

Exercise E.6 Word Choice

Edit the following paragraph for appropriate diction and connotation.

For help with this exercise, see Chapter 7 in *Successful College Writing*.

EXAMPLE:

➤ From middle-class to ~~rich~~ *wealthy* American communities, the disease known as anorexia is on the rise.

Americans have recently had their noses rubbed in the fact that anorexia nervosa, a disease of self-starvation, is becoming more widespread. Anorexia sufferers are overwhelmingly made up of teenage girls and young women. Most of them are white and come from middle-class or upper-class families. They are also usually sharp. They seem to other people to have pretty much every advantage. Their families and comrades ordinarily have a rough time comprehending why they will not eat. Because anorexia is a psychological disorder, the sufferers themselves may not catch on to what caused the onset of their illness. Anorexics have a weird body image. They often believe they are totally overweight unless they are dangerously slender. The disease is notoriously difficult to treat, even if the patient tries to go along with her doctors.

For help with this exercise, see Chapter 7 in *Successful College Writing*.

Exercise E.7 Concrete, Specific Detail

Revise the following sentences by adding concrete, specific details.

EXAMPLE:

➤ Learning about ~~standardized tests~~ may improve a student's performance on them.
the types of questions featured on standardized tests such as the SAT and ACT

1. Every year, a large number of high school students take standardized tests.

2. A good test score can help a student.

3. Test-preparation courses are becoming popular.

4. These courses are expensive.

5. Experts disagree about the value of such courses.

6. Many students get better scores after taking a course.

7. The amount of improvement is not always significant.

8. Opponents argue that the courses are unfair.

9. Others say that the courses make no real difference.

10. Many people continue to pay for test preparation.

Exercise E.8 Figures of Speech

Edit the following sentences to eliminate clichéd words and expressions.

For help with this exercise, see Chapter 7 in *Successful College Writing*.

EXAMPLE:

marathon runner heading uphill

➤ A woman athlete may have to work like a ~~mule~~ to earn her share of recognition.

1. For generations, women were considered to be delicate flowers too fragile for sports.

2. Many people thought that women would die like an old tree if they were too physically active.

3. Even though these mistaken beliefs were widespread, women athletes have moved forward by leaps and bounds.

4. Individual women athletes, like the track and golf star Babe Didrikson Zaharias, had to be as strong as an ox.

5. During World War II, a women's baseball league drew spectators like a snake in the grass when a shortage of male players depleted men's teams.

6. The end of the war nipped the women's league in the bud.

7. The American women's movement of the 1970s was the dawn of a new era for women in sports.

8. A "battle of the sexes" took place in tennis during that decade, when Billie Jean King, a star female player, made Bobby Riggs, an avowed "male chauvinist" who had challenged her, look as weak as the ocean tides.

9. In the following decades, some individual women became sports heroes, like Florence Griffith Joyner, who could run like the wind.

10. Finally, in the 1990s, the popularity of women's basketball and soccer spread like a disease in a crowded city.

For help with this
exercise, see
Chapter 7 in
*Successful College
Writing.*

Exercise E.9 Weak Verb/Noun Combinations

Edit the following sentences to eliminate weak verb/noun combinations.

EXAMPLE:

➤ For many years, mentally ill people were ~~given the same treatment~~ as criminals.
   treated the same

1. The treatment of mental illness has been troublesome to societies throughout history.

2. A thousand years ago, observers thought mental disturbance offered proof that the sufferer was possessed by demons.

3. Many mentally ill people suffered death in the course of treatment for demonic possession.

4. Belief in demonic possession eventually underwent a decrease in much of the world.

5. Instead, doctors and others made a classification of mental illness as a kind of disease.

6. Sufferers were frequently put into confinement and, often, forgotten.

7. Officials made the decision that mentally ill people were antisocial, not sick.

8. Most healthy people rarely gave any consideration to the mentally ill.

9. In the nineteenth century, a reformer, Dorothea Dix, made an investigation into the treatment of the mentally ill in Massachusetts.

10. Her report shocked people so much that Massachusetts, and soon other states, passed legislation requiring humane treatment for sufferers of mental illness.

Name _____ **Date** _____ **Section** _____

Exercise 1.1 Nouns, Pronouns, and Verbs

Identify the underlined word as a noun, a pronoun, or a verb.

For help with this exercise, see handbook sections 1a–1c in Successful College Writing.

EXAMPLE:

> pronoun
➤ Many Americans don't realize how much <u>their</u> ignorance of number concepts affects their lives.

1. The mathematician John Allen Paulos <u>claims</u> that too many Americans do not understand basic mathematical ideas.

2. Paulos calls this <u>lack</u> of understanding "innumeracy."

3. Innumerates may not <u>grasp</u> the idea of probability.

4. <u>Failing</u> to understand the likelihood of an event may cause poor judgment.

5. Unreasonable fears—for example, of being killed in a terrorist attack—may paralyze citizens <u>who</u> don't appreciate how unlikely such an event is.

6. A related misunderstanding is the failure to realize how common coincidences <u>are</u>.

7. For instance, the chance of two strangers on an airplane having <u>acquaintances</u> in common is surprisingly high.

8. In addition, probability shows that in any random group of twenty-three people, there is a 50 percent chance that two of <u>them</u> share a birthday.

9. People unfamiliar with rules of probability <u>may</u> be dangerously gullible.

10. Educational reforms and a systematic <u>attempt</u> to show the fun side of math could help Americans overcome their number resistance.

For help with this exercise, see handbook section 1c in *Successful College Writing*.

Exercise 1.2 Verb Form

Correct any errors in verb form in the following sentences. Some sentences may be correct as written.

EXAMPLE:

➤ In recent years, the study of detective stories ~~have~~ *has* become a legitimate academic
   pursuit.

1. Parents in the early twentieth century was warned that detective magazines
   could warp children's minds.

2. Pulp fiction about crime did indeed became rather lurid.

3. The detective story does, however, boast a literary past.

4. Many scholars have gave Edgar Allan Poe credit for being the first author to
   write detective fiction in English.

5. Poe's story "The Murders in the Rue Morgue" features an almost supernatu-
   rally clever detective.

6. Poe's detective clearly laid the foundation for the most famous literary
   sleuth, Sherlock Holmes.

7. In dozens of stories, Holmes, assisted by his friend Dr. Watson, uncovers the
   truth by careful observation.

8. Arthur Conan Doyle, the creator of Holmes and Watson, were amazed at the
   popularity of his fictional characters.

9. Some of the best-known writers of detective fiction in the twentieth century
   have been women.

10. While not all detective stories are worthy of serious study, the best ones are
    consider by scholars to be very rewarding.

Name _____ Date _____ Section _____

Exercise 1.3 Verb Tense

Identify the tense of each underlined verb.

For help with this exercise, see handbook section 1c in *Successful College Writing.*

EXAMPLE:

past perfect progressive

➤ By the spring of 1999, Wayne Gretzky <u>had been playing</u> professional hockey for over twenty years.

1. Wayne Gretzky <u>began</u> <u>playing</u> hockey in his native Canada at the age of three.

2. When he was five, he was frequently <u>scoring</u> goals against players several years older than he was.

3. Hockey fans <u>have known</u> Gretzky's name since his record-setting seasons with the Edmonton Oilers.

4. Before the Oilers traded him to Los Angeles, Gretzky <u>had acquired</u> his nickname, the "Great One."

5. Gretzky <u>holds</u> or shares more than sixty hockey records, an unprecedented number.

6. Several of his scoring records <u>will</u> probably always <u>stand</u>.

7. Gretzky's decision to retire in 1999 disappointed his fans, although they <u>had</u> perhaps <u>expected</u> the news.

8. When he retired, most of his fans <u>had been watching</u> him play for most of their lives.

9. Gretzky has said that he <u>will be spending</u> more time with his family now that his playing days are over.

10. In recognition of his achievements, the National Hockey League will never again <u>assign</u> a player Gretzky's number, 99.

For help with this exercise, see handbook section 1c in *Successful College Writing*.

Exercise 1.4 Verb Mood

Identify the mood — indicative, imperative, or subjunctive — of the underlined verb or verb phrase in each of the following sentences.

EXAMPLE:

➤ Charles Darwin's *The Origin of Species* <u>has inspired</u> *(indicative)* considerable discussion since its publication in 1859.

1. The study of biology <u>would be</u> very different today if Darwin had never written.

2. Although the mechanics of evolution <u>are</u> still <u>debated</u>, biologists all over the world accept Darwin's ideas.

3. Readers of Darwin's work in the nineteenth and early twentieth centuries <u>were</u> not easily <u>convinced</u>.

4. Many people wish that Darwin's theory <u>were</u> not widely accepted among scientists.

5. In the United States in 1925, a court of law told a Darwinian, "<u>Stop teaching</u> evolution."

6. In that famous trial, the Tennessee teacher J. T. Scopes <u>was tried</u> for telling his students to read about Darwin's theory.

7. Darrow argued that students <u>be</u> told.

8. The court ruled that the truth of evolutionary theory was not relevant, since Tennessee law <u>forbade</u> teaching it.

9. Scopes, who admitted teaching evolutionary theory, <u>lost</u> the case.

10. The Tennessee law forbidding the teaching of evolution <u>was</u> not <u>overturned</u> until 1967.

Name _____ Date _____ Section _____

Exercise 1.5 Adjectives and Adverbs

Identify the underlined word as an adjective or an adverb.

For help with this exercise, see handbook section 1d and 1e in *Successful College Writing*.

EXAMPLE:

➤ Education experts in the United States are debating the pros and cons of
    adjective
    <u>standardized</u> testing.

1. How <u>well</u> do American students compare with those in other industrialized nations?

2. A student who receives the <u>best</u> education the United States offers is likely to be very well prepared.

3. However, many students, especially those in <u>poorer</u> neighborhoods, get substandard training.

4. Education professionals agree that the U.S. <u>educational</u> system has problems.

5. <u>Unfortunately</u>, they cannot agree on what to do to solve this problem.

6. One <u>proposed</u> solution involves nationwide standards.

7. With nationwide standards, students across the country would be <u>responsible</u> for learning the same curriculum as all other students in the United States.

8. Students could prove they had met the standards by performing <u>satisfactorily</u> on a standardized test.

9. Supporters of <u>this</u> method claim that standards would force students to master knowledge before being promoted or graduating.

10. Some opponents argue that students learn <u>more</u> easily when teachers are able to use their own judgment about the curriculum.

For help with this exercise, see handbook sections 1f and 1g in *Successful College Writing*.

Exercise 1.6 Conjunctions and Prepositions

Identify the underlined word or words as a form of a conjunction or a preposition.

EXAMPLE:

preposition

➤ A new rapidly growing branch <u>of</u> physics is chaos theory.

1. <u>For</u> about the last twenty years, physicists have been analyzing chaos.

2. <u>In spite of</u> common perceptions, chaos may not be completely random.

3. The operations of some incompletely understood biological systems — brains, <u>for example</u> — may thrive in the gray area between order and chaos.

4. Some physicists believe that apparently chaotic behavior may actually act <u>according to</u> patterns.

5. <u>If</u> chaos is somehow systematic, it is nevertheless tremendously complex.

6. Finding the patterns of chaotic behavior is sometimes possible, <u>although</u> identifying them is difficult.

7. One difficulty lies <u>in</u> determining the type of model appropriate for a given complex system.

8. Understanding these complex systems <u>not only</u> is interesting in theory, <u>but also</u> has potential practical uses.

9. One group of physicists has tried to understand the abstractions of chaos theory <u>and</u> make concrete gains from their knowledge.

10. <u>As</u> part of an attempt to predict its future behavior, they are studying the complex and chaotic system known as the stock market.

SENTENCE STRUCTURE

Name _____ Date _____ Section _____

For help with this exercise, see handbook section 2a in *Successful College Writing*.

Exercise 2.1 Subjects and Predicates

Identify the underlined portion of each sentence as a simple subject, a simple predicate, a complete subject, or a complete predicate.

EXAMPLE:
simple subject
➤ <u>What</u> makes one violin sound different from another?

1. <u>The making of violins</u> is an art that has been practiced for centuries.

2. Modern technological <u>advances</u> have hardly touched violin makers, known as luthiers.

3. The greatest violin makers of all time <u>worked two to three hundred years ago in Italy</u>.

4. Modern luthiers <u>still do not know exactly how those great violin makers — notably Stradivarius and Amati — produced such perfect instruments</u>.

5. <u>Stradivarius violins, only about 150 of which are known to exist today,</u> can be worth over a million dollars each.

6. Stradivarius, who worked in Cremona, Italy, <u>invented</u> the proportions of the modern violin.

7. Some experts <u>believe</u> that the shape of his violins produces their exquisite tone.

8. Others argue that the precise shape could be reproduced by modern methods, yet nobody <u>has succeeded so far in duplicating the famous Stradivarius sound</u>.

9. Another <u>theory</u> is that the maple wood Stradivarius used, which came from ancient trees in short supply today, gives his violins their tone.

10. Chemists <u>are experimenting</u> with ways to treat newer wood that might give violins the elusive resonance of a Stradivarius.

For help with this exercise, see handbook section 2a in *Successful College Writing.*

Exercise 2.2 Objects and Complements

Identify each underlined word as a direct object, an indirect object, a subject complement, or an object complement.

EXAMPLE:

indirect object

➤ Can computers give adult <u>brains</u> new capacities for learning foreign languages?

1. Some kinds of learning get <u>easier</u> as people grow older.

2. But most adults find learning a foreign language extremely <u>difficult</u>.

3. At birth, babies' brains can distinguish every <u>sound</u> in every human language.

4. As they grow, children's brains become less <u>able</u> to recognize different sounds.

5. After the age of ten, most people cannot acquire a foreign <u>language</u> without an accent.

6. Adult brains reinforce familiar <u>sounds</u> when they hear unfamiliar ones.

7. This phenomenon actually makes adults less <u>likely</u> to distinguish unfamiliar sounds with increased exposure.

8. An experimental computer simulation may give <u>adults</u> new abilities to learn unfamiliar language sounds.

9. The computer offers <u>students</u> a chance to hear the unfamiliar sounds in an exaggerated way.

10. Perhaps someday adult learners will also be fluent, unaccented <u>speakers</u> of foreign languages.

Name _____ Date _____ Section _____

Exercise 2.3 Phrases

For help with this exercise, see handbook section 2b in *Successful College Writing*.

Identify the underlined phrase in each sentence as a prepositional phrase, a verbal phrase, an appositive phrase, or an absolute phrase.

EXAMPLE:

>   *verbal phrase*
>
> ➤   The science <u>of analyzing human DNA</u> has become very precise in recent years.

1. DNA, <u>the genetic code</u>, is a unique marker that is different in every human being.

2. DNA analysis can be used <u>as a crime-fighting tool</u>.

3. Like fingerprints, DNA <u>left at a crime scene</u> can help to identify a wrongdoer.

4. Today, most people contemplating a crime know how <u>to avoid leaving fingerprints</u>.

5. But criminals, <u>their DNA contained in every cell of their bodies</u>, can hardly avoid leaving identifying markers behind.

6. Any clue—<u>a single hair, a trace of saliva</u>—can eventually convict a criminal.

7. <u>A suspect having left a used coffee cup during questioning</u>, a police officer may not even need another sample to link him or her to the crime.

8. The good news <u>for some people</u> charged with or convicted of a crime is that DNA can also prove someone not guilty.

9. Some convicted criminals, <u>steadfastly maintaining their innocence</u>, have undergone new, sophisticated DNA analysis after years of imprisonment.

10. Recently, two men, <u>prisoners on death row</u>, were released after DNA tests proved they could not have committed the murder for which they were convicted.

For help with this exercise, see handbook section 2c in *Successful College Writing*.

Exercise 2.4 Subordinate Clauses

Underline the subordinate clause or clauses in each of the following sentences.

EXAMPLE:

➤ Superstitions, <u>which are irrational beliefs in charms and omens</u>, still have a hold on modern life.

1. Many superstitions date from classical or medieval times, when belief in witchcraft was widespread.

2. Superstitions were a way for people to explain whatever threatened them.

3. Because cats were believed to be witches in disguise, the fear of a black cat crossing one's path came about.

4. Walking under ladders has also long been considered unlucky; this superstition may survive because it protects pedestrians from falling objects.

5. Some people attribute to the Christian story of the Last Supper, where thirteen people were present, the origins of the superstitious fear of the number thirteen.

6. Wherever it began, fear of the number thirteen, or triskaidekaphobia, is still prevalent enough for many tall modern buildings not to have a thirteenth floor.

7. Early Romans believed that sneezing was a sign of the plague, so they feared it.

8. The method they invented to protect a sneezer was to say, "God bless you."

9. In the United States today, it is common to say "God bless you"—or "Gesundheit," which is German for "health"—following a sneeze.

10. Superstitions from the past may seem silly today, but who knows what strange customs of the present will be ridiculed in the future?

Name _____ Date _____ Section _____

Exercise 2.5 Sentence Types

Indicate whether each of the following sentences is a simple, a compound, a complex, or a compound-complex sentence.

For help with this exercise, see handbook section 2d in *Successful College Writing*.

EXAMPLE:

➤ While extremely muscular or very thin people are often portrayed as the American ideal, Americans are, on the average, heavier than ever. *complex*

1. Models and beauty contest winners in the United States have become much thinner in the last fifty years.

2. The weight that most people consider ideal for their height has also adjusted downward since the middle of the twentieth century.

3. More and better nutritional information is available today, and most Americans know the right things to eat.

4. Yet the number of people who actually make the right choices seems to have declined.

5. As medical experts have pointed out repeatedly, Americans are getting heavier, and more American children than ever are overweight.

6. Since people know what they should do and since the "perfect" bodies depicted in popular media are muscled or thin, why is there a national weight problem?

7. Part of the reason may be this nation's overall good fortune and abundance.

8. Most people rarely go without their favorite foods, and American favorites tend to be high in fat and calories.

9. In addition, the national fascination with cars and television has contributed to a sedentary lifestyle.

10. The result is a heavier America, but it is also a country where people feel free to make hurtful jokes about overweight people.

WRITING CORRECT SENTENCES

Name _____ Date _____ Section _____

For help with this exercise, see handbook section 3 in *Successful College Writing*.

Exercise 3.1 Sentence Fragments

Correct any sentence fragments in the following sentences. Some sentences may be correct as written.

EXAMPLE:

➤ Among the many treasures at Yale's library. ̭The Voynich manuscript stands out.

1. There are older and more valuable manuscripts. Than the Voynich.

2. However, there is none more mysterious. The Voynich still puzzling scholars many years after its discovery.

3. This manuscript was written in a code. So far unable to solve it.

4. Because the origins of the manuscript are unclear; the puzzle is doubly difficult.

5. No one knows. What country it came from.

6. Therefore, it very hard to determine the language the code represents. This makes decoding it even more troublesome.

7. Handwriting specialists can only guess at its age. It may date back to the Middle Ages.

8. The writing does not resemble. Any letters that can be traced to a known alphabet.

9. The manuscript which contains many beautiful illustrations. Of plants, people, and other seemingly unrelated images.

10. Because the Voynich manuscript is such an intriguing mystery. That some scholars might actually be disappointed to learn all of its secrets.

Name _____ Date _____ Section _____

Exercise 4.1 Run-On Sentences and Comma Splices

Correct any run-on sentences and comma splices in the following sentences.

For help with this exercise, see handbook section 4 in *Successful College Writing*.

EXAMPLE:

➤ Before her death in 1980, Mae West had become an institution; she had been in show business for seven decades.

1. Mae West began as a child star the career of "Baby Mae" took off when she performed at a local Brooklyn theater's amateur night.

2. At the age of nineteen, West began performing on Broadway she shocked audiences in 1911.

3. The voluptuous West became known for her suggestive clothing, even more famous were her suggestive wisecracks.

4. Attending black jazz clubs had introduced her to a new dance movement she performed this "shimmy" on Broadway, and it became a trademark for her.

5. West was not satisfied for long with the theatrical roles she was offered writing her own plays was one way to find good parts.

6. In 1925, she wrote a play called *Sex,* no producer she contacted would bring it to the stage.

7. The following year, West produced the play herself, advertisements for *Sex* were banned.

8. Nevertheless, the show played for nine months until it was closed down by the Society for the Suppression of Vice, West was arrested and spent eight days in jail.

9. In the 1930s and 1940s, Mae West took her naughty humor to Hollywood, while there she made a series of hit films and often wrote her own screenplays.

10. West made her final films in the 1970s by that time Americans found her less scandalous, but her name was still a household word.

For help with this exercise, see handbook section 5 in *Successful College Writing*.

Exercise 5.1 Subject-Verb Agreement

Correct any errors in subject-verb agreement in the following sentences. Some sentences may be correct as written.

EXAMPLE:

➤ African American heritage and the end of slavery is̲ *are* celebrated every year on June 19.

1. The festival called "Juneteenth," which people once recognized only in a few southern areas of the United States, are now much more widespread.

2. The events Juneteenth commemorates occurred after the end of the Civil War.

3. The surrender of the Confederate States were made official at Appomattox Courthouse on April 9, 1865.

4. From that day on, the Confederacy and the Union was again a single country.

5. Neither the northern states nor the southern states was now legally able to permit slave-owning, which had been officially outlawed in the United States several years earlier.

6. However, not all of the former slaves were aware they had been legally freed.

7. The story from those long-ago days go that in Texas, slave owners murdered the messengers bringing word of emancipation.

8. Not until June 19, 1865, were the news able to reach the last group of Texas slaves.

9. Therefore, festivities marking the end of slavery are held not on April 9 each year, the anniversary of the South's surrender, but on June 19.

10. Today, people celebrating Juneteenth attends concerts, films, and other cultural events.

Name _____ Date _____ Section _____

Exercise 6.1 Verb Forms

Correct any errors in verb form in the following sentences.

For help with this exercise, see handbook section 6 in *Successful College Writing*.

EXAMPLE:

➤ In 1915, a group of artists ~~had~~ decided to turn their backs on the traditional art world.

1. The horrors of World War I were convincing some artists that European society had to change radically.

2. Their reaction at first consist of musical and performance events they called the Cabaret Voltaire.

3. Soon, however, the most influential members of the group begun to focus on visual art.

4. The name *Dada* was chosen at random by the artists.

5. They rejected older artistic traditions, including avant-garde ideas that recently became popular.

6. Instead, the Dadaists challenging the whole concept of art.

7. Before the Dada movement had ended in 1923, several of the artists had experimented with random arrangements of materials.

8. Sometimes they chose the material they use from items discarded by other people.

9. One artist, Marcel Duchamp, even sat up ordinary objects at art shows, claiming that the act of choosing the objects made them art.

10. Dada was a rebellion, not an attempt to build a new tradition, so no identifiable stylistic legacy of the movement remain today.

For help with this exercise, see handbook sections 7a–7d in *Successful College Writing*.

Exercise 7.1 Pronoun Reference

Correct any instances of vague or unclear pronoun reference in the following sentences.

EXAMPLE:

and this attitude

➤ Many Americans express tremendous cynicism about the U.S. government, ~~which~~ is not good for the country.

1. In much political analysis, they say that public distrust of the U.S. government began with Watergate.

2. That scandal's continuing legacy may make it one of the most influential American events of the twentieth century.

3. Since the early 1970s, political scandals have rarely interested Americans; they often seem to have very little effect.

4. Journalists provided the American people with a lot of information about the Iran-Contra hearings, but they could not have cared less.

5. Most people were indifferent; could it have been the result of post–Watergate trauma?

6. If Americans expect politicians to be corrupt, it will not surprise or even interest them.

7. Ironically, the media's coverage of scandals seems to have made the public suspicious of them as well.

8. Cynicism about political and journalistic motives leads to apathy, and it can spread contagiously.

9. Many people are so apathetic that it makes them refuse to vote.

10. If people do not believe that they can make a difference in the political process, it makes the country less democratic.

Exercise 7.2 Pronoun-Antecedent Agreement

Correct any errors in pronoun-antecedent agreement in the following sentences. Some sentences may be correct as written.

For help with this exercise, see handbook sections 7c–7g in *Successful College Writing*.

EXAMPLE:

➤ Human ~~lives~~ *life* is important, and more lives could be protected if more were known about deadly storms.

1. Meteorology has made many advances in the past few decades, but they still cannot answer a number of questions about tornadoes.

2. Every tornado has their own unique characteristics.

3. The science of tornado watching has its own system, the Fujita scale, for measuring storms from weakest (F0) to strongest (F5).

4. An F4 tornado or an F5 tornado can destroy everything in their path.

5. Scientists cannot yet predict how strong any tornado will be before they happen.

6. One mystery about tornadoes involves the last step when it forms.

7. Specialists do not know if a tornado forms in a cloud and travels to the ground or if they begin on earth and spiral upward.

8. Improved meteorological technology and the skill to interpret data have made their contributions to tornado prediction.

9. Either a few extra minutes of warning or more information about a storm's power would prove their effectiveness in saving lives.

10. People who live in a tornado zone should always know where his or her nearest safe area is.

For help with this exercise, see handbook sections 7h–7m in *Successful College Writing*.

Exercise 7.3 Pronoun Case

Correct any errors in pronoun case in the following sentences. Some sentences may be correct as written.

EXAMPLE:

➤ Much of American mythology concerns heroes ~~whom~~ *who* solved problems by using violence.

1. Us residents of the United States are considered by much of the rest of the world to be an unusually violent people.

2. Many researchers have debated they're theories about violent behavior in this country.

3. Did the popular myth of the "Wild West" influence we and our ancestors?

4. Other industrialized nations and us have very different policies concerning guns.

5. Guns played an important part in Western settlement, but other machines may have been more significant than they.

6. Violence and justice are so intertwined for many Americans that disagreements between other people and they can erupt into fights.

7. American entertainment is frequently violent, too, and some people worry that such violence affects us and our children.

8. There are defenders of violent films, TV shows, and video games whom claim that entertainment reflects our tastes rather than influencing them.

9. What makes us Americans so prone to violence?

10. Sometimes it seems that our worst enemies are us.

Exercise 8.1 Shifts

Correct any inappropriate shifts in the following sentences.

For help with this exercise, see handbook sections 8a–8g in *Successful College Writing*.

EXAMPLE:

➤ Some scholars have asked ~~did~~ *whether* African folk traditions influence*d* African American folklore.

1. West African villages have strong oral traditions in which the younger people are told stories by their parents and grandparents.

2. Way back before the Revolutionary War, slave traders forced ancestors of the people from those villages to come to the United States.

3. In their difficult new situation in this country, the Africans adapted their stories so that you could learn from them.

4. Although different stories had different messages, one kind of character comes up over and over again.

5. The character is cunning and clever; call him a "trickster."

6. The stories about Br'er Rabbit are good examples of folktales whose hero was a trickster.

7. Many of the other animals want to gobble up Br'er Rabbit, who has only his wits to protect him.

8. Yet in every story, Br'er Rabbit not only escapes, but his enemies are made to appear foolish by him as well.

9. Trickster characters like Br'er Rabbit showed slaves who heard these stories that they, too, could triumph by using cleverness when foes surround them.

10. Today, folklorists are exploring how did early African Americans encourage each other by telling stories of tricksters outsmarting powerful enemies.

For help with this exercise, see handbook sections 8h–8j in *Successful College Writing*.

Exercise 8.2 Mixed Constructions

Correct any mixed constructions in the following sentences.

EXAMPLE:

➤ A common misconception is the ~~ability~~ *idea that it is easy* to identify when someone is telling a lie.

1. Most people think perceiving falsehoods are easy to spot.

2. They think that interpreting nonverbal signals shows when someone is lying.

3. The fact that these signals, such as avoiding eye contact or hesitating before answering a question, are habits of truthful people as well.

4. The reason liars are hard to identify is because no single trait always proves that a person is lying.

5. Truthful people who are afraid they will not be believed may act suspiciously is one problem with lie detection.

6. There are a few people are unusually good at identifying liars.

7. However, perhaps because these people are attuned to deceitful behavior may explain why they are not especially good at identifying truth-tellers.

8. Listening to a stranger's lies may be easier to detect than a loved one's.

9. The better someone knows and likes another person seems to make spotting lies more difficult.

10. Someone who finds it hard to believe that her friends would try to deceive her is an understandable human characteristic.

Name _____ Date _____ Section _____

Exercise 9.1 Adjectives and Adverbs

Correct any errors in the use of adjectives or adverbs in the following sentences.

For help with this exercise, see handbook section 9 in *Successful College Writing*.

EXAMPLE:

➤ People think of beauty different in different cultures.
   (*ly* inserted above "different"; caret below)

1. Many people go to a lot of trouble to look attractively.

2. In the United States, no one thinks a woman wearing high heels is dressed strange.

3. Many Americans even go to real extreme lengths, such as having surgery, to be beautiful.

4. People can see the strangeness of beauty rituals clearer if the rituals are unfamiliar.

5. For example, in China in past centuries, beautiful women had to have the tiniest feet.

6. To achieve this goal, families bound their daughters' feet so tight that the feet could not grow.

7. Subcultures within the United States also have their own standards of beauty that may seem odder to people who are not part of the subculture.

8. For many young Americans, tattoos and body piercing were the trendier fashion statements of the 1990s.

9. They might have argued that such beautification was no unusualer than plucking out one's eyebrows.

10. Parents, however, often felt vastly relief if their children reached adulthood without tattoos.

For help with this exercise, see handbook section 10 in *Successful College Writing.*

Exercise 10.1 Misplaced and Dangling Modifiers

Correct any misplaced or dangling modifiers in the following sentences.

EXAMPLE:

➤ The sports world has changed to reflect the number of young athletes. ~~rapidly growing.~~ *rapidly growing*

1. Recently, several sports have gained popularity that no one had heard of thirty years ago.

2. With a name that suggests their dangerous allure, members of Generation X are attracted to these athletic events.

3. These "Generation X" games often involve going to inaccessible places, which include snowboarding and sky-surfing.

4. Snow activities are especially popular that can be done on remote mountain-tops.

5. Some of these sports have become so widely accepted that participants can now compete in the Olympics, such as freestyle skiing and snowboarding.

6. Gasping at the antics of snowboarders, mountain bikers, and other athletes, these daredevils prove that the sports world really has changed.

7. Only these "in-your-face" athletes are a small part of what is interesting about the changes taking place in sports today.

8. Occasionally, even fans of extreme sports know that the quest for adventure leads people into dangerous situations.

9. Environmentalists also point out unfortunately that in some remote wilderness areas, extreme sports are taking their toll on nature.

10. Probably, whether people love them or hate them, extreme sports will continue to inspire extreme reactions.

PUNCTUATION

Name _____ Date _____ Section _____

For help with this exercise, see handbook section 11 in *Successful College Writing*.

Exercise 11.1 End Punctuation

Correct any errors in the use of end punctuation marks in the following sentences. Some sentences may be correct as written.

EXAMPLE:

➤ No one knows what kind of undiscovered life forms exist at the bottom of the ocean?.
                                              ^

1. In some places, the ocean is more than seven miles deep!

2. Enormous pressure and complete darkness in the depths make it difficult for humans to discover what is down there?

3. When deep-sea fishing boats haul up their nets, they sometimes find creatures never before seen or prehistoric life forms that were believed to be extinct.

4. The sheer size of the ocean depths indicates that there may be many more species down there than are found on land!

5. Could there be millions of unknown species living in the deepest ocean trenches?

6. Scientists wonder what the implications of new species might be for human beings.

7. Is it also possible that the actions of humans are affecting life at the bottom of the sea.

8. Biologists who have recently measured the food supply on the ocean floor might be moved to exclaim, "It seems to be dwindling?"

9. Most of the food that reaches the bottom comes from near the surface, where there is light?

10. Warmer surface temperatures may be reducing the food supply at the bottom, and who has more influence on global warming than human beings.

Name _____ Date _____ Section _____

For help with this exercise, see handbook section 12 in *Successful College Writing*.

Exercise 12.1 Adding Commas

Add or omit commas as necessary in the following sentences. Some sentences may be correct as written.

   EXAMPLE:

➤ Horse racing‸which has been a spectator sport for centuries‸still delights fans.

1. Breeders have long prized their swiftest, most graceful horses, and raced them.

2. Horse racing in the United States generally means either thoroughbred racing or harness racing.

3. Harness racehorses pull small lightweight vehicles, handled by a driver.

4. Harness racing falls into the two categories of trotting, and pacing.

5. The most famous event in harness racing the Hambletonian, is a mile-long trotting race.

6. Harness racing may be known mainly to enthusiasts but even people who appreciate very little about horse racing are familiar with thoroughbred racing.

7. Thoroughbred racehorses, unlike harness racehorses, carry a rider.

8. The best-known events in thoroughbred racing, the Kentucky Derby, the Preakness Stakes, and the Belmont Stakes, are the three races, that make up the Triple Crown.

9. All of the Triple Crown races which vary in length are for three-year-old horses.

10. In the twentieth century only eleven horses won thoroughbred racing's Triple Crown.

Exercise 12.2 Working with Commas

Add or omit commas as necessary in the following sentences. Some sentences may
be correct as written.

For help with this
exercise, see
handbook section
12 in *Successful
College Writing*.

EXAMPLE:

➤ There are many theories/about the kinds of police work that are the most
effective/at reducing crime.

1. Several years ago, many police departments ignored minor violations of the
    law, and concentrated on bigger crime problems.

2. Today, however, the "broken window" theory, is widely accepted.

3. According to this popular theory allowing broken windows to remain, unre-
    paired, leads to a loss of hope in a community.

4. Frequently, buildings that look neglected make neighbors feel that no one
    cares what goes on in the area.

5. Similarly, if petty crimes are ignored in a neighborhood people there may
    feel that larger crimes are acceptable as well.

6. Community policing is one result of the new emphasis on stopping "victim-
    less" crimes such as loitering and panhandling.

7. But, can a police officer, walking a beat, really be more effective than a
    patrol car?

8. Some experts believe that police should be required to live in the communi-
    ties, that they serve.

9. Police who live elsewhere may not understand the needs of the community,
    and they will certainly know less about the people living in the community.

10. Different methods of community policing may work in different areas but
    the goal should always be to keep communications open between the public
    and the police.

For help with this exercise, see handbook section 13 in *Successful College Writing*.

Exercise 13.1 Semicolons

Correct any errors in the use of semicolons in the following sentences. Some sentences may be correct as written.

EXAMPLE:

➤ The anti-Communist hysteria of the Cold War era marks one of the lowest points in American history; when fear led to persecution of some citizens.

1. Many Americans think of the years after World War II as a golden era; a time before modern complexities made life more difficult.

2. Even without considering the quality of life at that time for women and minorities; an idyllic view of the mid-twentieth century ignores other issues.

3. The late 1940s and 1950s marked the height of the Cold War era; many Americans were frightened about what might happen in the future.

4. The Soviet Union, an ally of the United States during World War II, took control of the governments of neighboring countries, China, after a civil war, fell under Communist rule, and the Korean conflict, in which Americans were involved, seemed to prove that Communists wanted to take over as much land as possible.

5. Americans reacted to Communist activities elsewhere in the world, and part of their reaction included fear of communism at home.

6. Senator Joseph McCarthy may have shared this fear, he certainly capitalized on it to advance his political career.

7. In 1950, McCarthy announced that he had a list of Communists; who held positions in the U.S. State Department.

8. At about the same time, the House Un-American Activities Committee began investigating Hollywood; many stars were asked to testify about suspected Communists in the film industry.

9. Eventually, more than 150 film workers, including; performers, directors, and writers, were blacklisted by the Hollywood studios.

10. For the first half of the 1950s, anti-Communist leaders were very powerful in the United States; however, by 1955 McCarthy was in disgrace; and in 1957 the courts determined that membership in the Communist Party should no longer be a criminal offense in this country.

For help with this exercise, see handbook section 14 in *Successful College Writing*.

Exercise 14.1 Colons

Correct any errors in the use of colons in the following sentences. Some sentences may be correct as written.

EXAMPLE:

➤ Near the end of the expedition, Scott and his men were̷ cold, hungry, and exhausted.

1. In 1910, Robert Falcon Scott led his second expedition to Antarctica with two objectives to collect scientific data and to be the first humans at the South Pole.

2. The years before World War I were a heady time for: exploration of the frozen Antarctic continent.

3. The story of Scott's difficult journey continues to fascinate armchair adventurers: even though the expedition was, in many ways, a failure.

4. After arriving in Antarctica, Scott's scientists began their work, they collected specimens, surveyed the land, and recorded twelve volumes of data.

5. In 1911, Scott learned that the Norwegian explorer Roald Amundsen had decided to try to reach the South Pole as well.

6. Scott stuck to his original timetable for the South Pole journey, he did not want to engage in a race.

7. Scott and his men set out for the South Pole in the Antarctic summer of 1911: which is the winter season in the Northern Hemisphere.

8. In January 1912, Scott and the four companions who had traveled to the Pole with him were disappointed to learn that Amundsen's men had arrived a month earlier.

9. As they traveled back to their base camp, death took all five men Scott, Titus Oates, Edgar Evans, Henry Bowers, and Edward Wilson.

10. *Scott's Last Expedition: The Journals* records the explorer's last diary entry: "I do not think we can hope for any better things now. We shall stick it out to the end, but we are getting weaker, of course, and the end cannot be far. It seems a pity, but I do not think I can write more."

Exercise 15.1 Quotation Marks

Correct any errors in the use of quotation marks in the following sentences.

For help with this exercise, see handbook section 15 in *Successful College Writing*.

EXAMPLE:

➤ Is Hamlet contemplating suicide when he says, "To be, or not to be, that is the

question?"?

1. The film producer shouted excitedly, "Everyone loves Shakespeare because he used so many familiar quotations"!

2. "When we make movies based on Shakespeare plays", he added "we don't have to pay royalties to the writer."

3. Films based on Shakespeare plays try to reveal the relevance of his work to a "modern" audience.

4. Although Shakespeare lived four hundred years ago, his work is currently "in demand" in Hollywood.

5. "Hamlet," "A Midsummer Night's Dream," and "Romeo and Juliet" are just a few of the Shakespeare plays filmed in the 1990s.

6. The producer commented, "When I hear that a new film will be based on Shakespeare, I wonder, like Juliet, "What's in a name?" "

7. If the name Shakespeare were not involved, would filmmakers be as interested in the material?

8. Shakespeare's plays are frequently performed in theaters, too, and several young playwrights recently wrote works based on his "sonnets."

9. Hamlet, perhaps Shakespeare's most famous character, laments Alas, poor Yorick! I knew him, Horatio, a fellow of infinite jest, of most excellent fancy.

10. Othello, one of Shakespeare's most complex characters, laments that he "loved not wisely, but too well".

For help with this exercise, see handbook section 16 in *Successful College Writing*.

Exercise 16.1 Ellipsis Marks

Shorten each quotation below by replacing the underlined portions with ellipsis marks, if appropriate. In some cases, an omission may be inappropriate.

EXAMPLE:

➤ "Don't tell me to get ready to die. ~~I know not what shall be~~. The only preparation I can make is by fulfilling my present duties" (Emerson 365).

1. "A writer who keeps her audience in mind cannot fail to be effective."

2. "We hold these truths to be self-evident: that all men are created equal, that they are endowed by their creator with certain inalienable rights, that among these are life, liberty, and the pursuit of happiness."

3. "Thomas Jefferson wanted the Declaration of Independence to say that men were 'created independent,' even though he himself owned slaves."

4. Elizabeth Cady Stanton's "Declaration of Sentiments" announces, "In entering upon the great work before us, we anticipate no small amount of misconception, misrepresentation, and ridicule, but we shall use every instrumentality within our power to effect our object."

5. "Stanton's 'Declaration of Sentiments' was based quite consciously on the language Jefferson had used in the Declaration of Independence."

6. "It may seem strange that any men should dare to ask a just God's assistance in wringing their bread from the sweat of other men's faces; but let us judge not that we be not judged," Lincoln said in his second inaugural address.

7. "Allusions to the language of familiar literature, such as the Bible or the Declaration of Independence, can lend authority to a text that uses them well."

8. Lincoln went on, "Fondly do we hope—fervently do we pray—that this mighty scourge of war may speedily pass away."

9. Martin Luther King Jr. expressed the wish that his children would be judged "not by the color of their skin, but by the content of their character."

10. "Repetition of structure can be an effective rhetorical device. This is true whether the work is intended for an audience of readers or listeners."

Exercise 17.1 Apostrophes

Correct any errors in the use of apostrophes in the following sentences. Some sentences may be correct as written.

For help with this exercise, see handbook section 17 in *Successful College Writing*.

EXAMPLE:

➤ Some explorer/s' ideas about the ruins in Mashonaland were incorrect.

1. African chief's stories led a German explorer to the stone ruins in Mashonaland, now in Zimbabwe, in 1871.

2. The explorer, who's name was Karl Mauch, tried to find out who had built the once-great city.

3. The tribes nearby could not answer Mauches' question, but they knew gold had been found there.

4. The African's called the site *Zimbabwe*.

5. Mauch became convinced that the city was Ophir, the source of the gold brought back to King Solomon's Israel around 1000 B.C.E.

6. He thought perhaps the cities' builder was the Queen of Sheba.

7. An archeologists' findings later demonstrated that the city was about six hundred years old and that it had been built by African natives.

8. The Shona tribe probably built the first walls on the site, but it's more complex structures were added later by the Rozwi tribe.

9. The Rozwi probably erected the temple, which was inhabited by Rozwi ruler-priests until their empire's end in the 1830's.

10. The legends about the origins of the city persisted for a long time, perhaps because of white South Africans and Europeans' resistance to the idea that black Africans had built the impressive structures.

For help with this exercise, see handbook section 18 in *Successful College Writing*.

Exercise 18.1 Parentheses and Brackets

Correct any errors in the use of parentheses or brackets in the following sentences.

EXAMPLE:

➤ The film poster announced, "The monster takes its revenge⸓ [sic]."

1. Bad movies, (some of which are quite enjoyable to watch), often have a cult following.

2. Some films routinely make every critic's list of worst films (Usually, these movies are so bad they are funny.).

3. A few filmmakers [like Ed Wood] and movie companies [like American International Pictures] have acquired fame among fans of bad movies.

4. Roger Corman's American International Pictures [AIP] churned out innumerable inexpensive, quickly made films.

5. One Corman film, *Little Shop of Horrors,* (1960) was filmed in less than three days.

6. But the director Edward D. Wood Jr. [1924–1978] has a special place in the world of bad movies.

7. Wood gained new fame with Tim Burton's film biography, *Ed Wood,* (1994).

8. Like Corman's movies, Wood's were made very quickly, but Wood, (unlike Corman), thought he was making great films.

9. Wood's "masterpiece," *Plan 9 from Outer Space,* (Bela Lugosi's last film) is a science fiction and horror film with bad acting, dreadful writing, and laughable special effects.

10. Wood said that *"Plan 9* (was his) pride and joy."

Exercise 19.1 Dashes

In the following sentences, add a dash or pair of dashes where they might be effective, and correct any errors in the use of dashes and other punctuation.

For help with this exercise, see handbook section 19 in *Successful College Writing*.

EXAMPLE:

➤ A backyard bird count takes place ⫽ at the end of every year.

1. Songbirds are a part of our national heritage, each state has its own official bird.

2. Some states have official birds — unique to the region.

3. The nene — Hawaii's state bird, is a goose found only on those islands.

4. In Salt Lake City, a statue of a seagull — which is Utah's state bird—honors the birds that ate a huge swarm of locusts — without the birds, most crops would have been eaten by the insects.

5. Other states share popular state birds, the cardinal, the meadowlark, and the mockingbird are all official birds in at least five states.

6. When Americans think of spring — they often think of songbirds chirping in the trees.

7. For many years the Audubon Society, an organization devoted to nature study — has studied populations of songbirds.

8. Birdwatchers — mainly trained volunteers count birds in small local areas during the year-end holiday season.

9. The numbers of some songbirds — though fortunately not all have declined alarmingly.

10. Although most people appreciate the sights and sounds of songbirds—they may not realize how modern human habits interfere with many birds' lives.

Name _____ Date _____ Section _____

For help with this exercise, see handbook section 20 in *Successful College Writing*.

Exercise 20.1 Capitalization

Correct any errors in capitalization in the following sentences.

EXAMPLE:

➤ Some historians believe that the ͭTwentieth ͨCentury will be remembered as America's century.

1. At the turn of a new century and a new Millennium, many people reflected on historical changes that had taken place in the previous hundred years.

2. In the late 1990s, Americans began making lists reflecting their choices of the greatest Events, Literature, people, and Films of the century.

3. Most Americans would agree that the two World Wars shaped the twentieth century and this country's role in it.

4. List makers might, however, dispute the importance of *Ulysses* or *Gone with the wind*.

5. Between the beginning and the end of the twentieth century, the United States changed from a minor player in global politics into the single undisputed World Power.

6. Technology also advanced dramatically in the century of television, the *apollo* space missions, and personal computers.

7. Of course, technology was sometimes used for evil purposes, as the holocaust and nuclear weapons proved.

8. Some people would even argue that a significant feature of the century was an increasing concern for the environment—In the United States, in Europe, and in parts of the Former Soviet Union, among other places.

9. The trend toward urbanization saw people moving from rural areas to cities, with the result in this country that the great plains grew emptier while the Coasts' population increased.

10. Only historical distance will reveal whether the twentieth century was "The best of times" or "The worst of times."

Exercise 21.1 Abbreviations

Correct any errors in the use of abbreviations in the following sentences.

For help with this exercise, see handbook section 21 in *Successful College Writing.*

EXAMPLE:

➤ Humanitarian ~~orgs.~~ *organizations* provide relief in disaster areas worldwide.

1. When disasters strike, victims count on international organizations like the Red Cross, Doctors without Borders, etc.

2. A Dr.'s help is often the most desperately needed form of aid.

3. People often offer canned goods and blankets, while major corps. receive tax benefits for donations of drugs and other medical supplies.

4. When Hurricane Mitch devastated Honduras, many U.S. cits. were quick to help.

5. An R.N. who is willing to travel to the disaster area can provide needed services.

6. For several years, volunteer doctors have tried to alleviate the AIDS crisis in Afr.

7. In some situations, e.g. during outbreaks of deadly diseases or in war-torn areas, medical personnel risk their own lives.

8. Doctors from the Atlanta, Ga.-based Centers for Disease Control travel the globe to isolate and study dangerous viruses.

9. The CDC doctors do not provide medical assistance in war zones, but other orgs. do.

10. In the aftermath of bloody fighting, a U.N. peacekeeping force may arrive to find intl. doctors already at work.

For help with this exercise, see handbook section 22 in *Successful College Writing*.

Exercise 22.1 Numbers

Correct any errors in the use of numbers in the following sentences.

EXAMPLE:

➤ The Beatles had more number *one* 1 hits than any other group in pop history.

1. John Lennon, Paul McCartney, George Harrison, and Ringo Starr were 4 young men from Liverpool, England, who formed what would become the most popular rock band of all time.

2. On January twenty-five, 1964, the Beatles' first hit entered the U.S. charts.

3. The song "I Want to Hold Your Hand" spent seven weeks at number one and 14 weeks in the top 40.

4. Almost immediately, the Beatles began to attract 1000s of screaming fans everywhere they went.

5. Throughout the nineteen-sixties, the Beatles were the world's most popular group.

6. During the eight years of the Beatles' reign on the charts, they had more than forty three-minute pop hits.

7. By the 2nd half of the decade, the Beatles had stopped touring.

8. They performed live together for the last time on the roof of Three Savile Row, the headquarters of their doomed record company, Apple.

9. 150 employees worked for Apple, which eventually went bankrupt.

10. By no means did each Beatle earn twenty-five percent of the group's profits, for Lennon and McCartney wrote more than ninety percent of the songs.

Name _____ Date _____ Section _____

Exercise 23.1 Italics and Underlining

For help with this exercise, see handbook section 23 in *Successful College Writing*.

Correct any errors in the use of italics in the following sentences.

EXAMPLE:

➤ <u>Information overload</u>, a condition that makes people feel overwhelmed in the face of almost unlimited information, affects many Americans.

1. Americans today get their information from 60 Minutes, the New York Times, electronic sources, and thousands of other places.

2. Once, choices were limited: to find out about raising a child, for example, parents consulted Dr. Spock's book "Baby and Child Care."

3. Now, magazines like Parenting compete with the new edition of *Dr. Spock* and dozens of other titles.

4. Obscure information is more accessible than ever, so a fan of the song *Telstar* can find *The Joe Meek Story,* a full-length biography of its producer.

5. A student wanting to learn about the dead language called Old English could consult Web sites like the one maintained by *Georgetown University.*

6. It may no longer be possible for a single person to know all about, for example, *biology.*

7. Once, the term Renaissance man or Renaissance woman referred to a person well educated and talented in many subjects.

8. Leonardo da Vinci, the original Renaissance man, not only painted the "Mona Lisa" but also wrote botanical treatises and devised remarkable engineering plans.

9. Today, we do not expect the builder of the ocean liner Queen Elizabeth II to know other subjects.

10. A lifetime of study may lie behind a single article in the New England Journal of Medicine.

For help with this exercise, see handbook section 24 in *Successful College Writing*.

Exercise 24.1 Hyphens

Correct any errors in the use of hyphens in the following sentences.

EXAMPLE:

➤ Buying lottery/tickets is an extremely inefficient way to gain additional income.

1. Does buying lottery tickets and entering sweepstakes make a person selfemployed?

2. The odds of winning a major lottery prize are often over a million-to-one.

3. Yet many people, including desperately-poor ones who cannot afford the tickets, buy large numbers of them when the jackpot is high and the odds are worst.

4. A sensible approach to such sky high odds would be not to enter the lottery at all.

5. Sweepstakes are well-known to anyone with a mailbox.

6. Unlike lotteries, apparently-free sweepstakes do not require any cash investment other than the price of a stamp.

7. Yet many sweepstakes imply that buying a magazine-subscription or a product improves the chances of winning.

8. Some sweepstakes companies have been accused of trying to dupe customers who do not read the fine-print.

9. Some elderly people have thrown away their great grandchildren's inheritance, buying hundreds of products they don't need from sweepstakes advertisers.

10. The idea of getting rich with minimal work or investment is so strikingly-attractive that many people put logic aside and come up with the money.

Exercise 25.1 Spelling

Correct any spelling errors in the following paragraph.

For help with this exercise, see handbook section 25 in *Successful College Writing*.

EXAMPLE:

➤ It sometimes ~~seams~~ *seems* as if every business ~~dicision~~ *decision* today has to go through a focus group.

Focus groups consist of people selected to express there opinions about products rangeing from sneakers and gum to movies. Some times people who are supposed to be experts on a subject are selected. When companys test a new product, they choose people who might realisticly be expected to by it. If marketers are tring out a new soft drink, for example, they might ask teen agers for their advise. A company makeing a luxery car would be more inclined to seek the veiws of upper-middle-class buyers. On other ocasions, a focus group is picked at random. To find out how much consumors like a new TV show, a network might ask shoppers at a mall to watch an episode and discuss it with other participents. The network could than learn not only what viewers like and dislike about the show, but also which groups are most likly to watch it. This information helps the network determine what changes to make in the show and what sponsers to approach. Of course, sense many people perfer the familiar, focus groups sometimes insure that tryed and true formulas ocurr again and again at the expense of new ideas.

Name _____ Date _____ Section _____

For help with this
exercise, see
handbook section
26 in *Successful
College Writing*.

Exercise 26.1 Nouns and Articles

Correct any errors in the use of nouns or articles in the following sentences.

EXAMPLE:

> ~~National~~ *The national* parks of the United States remind visitors of the great natural ~~beauties~~ *beauty* of this country.

1. The first American land set aside for a national public park was Yellowstone National Park, which was established in 1872 by a President Ulysses S. Grant.

2. Yellowstone National Park has not only the beautiful scenery but also the strange results of ancient volcanoes.

3. Underground lava left from the millions of years ago heats cold ground-water.

4. This heating results in hot springs, geysers, and the boiling muds.

5. Sequoia National Park, second national park established in the United States, is the home of many giant sequoia trees.

6. To the north of the Sequoia National Park is the third oldest national park, Yosemite National Park.

7. Like Sequoia National Park, Yosemite National Park offers the area of incredible beauty.

8. A waterfalls are found in some of our nation's oldest parks, such as Yosemite National Park and Niagara Reservation State Park.

9. Many other national parks have unusual natural formations; Denali National Park, for example, contains a highest mountain in North America.

10. A visitor who takes the time to see America's national parks will have a experience he or she will never forget.

Exercise 26.2 Count and Noncount Nouns

In each sentence, circle the correct count or noncount noun in parentheses.

For help with this exercise, see handbook section 26 in *Successful College Writing*.

EXAMPLE:

➤ Arielle got her (nail, (nails)) manicured for the wedding.

1. I plan to serve (shrimp, shrimps) at our party tomorrow night.

2. When you go to the store later, please pick up two pints of (cream, creams).

3. Please make the three (bed, beds) upstairs before you leave.

4. Did someone dust the (furniture, furnitures) in the living room?

5. The (smoke, smokes) from Paulie's cigar made me cough.

6. Please put the (book, books) back on the shelves where they belong.

7. I will sweep up the (sand, sands) in the front hall.

8. Tell Daniel that he must put all of his (tool, tools) back in the garage.

9. I don't want any of his (equipment, equipments) lying around when the guests arrive.

10. Let's check yesterday's and today's (mail, mails) to see who is coming to the party.

For help with this exercise, see handbook section 27 in *Successful College Writing*.

Exercise 27.1 Verbs

Correct any errors in the use of the underlined verbs in the following sentences. Some sentences may be correct as written.

EXAMPLE:

➤ Carlos Santana <u>have</u> some American radio hits with English lyrics and some with Spanish lyrics.

has had (above "have")

1. As a young boy in Mexico, Carlos Santana learned <u>playing</u> the clarinet and violin.

2. From his early years, Carlos Santana never stopped <u>to play</u> instruments.

3. When Santana was fourteen, he <u>taked</u> up the guitar.

4. The Santana family <u>was moving</u> to San Francisco in 1962, when Carlos was fifteen.

5. By 1967, Santana <u>has formed</u> a band.

6. The Santana Blues Band <u>begun</u> to make a name in San Francisco clubs.

7. San Francisco in the late 1960s <u>had been</u> a center for new musical talent, and Santana's band attracted attention.

8. The promoters of the 1969 Woodstock Music Festival asked the band, now called Santana, <u>playing</u> at their three-day outdoor concert.

9. Carlos Santana, who <u>just turned</u> twenty-two, led his band through a long composition called "Soul Sacrifice."

10. The crowds <u>were</u> delighted, and Santana <u>became</u> a star.

Name _____ Date _____ Section _____

Exercise 27.2 Infinitives and Gerunds

For help with this exercise, see handbook section 27 in *Successful College Writing*.

For each of the following sentences, fill in the blank with the appropriate infinitive or gerund formed from the verb in parentheses.

Example:

➤ It is easy to understand foreign students' _____*being*_____ (be) confused about grades in American university classes.

1. Most U.S. professors prefer their students _____ (work) independently, but professors do offer help to students who need it.

2. University policies forbid _____ (share) answers to a test.

3. However, instructors often encourage their students _____ (collaborate) in teams on projects other than tests and papers.

4. Universities consider _____ (plagiarize) written work as grounds for expulsion.

5. Dishonest students may jeopardize their relationship with other students who resent their _____ (cheat).

6. Instructors expect students _____ (do) the work for a class even if the work is not graded.

7. Some teachers believe that not grading an assignment enables students _____ (judge) their own work.

8. If students want to improve their grades, professors often support students' _____ (work) with a tutor.

9. But most professors don't appreciate their students' _____ (ask) about grades on a test or paper in the middle of class.

10. Students who want class time to discuss grades risk _____ (anger) their professors.

For help with this exercise, see handbook section 27 in *Successful College Writing*.

Exercise 27.3 Modal Verbs

In the exercise below, circle the correct modal auxiliary.

EXAMPLE:

➤ May/(Would) you help me complete the assignment?

1. It doesn't rain very often in Arizona, but today it looks like it (can/might).

2. I know I (will/ought to) call my aunt on her birthday, but I always find an excuse.

3. Sarah (should/must) study for her English exam, but she is happier spending time with her friends.

4. John (can/would) be the best person to represent our class.

5. Since the close presidential election of 2000, many people now believe they (could/should) vote in every election.

6. All students (will/must) bring two pencils, a notebook, and a dictionary to class every day.

7. (Would/May) you show me the way to the post office?

8. I (could/should) not ask for more than my health, my family, and my job.

9. Do you think they (could/can) come back tomorrow to finish the painting job?

10. A dog (should/might) be a helpful companion for your disabled father.

Exercise 28.1 The Prepositions *in, on,* and *at*

Fill in each blank with the correct preposition: *in, on,* or *at.*

For help with this exercise, see handbook section 28 in *Successful College Writing.*

EXAMPLE:

➤ Putting fresh vegetables __*in*__ a salad makes a tremendous difference.

1. For many people, a feature of modern life is eating food that comes _____ cans or boxes.

2. _____ dinnertime, the convenience of frozen and canned food is undeniable, but there is a trade-off.

3. Many Americans have grown dissatisfied with the convenience foods available _____ the supermarket.

4. Frequently, shoppers are willing to look harder for foods grown _____ local farms.

5. Both farmers and city dwellers benefit when agricultural products are available _____ urban areas.

6. Farmers get extra money _____ their pockets, and city people get delicious vegetables.

7. Why should rural dwellers be the only ones to enjoy an ear of sweet corn _____ a July day?

8. Farm products grown nearby also retain more vitamins than foods that have traveled long distances _____ a truck or train.

9. Decades ago, when most Americans sat _____ the dinner table, the foods they ate were likely to come from local growers.

10. _____ the United States today, regional foods and local produce are making a healthy comeback.

For help with this exercise, see handbook section 29 in *Successful College Writing*.

Exercise 29.1 Adjectives

Correct any errors in the use of adjectives in the following sentences. Some sentences may be correct as written.

EXAMPLE:

➤ ~~Brightly colored,~~ *f*luffy quilts are great to have in the autumn and winter ~~cold~~ weather.

F , brightly colored ... *cold*

1. The three first quilts that I made were not very intricate.

2. My fourth quilt's pattern, however, comprised 2,000 two-inch squares of multicolored fabric.

3. I found inspiration for the pattern in a short magazine article about memory quilts.

4. The article said that the most best memory quilts don't have fabric new in them.

5. To make the squares for my memory quilt, I cut up my old son's shirts and boxer shorts.

6. He has many drawers full of clothing that he has outgrown.

7. Assembling a memory quilt from these items was an opportunity good for me to make space in his bureau and to practice my sewing.

8. It was also an opportunity good for me to preserve his memories childhood.

9. My son considers it a treasured heirloom.

10. He thought the wonderful quilt was an idea, and he now wants me to make one bigger.

Exercise 30.1 Common Sentence Problems

Correct any common sentence problems in the following sentences.

For help with this exercise, see handbook section 30 in *Successful College Writing.*

EXAMPLE:

➤ Contagious diseases have frightened *people around the world* throughout history ~~people around the world.~~

1. Many people once believed that the twentieth century would produce medical miracles would bring an end to infectious diseases.

2. Medical research had not made at the end of the twentieth century this wish a reality.

3. Vaccines removed from the list of childhood diseases some terrible illnesses, such as polio.

4. One dangerous disease completely disappeared in the twentieth century was smallpox.

5. However, a few laboratories can still provide to trusted researchers access to samples of the virus.

6. Ordinary people forgot about smallpox their fears, but other diseases soon took its place.

7. The AIDS epidemic struck in the 1980s many previously healthy young people.

8. AIDS proved that medical science could declare total victory never over disease.

9. In the same decade, other terrifying new viruses that their existence was until recently unknown, such as Ebola, raced through local populations.

10. Medicine today can reveal much more about diseases than people knew during medieval plagues, but not always can this knowledge save the lives of sick people.

For help with this Exercise, see handbook section 30 in *Successful College Writing.*

Exercise 30.2 Forming Negative Sentences

Rewrite each sentence in the space provided so that it correctly expresses a negative statement.

EXAMPLE:

➤ The president will veto the tax bill.

The president will not veto the tax bill. _____

1. Speed limits are a good idea.

   _____

2. Hector knows the baseball scores.

   _____

3. He is a baseball fan.

   _____

4. Olga understands the importance of math class.

   _____

5. Medical careers are where math skills make the most difference.

   _____

6. Conversation is acceptable in the library.

   _____

7. Morning is the hardest time for Julia to concentrate.

   _____

8. Young hunters can shoot safely.

   _____

9. Marco always worries about the health of his relatives in Brazil.

   _____

10. The high school may build a new gymnasium.

    _____

ANSWERS TO EXERCISES

Exercise P.1 Possible Answers (page 1)

1. Given that the French diet is full of red meat, butter, and cheese, Americans are right to wonder why the French don't seem to get fat.
2. Studies show that many children who are patients in hospitals enjoy visits from trained pet therapists.
3. Though I didn't finish the race, running in the Boston Marathon taught me a lot about determination and friendship.
4. Effective
5. Because it's very difficult to evaluate someone's character online, people ought to be very cautious when participating in Internet dating.
6. Effective
7. Keeping up with the intimate details of movie stars' lives has become more important to some American teenagers than knowing the crucial details of American history.
8. One of the places where we can still find harmful stereotypes of African Americans, Native Americans, and Arabs is in Disney movies.
9. Like many other supposedly public places, national parks now charge fees that are far too high for the average visitor.
10. Effective

Exercise P.2 Possible Answers (page 3)

1. Most ordinary Americans, however, like their government, need to borrow money in order to survive economically.
2. Modern technology, however, has made it possible for many Americans to avoid the exercise that was once a part of daily life in this country.
3. Therefore, parents who want to give their child a head start should begin to play classical music for the child even before the baby's birth.

Exercise P.3 Answers (page 5)

1. (5) Interestingly, the word *bagatelle* can also refer to a short poem or piece of music. (10) However, video games are probably more popular than pinball today.
2. (4) According to folklore, when observers see one of these "shooting stars," they should make a wish. (5) Vaporized matter from burned-out meteors adds about ten tons to the mass of the earth every day.
3. (3) Running a family farm has never been easy. (7) The expense of new harvesting machines, called combines, and the need to get the harvest in as quickly as possible are major reasons farmers hire custom cutters rather than doing the work themselves.

Exercise P.4 Answers (page 7)

1. One alternative to drugs for treating depression is the controversial Eye Movement Desensitization and Reprocessing or EMDR. This treatment is particularly useful for people who are depressed as a result of a traumatic event. ~~Prozac is also useful for treat-~~

ing depression. ~~For those who don't respond to Prozac, doctors often recommend Zoloft.~~ In an EMDR session, the therapist makes hand motions or flashes a light in front of the patient's face while he or she talks about an upsetting experience. ~~People who have experienced trauma often need a lot of support.~~ Many people have found this nontraditional therapy to be very helpful in processing their experiences, though no one knows for sure why EMDR works. ____*not unified*____

2. The advertisements that now appear before the movie are not effective because they only make moviegoers irritable. ~~Coke is one of the most frequently advertised products and one of the most recognized American brands. People often drink Coke or other soft drinks when they go to the movies.~~ Ads take away from the otherwise enjoyable experience of seeing a movie in the theater. These days, you have to sit through ten minutes of commercials before the previews start. ~~Advertisers also use product placement as a way to increase their product's visibility.~~ By the time the movie begins, you may already have been in your seat for half an hour. Because of this inconvenience, people may decide that it's worthwhile to wait for the DVD and skip the ads. Movie-theater owners would be wise to remember their paying audience and reconsider this partnership with advertisers. ____*not unified*____

3. Unified

4. One of America's most well known and important court cases is the Scopes "Monkey Trial." ~~Students should learn their country's history at an early age. Knowing the past can help us predict the future.~~ In 1925, John Scopes, a high school biology teacher, was charged with violating state law by teaching the theory of evolution to his students. He believed he was teaching an important scientific theory, but others believed that evolution contradicted the story of creation told in the Bible. The trial became famous because so many people had such strong feelings on both sides. It has also remained relevant because we haven't come to a definitive conclusion about which ideas students should or should not learn in school. ~~There are many old conflicts that remain unresolved. For instance, people have been arguing for decades over whether or not abortion should be legal.~~ ____*not unified*____

5. More animal shelters should adopt a "no kill" policy. Controlling the stray animal population by euthanizing is not the best solution. Killing unwanted pets solves the problem of overpopulation only temporarily, and it creates a bigger problem because it teaches people that animals are disposable. ~~Many people don't consider snakes, iguanas, and other reptiles as pets. When I was seven, I adopted a snake from our local shelter, and he turned out to be a wonderful pet.~~ We need to learn to be kinder and more responsible when it comes to animals. We need to have pets fixed and accept them even when they have special needs. ~~We need to accept humans with special needs as well.~~ Many of the animals in shelters are there because they were neglected or mistreated. If we change our own behavior, fewer animals will end up abused and unwanted. ____*not unified*____

6. Buying a house is not always a good investment. People who sell their houses after owning them for only a couple of years often lose money. ~~Spending money on a computer is not always a good investment either. Computers lose their value very quickly. Unless the buyer uses the computer for work, money spent on a computer is money lost.~~ People who don't buy enough insurance for their homes can lose money if there is a fire, flood, or other disaster. Houses also require a lot of maintenance. When people sell their houses,

often they find it difficult to make back the money they spent fixing up the house. Sometimes people are better off investing their money in something that does not cost so much. _not unified_

7. Unified

8. Hilary Swank is a positive role model for young actresses. ~~Jennifer Lopez is a good role model for future dancers and singers. Many girls look up to their mothers as well.~~ Unlike many successful women in the movie industry, Swank is not afraid to challenge herself when choosing roles. In both *Boys Don't Cry* and *Million Dollar Baby,* Swank focuses not on looking pretty but on inhabiting her characters and their difficult lives. Her determination and willingness to take these risks may come in part from her background. She was not born into a rich or privileged family and, like some of the characters she plays, she has had to work very hard to achieve her goals. ~~Many famous people have rough starts. Jennifer Lopez did not come from a rich family.~~ It's important for young girls to see a successful movie star who has dedication, integrity, and a real love of acting. _not unified_

Exercise P.5 Possible Revisions (page 11)

1. A family gathering is supposed to fill us with a joyful sense of belonging, but it may not. Getting together for a family event, such as Thanksgiving dinner, can produce anxiety, anger, or depression just as often as it results in a warm, satisfied glow. People who are thrown together because they are related — by blood or by marriage — don't necessarily understand or like each other especially well. When relatives and in-laws get together, there are bound to be members of the group who don't get along. In my family, for example, my brother Philip and my aunt Julia are likely to get into an argument about some topic. Because family members are supposed to love each other, Philip and Julia usually try to talk with each other politely, never going into much depth or discussing dangerous topics such as politics, but the strain of trying to be nice can make them tense. And if they both have a few beers, the two of them don't even really try to chat any longer; they just glare at one another from their respective corners of the long dining-room table. Finally, Philip makes a sarcastic remark, Julia spits back a furious reply, and the rest of us feel embarrassed.

2. A movie can't be good unless all of the pieces — from the directing and screenwriting to the casting and music — come together successfully. I recently saw *Titanic* and thought that the concept and special effects were great, but the script was padded with laughable lines and two completely unnecessary gunfights. The script isn't always the problem; in *She's Gotta Have It,* for example, there was some fine writing, but the lead actress, Tracy Camilla Johns, never let the audience forget she was only playing a role. In contrast, Sean Penn and Christopher Walken were convincing as father and son in *At Close Range,* but the events in that movie happened so slowly that I wondered what the director, James Foley, was thinking. Even if everything else is on target, overbearing music can ruin a good scene, as in parts of *Saving Private Ryan,* where composer John Williams doesn't seem to trust the audience to know what to feel. With so many variables, it's a wonder that any good movies exist. They do, of course; *Rushmore* and *Big Night* are just two examples of recent films whose witty scripts, fine acting, crisp pace, and mood-enhancing music made audiences feel that everything about them was right.

3. Children should have a dog or cat as soon as they are old enough to play gently with it and avoid hurting it. Feeding and cleaning up after a pet is a good experience for any child. If parents are firm with their children and don't do their animal-care chores for them, the children will learn how to behave responsibly; it's hard to ignore or forget a beloved dog waiting for his little owner to feed and walk him. Additionally, having a pet can teach children about loving and protecting a creature weaker than themselves; any child who has ever held a contented, purring cat will find it very hard to be cruel to any animal. Responsibility and empathy are valuable lessons for children to learn and can help them grow into humane, decent adults. Finally, having a dog or cat can be a reward in itself—the animal returns affection and can actually make a child's life happier. At times, such as when parents or friends have disappointed a child, the family dog or cat will be a steadfast companion. Most adults who had a pet in childhood have wonderful memories of a much-loved Fido or Fluffy.

Exercise P.6 Answers (page 12)

1. Underdeveloped
2. Underdeveloped
3. Well developed
4. Underdeveloped
5. Well developed
6. Underdeveloped
7. Underdeveloped
8. Underdeveloped

Exercise P.7 Possible Revisions (page 17)

1. The French may still have the international reputation of being the people most interested in gourmet food, **but** Americans are quickly gaining **gastronomical ground. Once,** "American food" meant fast foods like hamburgers and hot dogs, **and in fact,** people around the world still associate these foods with American culture. **That perception is not entirely accurate now**: U.S. food lovers may seek out the best burgers, fries, and barbecue foods, **but** they also want to sample foods from ethnic cultures within the United States and **from** other countries. **Today,** people want the best of what American produce has to offer and will go far to find fresh, local ingredients that are expertly prepared.

2. Modern conceptions of timekeeping owe a lot to the ancient Babylonians. **They** gave people today the twelve-month year, the twenty-four-hour day, the sixty-minute hour, and the sixty-second minute. The number *twelve* was significant to the **Babylonian culture because the people** noticed that there were usually twelve full moons in a year. **Therefore**, the Babylonian calendar contained twelve months of thirty days each. **Because** five days were left over each year, every six years they had to add an extra month to the year. **Continuing to emphasize the mystical number** *twelve*, **the Babylonians** divided the day and night into twelve hours each. **In addition to** *twelve*, the number *sixty* was important to **this culture because it** can be evenly divided by many integers—two, three, four, five, six, ten, twelve, fifteen, twenty, and thirty. **Consequently, Babylonian time** divided each

hour into sixty minutes and each minute into sixty seconds. **Later**, the Romans changed the length of some Babylonian months from thirty to thirty-one or twenty-eight days, **but** the Babylonians' other time measurements survive to this day.

3. The Restoration period in England, which began with the return of the monarchy in 1660, was marked by the kind of public behavior on the part of aristocrats and courtiers that would still provoke a shocked reaction today. **The Restoration king**, Charles II, served as the model of moral—or immoral—behavior for members of his court. **Charles had** no children by his wife, **but** he had a large number of children by his several mistresses. **Following the king's example**, young male courtiers boasted of numerous love affairs. **To please these aristocrats**, court poets and dramatists composed bawdy, amoral literary works. Many **of these works** contained words and suggestions that even modern newspapers would not print. **During the Restoration**, the public loved to attend performances of plays **even though** simply being seen at a theater could give a person a questionable reputation. The clergy and other representatives of moral authority protested the literary, theatrical, and personal misbehavior of the aristocrats. **Eventually**, bawdiness became less fashionable, **and** a much more conservative age followed the Restoration.

Exercise P.8 Answers (page 19)

Title	**More Than Just a Place to Sleep**
Introduction	*Thesis:* Though it requires some preparation and adaptability, staying at a traditional Japanese hotel, or *ryokan,* is an enjoyable and worthwhile way for a Western visitor to learn about Japanese culture.
Body Paragraph 1	Finding a *ryokan*

- locate Web sites that list *ryokan*s (6)
- determine your price range
- decide how formal or informal a *ryokan* you'd like (2)
- make advance reservations

Body Paragraph 2 Apparel etiquette in a *ryokan*

- take off your shoes when you enter the *ryokan* and put on slippers
- take off the slippers when walking on the tatami mats (3)
- wear *geta* (wooden clogs) if you stroll around the *ryokan* grounds
- wear your *yukata* (robe provided by the *ryokan*) when in the *ryokan* (4)
- *yukatas* should be worn left side over right; right side over left is for funerals (7)
- wear a *tanzen* (outer robe) over your *yukata* if you get cold

Body Paragraph 3 Japanese bath etiquette

- Japanese often bathe before dinner
- in changing room, put *yukata* in basket provided
- wash yourself in the bathing area using shower or basin before entering the public bath (9)
- do not drain the water from the tub when finished
- dry yourself thoroughly before returning to the changing room (8)

Body Paragraph 4	Engaging with your host or hosts
	• learn a few key phrases in Japanese
	• ask about the building and garden
	• ask about the best sights to see in their town (5)
Body Paragraph 5	A day in the life of a different culture
	• be willing to try unusual breakfast foods, like cold squid and miso soup (1)
	• enjoy the serenity of life without television
	• try meditating
	• adjust to the firmness of a futon mattress (10)
Conclusion	While staying in a familiar Western-style hotel might feel easier, after a night or two in a *ryokan,* you'll find yourself more mindful of Japanese culture and traditions, and remarkably refreshed.

Exercise E.1 Possible Answers (page 21)

1. American parents choose carefully when naming their children.
2. Comparing popular names of today and of the past shows how much our ideas about naming children have changed.
3. Girls' names have changed the most.
4. Forty years ago, most baby girls received traditional names rather than unusual ones.
5. Some of the older names gradually became less popular, and newer names, like Jennifer, now a perennial favorite, took their place.
6. Today, parents often give their daughters names that were once considered masculine, like Sidney or Taylor.
7. Some parents try to make their daughters' names seem unusual by spelling a traditional name in a nontraditional way.
8. Boys' names, however, have not changed as noticeably.
9. For decades the most popular boys' name has been Michael.
10. Perhaps, as the results of a recent poll suggest, parents think having an unusual name helps girls and harms boys.

Exercise E.2 Possible Answers (page 22)

1. Nicotine, which is an addictive drug, is an ingredient in cigarettes.
2. No smoker sets out to become addicted to cigarettes, but most people have difficulty stopping once they start smoking.
3. Movies can affect young people profoundly; they often portray smokers as glamorous and sexy.
4. Many thirty-year-old people who do not smoke are unlikely to begin smoking.
5. The tobacco companies need new customers, and they are more apt to find such customers among the younger generations.
6. When some teenagers take up smoking, they don't consider the possible consequences.
7. The Joe Camel cartoon advertisements were controversial because cartoons often appeal to children.

8. The Joe Camel advertising campaign was withdrawn, and new restrictions have been placed on tobacco ads.
9. Smoking can be unsightly and unhealthy, but it is legal.
10. The number of lawsuits against tobacco companies has risen recently; families have argued that tobacco companies are to blame for the deaths of their loved ones.

Exercise E.3 Possible Answers (page 23)

1. In the nineteenth century, criminal tendencies were mistakenly thought to be related to physical traits.
2. Phrenologists, who studied bumps on the skull, mapped the human head for anti-social protrusions.
3. They hoped that they could identify potential criminals before crimes occurred.
4. Carefully recording their findings, other researchers, followers of a pseudoscience called craniometry, measured the proportions of the human head.
5. Using measurements of skull circumference, craniometrists inferred conclusions about brain size and intelligence as well as criminality.
6. From the beginning, these scientists' studies were fatally flawed because they found what they expected to find.
7. Since these "sciences" fell out of favor in the mid-twentieth century, researchers have been focusing on psychology as a means of understanding criminal actions.
8. The debate over which influence is stronger, heredity or environment, continues among social scientists.
9. One of the key controversies among scientists, the issue may never be resolved to everyone's satisfaction.
10. In scientific inquiry, however, important questions generate useful research as well as theories that are later discredited.

Exercise E.4 Answers (page 25)

1. The United States uses large amounts of energy, **depends** heavily on oil, and imports much of that oil.
2. Burning oil for energy pollutes the air, destroys an irreplaceable commodity, and **wastes** resources.
3. During the 1970s, an embargo made oil expensive and **difficult** to get.
4. The oil crisis led to a wider interest in alternative energy sources that would be renewable, environmentally sound, and **less expensive** than oil.
5. Some new homes used solar heating, although it was expensive to install and still relatively untested.
6. Many Americans expected electric cars to be perfected and widely available by the end of the twentieth century.
7. Instead, the embargo ended, the cost of oil dropped, and gasoline prices **declined**.
8. At the same time, money to invent alternative energy technologies, to develop new products, and **to market** the products dried up.

9. Scientists and **environmentalists** who study the environment hope that there will be plentiful renewable energy sources someday.

10. It would be better to have alternative energy possibilities soon than **to wait** for the world's oil reserves to run dry.

Exercise E.5 Possible Answers (page 26)

1. Annual "Fashion Week" events in American and European cities draw big crowds.

2. Photographers, journalists, models, and celebrities attend shows by new and established designers.

3. Many people in the audience show off their model-thin bodies and photogenic faces.

4. Often, *haute couture* shows with their expensive, trend-setting fashions entice the largest numbers of eager spectators.

5. Designers do not expect ordinary people to wear *haute couture* garments.

6. Designers frequently consider their *haute couture* creations to be works of art rather than mere outfits.

7. Only runway models can wear such clothing in public.

8. Other people attract ridicule in *haute couture* clothes.

9. Dressers can drape clothes more easily on models who have very thin bodies.

10. The spectacle impresses some people more than the clothes do.

Exercise E.6 Possible Answers (page 27)

Americans have recently been **forced to accept** the fact that anorexia nervosa, a disease of self-starvation, is becoming more widespread. Anorexia sufferers are overwhelmingly made up of teenage girls and young women. Most of them are white and come from middle-class or upper-class families. They are also usually **intelligent**. They seem to other people to have **nearly** every advantage. Their families and **friends** ordinarily have a **difficult** time comprehending why they will not eat. Because anorexia is a psychological disorder, the sufferers themselves may not **understand** what caused the onset of their illness. Anorexics have a **distorted** body image. They often believe they are **extremely** overweight unless they are dangerously **thin**. The disease is notoriously difficult to treat, even if the patient tries to **cooperate with** her doctors.

Exercise E.7 Possible Answers (page 28)

1. Every year, almost all college-bound high school juniors take one or more college admissions tests.

2. A high test score can help a student gain admission to a prestigious college.

3. Test-preparation courses, which give students practice exams to measure their progress, are becoming popular.

4. These courses can cost hundreds of dollars.

5. Educators disagree about whether test-preparation courses actually help students prepare for the exam and for college work.

6. Many students who take a standardized test before and after a test-preparation course show at least some improvement in their scores after the course.

7. The amount of improvement may be only a few percentage points.

8. Opponents of the courses argue that by taking them, wealthy students can, in effect, buy a better score.

9. Others say that the scores of students who take test-preparation courses are not significantly higher than the scores of students who don't.

10. Many worried parents continue to pay for test preparation, reasoning that it can't hurt their children's chances.

Exercise E.8 Possible Answers (page 29)

1. For generations, women were considered to be spun-glass angels too fragile for sports.

2. Many people thought that women would die like a butterfly in a whirlwind if they were too physically active.

3. Even though these mistaken beliefs were widespread, women athletes have moved forward, hurdling over all obstacles.

4. Individual women athletes, like the track and golf star Babe Didrikson Zaharias, had to be as strong as a well-toned muscle.

5. During World War II, a women's baseball league drew spectators like bees to a field of poppies when a shortage of male players depleted men's teams.

6. The end of the war drained the blood from the women's league.

7. The American women's movement of the 1970s was the beginning of a new season for women in sports.

8. A "battle of the sexes" took place in tennis during that decade, when Billie Jean King, a star female player, made Bobby Riggs, an avowed "male chauvinist" who had challenged her, look as weak as a newborn baby's grip.

9. In the following decades, some individual women became sports heroes, like Florence Griffith Joyner, who could run like a cheetah.

10. Finally, in the 1990s, the popularity of women's basketball and soccer spread like the "wave" in a packed stadium.

Exercise E.9 Possible Answers (page 30)

1. The treatment of mental illness has troubled societies throughout history.

2. A thousand years ago, observers thought mental disturbance proved that the sufferer was possessed by demons.

3. Many mentally ill people died in the course of treatment for demonic possession.

4. Belief in demonic possession eventually decreased in much of the world.

5. Instead, doctors and others classified mental illness as a kind of disease.

6. Sufferers were frequently confined and, often, forgotten.

7. Officials decided that mentally ill people were antisocial, not sick.

8. Most healthy people rarely considered the mentally ill.

9. In the nineteenth century, a reformer, Dorothea Dix, investigated the treatment of the mentally ill in Massachusetts.

10. Her report shocked people so much that Massachusetts, and soon other states, legislated humane treatment for sufferers of mental illness.

Exercise 1.1 Answers (page 31)

1. Verb
2. Noun
3. Verb
4. Noun
5. Pronoun
6. Verb
7. Noun
8. Pronoun
9. Verb
10. Noun

Exercise 1.2 Answers (page 32)

1. Parents in the early twentieth century **were** warned that detective magazines could warp children's minds.
2. Pulp fiction about crime did indeed **become** rather lurid.
3. Correct
4. Many scholars have **given** Edgar Allan Poe credit for being the first author to write detective fiction in English.
5. Correct
6. Correct
7. Correct
8. Arthur Conan Doyle, the creator of Holmes and Watson, **was** amazed at the popularity of his fictional characters.
9. Correct
10. While not all detective stories are worthy of serious study, the best ones are **considered** by scholars to be very rewarding.

Exercise 1.3 Answers (page 33)

1. Simple past
2. Past progressive
3. Present perfect
4. Past perfect
5. Simple present
6. Simple future
7. Past perfect
8. Past perfect progressive
9. Future progressive

10. Simple future

Exercise 1.4 Answers (page 34)

1. Subjunctive
2. Indicative
3. Indicative
4. Subjunctive
5. Imperative
6. Indicative
7. Subjunctive
8. Indicative
9. Indicative
10. Indicative

Exercise 1.5 Answers (page 35)

1. Adverb
2. Adjective
3. Adjective
4. Adjective
5. Adverb
6. Adjective
7. Adjective
8. Adverb
9. Adjective
10. Adverb

Exercise 1.6 Answers (page 36)

1. Preposition
2. Preposition
3. Conjunction
4. Preposition
5. Conjunction
6. Conjunction
7. Preposition
8. Conjunction
9. Conjunction
10. Preposition

Exercise 2.1 Answers (page 37)

1. Complete subject

2. Simple subject
3. Complete predicate
4. Complete predicate
5. Complete subject
6. Simple predicate
7. Simple predicate
8. Complete predicate
9. Simple subject
10. Simple predicate

Exercise 2.2 Answers (page 38)

1. Subject complement
2. Object complement
3. Direct object
4. Subject complement
5. Direct object
6. Direct object
7. Object complement
8. Indirect object
9. Indirect object
10. Subject complement

Exercise 2.3 Answers (page 39)

1. Appositive phrase
2. Prepositional phrase
3. Verbal phrase
4. Verbal phrase
5. Absolute phrase
6. Appositive phrase
7. Absolute phrase
8. Prepositional phrase
9. Verbal phrase
10. Appositive phrase

Exercise 2.4 Answers (page 40)

1. Many superstitions date from classical or medieval times, <u>when belief in witchcraft was widespread</u>.
2. Superstitions were a way for people to explain <u>whatever threatened them</u>.
3. <u>Because cats were believed to be witches in disguise</u>, the fear of a black cat crossing one's path came about.

4. Walking under ladders has also long been considered unlucky; this superstition may survive <u>because it protects pedestrians from falling objects</u>.

5. Some people attribute to the Christian story of the Last Supper, <u>where thirteen people were present</u>, the origins of the superstitious fear of the number thirteen.

6. <u>Wherever it began</u>, fear of the number thirteen, or triskaidekaphobia, is still prevalent enough for many tall modern buildings not to have a thirteenth floor.

7. Early Romans believed <u>that sneezing was a sign of the plague</u>, so they feared it.

8. The method <u>they invented</u> to protect a sneezer was to say, "God bless you."

9. In the United States today, it is common to say "God bless you" — or "Gesundheit," <u>which is German for "health"</u> — following a sneeze.

10. Superstitions from the past may seem silly today, but <u>who knows what strange customs of the present will be ridiculed in the future</u>?

Exercise 2.5 Answers (page 41)

1. Simple
2. Complex
3. Compound
4. Complex
5. Compound-complex
6. Complex
7. Simple
8. Compound
9. Simple
10. Compound-complex

Exercise 3.1 Possible Answers (page 42)

1. There are older and more valuable manuscripts than the Voynich.

2. However, there is none more mysterious. The Voynich is still puzzling scholars many years after its discovery.

3. This manuscript was written in a code. So far, no one has been able to solve it.

4. Because the origins of the manuscript are unclear, the puzzle is doubly difficult.

5. No one knows what country it came from.

6. Therefore, it is very hard to determine the language the code represents. This makes decoding it even more troublesome.

7. Correct

8. The writing does not resemble any letters that can be traced to a known alphabet.

9. The manuscript contains many beautiful illustrations. It depicts plants, people, and other seemingly unrelated images.

10. The Voynich manuscript is such an intriguing mystery that some scholars might actually be disappointed to learn all of its secrets.

Exercise 4.1 Possible Answers (page 43)

1. Mae West began as a child star. The career of "Baby Mae" took off when she performed at a local Brooklyn theater's amateur night.

2. At the age of nineteen, West began performing on Broadway; she shocked audiences in 1911.

3. The voluptuous West became known for her suggestive clothing and even more famous for her suggestive wisecracks.

4. Attending black jazz clubs had introduced her to a new dance movement. She performed this "shimmy" on Broadway, and it became a trademark for her.

5. West was not satisfied for long with the theatrical roles she was offered; writing her own plays was one way to find good parts.

6. In 1925, she wrote a play called *Sex*, but no producer she contacted would bring it to the stage.

7. The following year, when West produced the play herself, advertisements for *Sex* were banned.

8. Nevertheless, the show played for nine months until it was closed down by the Society for the Suppression of Vice. West was arrested and spent eight days in jail.

9. In the 1930s and 1940s, Mae West took her naughty humor to Hollywood. While there she made a series of hit films and often wrote her own screenplays.

10. West made her final films in the 1970s. By that time Americans found her less scandalous, but her name was still a household word.

Exercise 5.1 Answers (page 44)

1. The festival called "Juneteenth," which people once recognized only in a few southern areas of the United States, **is** now much more widespread.

2. Correct

3. The surrender of the Confederate States **was** made official at Appomattox Courthouse on April 9, 1865.

4. From that day on, the Confederacy and the Union **were** again a single country.

5. Neither the northern states nor the southern states **were** now legally able to permit slave-owning, which had been officially outlawed in the United States several years earlier.

6. Correct

7. The story from those long-ago days **goes** that in Texas, slave owners murdered the messengers bringing word of emancipation.

8. Not until June 19, 1865, **was** the news able to reach the last group of Texas slaves.

9. Correct

10. Today, people celebrating Juneteenth **attend** concerts, films, and other cultural events.

Exercise 6.1 Answers (page 45)

1. The horrors of World War I **convinced** some artists that European society had to change radically.

2. Their reaction at first **consisted** of musical and performance events they called the Cabaret Voltaire.

3. Soon, however, the most influential members of the group **began** to focus on visual art.

4. **The artists chose** the name *Dada* at random.

5. They rejected older artistic traditions, including avant-garde ideas that **had** recently **become** popular.

6. Instead, the Dadaists **challenged** the whole concept of art.

7. Before the Dada movement **ended** in 1923, several of the artists had experimented with random arrangements of materials.

8. Sometimes they chose the material they **used** from items discarded by other people.

9. One artist, Marcel Duchamp, even **set** up ordinary objects at art shows, claiming that the act of choosing the objects made them art.

10. Dada was a rebellion, not an attempt to build a new tradition, so no identifiable stylistic legacy of the movement **remains** today.

Exercise 7.1 Possible Answers (page 46)

1. Many political analysts say that public distrust of the U.S. government began with Watergate.

2. That scandal's continuing legacy may make Watergate one of the most influential American events of the twentieth century.

3. Since the early 1970s, political scandals have rarely interested Americans; the scandals often seem to have very little effect.

4. Journalists provided the American people with a lot of information about the Iran-Contra hearings, but the public could not have cared less.

5. Could the indifference of most people have been the result of post–Watergate trauma?

6. If Americans expect politicians to be corrupt, government scandals will not surprise or even interest the public.

7. Ironically, the media's coverage of scandals seems to have made the public suspicious of journalists as well.

8. Cynicism about political and journalistic motives, which can spread contagiously, leads to apathy.

9. Many people are so apathetic that they refuse to vote.

10. If people do not believe that they can make a difference in the political process, the country becomes less democratic.

Exercise 7.2 Answers (page 47)

1. Meteorology has made many advances in the past few decades, but **it** still cannot answer a number of questions about tornadoes.

2. Every tornado has **its** own unique characteristics.

3. Correct

4. An F4 tornado or an F5 tornado can destroy everything in **its** path.

5. Scientists cannot yet predict how strong any tornado will be before **it** happens.
6. One mystery about tornadoes involves the last step when **they** form.
7. Specialists do not know if a tornado forms in a cloud and travels to the ground or if **it begins** on earth and **spirals** upward.
8. Correct
9. Either a few extra minutes of warning or more information about a storm's power would prove **its** effectiveness in saving lives.
10. People who live in a tornado zone should always know where **their** nearest safe area is.

Exercise 7.3 Answers (page 48)

1. **We** residents of the United States are considered by much of the rest of the world to be an unusually violent people.
2. Many researchers have debated **their** theories about violent behavior in this country.
3. Did the popular myth of the "Wild West" influence **us** and our ancestors?
4. Other industrialized nations and **we** have very different policies concerning guns.
5. Correct
6. Violence and justice are so intertwined for many Americans that disagreements between other people and **them** can erupt into fights.
7. Correct
8. There are defenders of violent films, TV shows, and video games **who** claim that entertainment reflects our tastes rather than influencing them.
9. Correct
10. Sometimes it seems that our worst enemies are **we**.

Exercise 8.1 Possible Answers (page 49)

1. West African villages have strong oral traditions in which parents and grandparents tell the younger people stories.
2. Before the Revolutionary War, slave traders forced ancestors of the people from those villages to come to the United States.
3. In their difficult new situation in this country, the Africans adapted their stories so that people could learn from them.
4. Although different stories had different messages, one kind of character came up over and over again.
5. The character is cunning and clever; he is a "trickster."
6. The stories about Br'er Rabbit are good examples of folktales whose hero is a trickster.
7. Many of the other animals want to eat Br'er Rabbit, who has only his wits to protect him.
8. Yet in every story, Br'er Rabbit not only escapes, but he makes his enemies appear foolish as well.
9. Trickster characters like Br'er Rabbit showed slaves who heard these stories that they, too, could triumph by using cleverness when foes surrounded them.

10. Today, folklorists are exploring how early African Americans encouraged each other by telling stories of tricksters outsmarting powerful enemies.

Exercise 8.2 Possible Answers (page 50)

1. Most people think falsehoods are easy to spot.
2. They think that nonverbal signals show when someone is lying.
3. These signals, such as avoiding eye contact or hesitating before answering a question, are habits of truthful people as well.
4. Liars are hard to identify because no single trait always proves that a person is lying.
5. One problem with lie detection is that truthful people who are afraid they will not be believed may act suspiciously.
6. A few people are unusually good at identifying liars.
7. However, perhaps because these people are attuned to deceitful behavior, they are not especially good at identifying truth-tellers.
8. A stranger's lies may be easier to detect than a loved one's.
9. The better someone knows and likes another person, the more difficult it seems to be to spot his or her lies.
10. Finding it hard to believe that one's friends would try to deceive one is an understandable human characteristic.

Exercise 9.1 Possible Answers (page 51)

1. Many people go to a lot of trouble to look **attractive**.
2. In the United States, no one thinks a woman wearing high heels is dressed **strangely**.
3. Many Americans even go to **really** extreme lengths, such as having surgery, to be beautiful.
4. People can see the strangeness of beauty rituals **more clearly** if the rituals are unfamiliar.
5. For example, in China in past centuries, beautiful women had to have **tiny** feet.
6. To achieve this goal, families bound their daughters' feet so **tightly** that the feet could not grow.
7. Subcultures within the United States also have their own standards of beauty that may seem **odd** to people who are not part of the subculture.
8. For many young Americans, tattoos and body piercing were the **trendiest** fashion statements of the 1990s.
9. They might have argued that such beautification was no **more unusual** than plucking out one's eyebrows.
10. Parents, however, often felt **vast** relief if their children reached adulthood without tattoos.

Exercise 10.1 Possible Answers (page 52)

1. Recently, several sports that no one had heard of thirty years ago have gained popularity.

2. With a name that suggests their dangerous allure, extreme sports are attracting members of Generation X.
3. These "Generation X" games, which include snowboarding and sky-surfing, often involve going to inaccessible places.
4. Snow activities that can be done on remote mountaintops are especially popular.
5. Some of these sports, such as freestyle skiing and snowboarding, have become so widely accepted that participants can now compete in the Olympics.
6. Gasping at the antics of snowboarders, mountain bikers, and other athletes, fans can see that the sports world really has changed.
7. These "in-your-face" athletes are only a small part of what is interesting about the changes taking place in sports today.
8. Even fans of extreme sports know that the quest for adventure occasionally leads people into dangerous situations.
9. Environmentalists also point out that in some remote wilderness areas, extreme sports are unfortunately taking their toll on nature.
10. Whether people love them or hate them, extreme sports will probably continue to inspire extreme reactions.

Exercise 11.1 Answers (page 53)

1. In some places, the ocean is more than seven miles deep.
2. Enormous pressure and complete darkness in the depths make it difficult for humans to discover what is down there.
3. Correct
4. The sheer size of the ocean depths indicates that there may be many more species down there than are found on land.
5. Correct
6. Correct
7. Is it also possible that the actions of humans are affecting life at the bottom of the sea?
8. Biologists who have recently measured the food supply on the ocean floor might be moved to exclaim, "It seems to be dwindling!"
9. Most of the food that reaches the bottom comes from near the surface, where there is light.
10. Warmer surface temperatures may be reducing the food supply at the bottom, and who has more influence on global warming than human beings?

Exercise 12.1 Answers (page 54)

1. Breeders have long prized their swiftest, most graceful horses and raced them.
2. Correct
3. Harness racehorses pull small, lightweight vehicles handled by a driver.
4. Harness racing falls into the two categories of trotting and pacing.
5. The most famous event in harness racing, the Hambletonian, is a mile-long trotting race.

6. Harness racing may be known mainly to enthusiasts, but even people who appreciate very little about horse racing are familiar with thoroughbred racing.

7. Correct

8. The best-known events in thoroughbred racing, the Kentucky Derby, the Preakness Stakes, and the Belmont Stakes, are the three races that make up the Triple Crown.

9. All of the Triple Crown races, which vary in length, are for three-year-old horses.

10. In the twentieth century, only eleven horses won thoroughbred racing's Triple Crown.

Exercise 12.2 Answers (page 55)

1. Several years ago, many police departments ignored minor violations of the law and concentrated on bigger crime problems.

2. Today, however, the "broken window" theory is widely accepted.

3. According to this popular theory, allowing broken windows to remain unrepaired leads to a loss of hope in a community.

4. Correct

5. Similarly, if petty crimes are ignored in a neighborhood, people there may feel that larger crimes are acceptable as well.

6. Correct

7. But can a police officer walking a beat really be more effective than a patrol car?

8. Some experts believe that police should be required to live in the communities that they serve.

9. Correct

10. Different methods of community policing may work in different areas, but the goal should always be to keep communications open between the public and the police.

Exercise 13.1 Answers (page 56)

1. Many Americans think of the years after World War II as a golden era, a time before modern complexities made life more difficult.

2. Even without considering the quality of life at that time for women and minorities, an idyllic view of the mid-twentieth century ignores other issues.

3. Correct

4. The Soviet Union, an ally of the United States during World War II, took control of the governments of neighboring countries; China, after a civil war, fell under Communist rule; and the Korean conflict, in which Americans were involved, seemed to prove that Communists wanted to take over as much land as possible.

5. Correct

6. Senator Joseph McCarthy may have shared this fear; he certainly capitalized on it to advance his political career.

7. In 1950, McCarthy announced that he had a list of Communists who held positions in the U.S. State Department.

8. Correct

9. Eventually, more than 150 film workers, including performers, directors, and writers, were blacklisted by the Hollywood studios.

10. For the first half of the 1950s, anti-Communist leaders were very powerful in the United States; however, by 1955 McCarthy was in disgrace, and in 1957 the courts determined that membership in the Communist Party should no longer be a criminal offense in this country.

Exercise 14.1 Answers (page 58)

1. In 1910, Robert Falcon Scott led his second expedition to Antarctica with two objectives: to collect scientific data and to be the first humans at the South Pole.

2. The years before World War I were a heady time for exploration of the frozen Antarctic continent.

3. The story of Scott's difficult journey continues to fascinate armchair adventurers even though the expedition was, in many ways, a failure.

4. After arriving in Antarctica, Scott's scientists began their work: they collected specimens, surveyed the land, and recorded twelve volumes of data.

5. Correct

6. Scott stuck to his original timetable for the South Pole journey: he did not want to engage in a race.

7. Scott and his men set out for the South Pole in the Antarctic summer of 1911, which is the winter season in the Northern Hemisphere.

8. Correct

9. As they traveled back to their base camp, death took all five men: Scott, Titus Oates, Edgar Evans, Henry Bowers, and Edward Wilson.

10. Correct

Exercise 15.1 Answers (page 59)

1. The film producer shouted excitedly, "Everyone loves Shakespeare because he used so many familiar quotations!"

2. "When we make movies based on Shakespeare plays," he added, "we don't have to pay royalties to the writer."

3. Films based on Shakespeare plays try to reveal the relevance of his work to a modern audience.

4. Although Shakespeare lived four hundred years ago, his work is currently in demand in Hollywood.

5. *Hamlet, A Midsummer Night's Dream,* and *Romeo and Juliet* are just a few of the Shakespeare plays filmed in the 1990s.

6. The producer commented, "When I hear that a new film will be based on Shakespeare, I wonder, like Juliet, 'What's in a name?'"

7. If the name "Shakespeare" were not involved, would filmmakers be as interested in the material?

8. Shakespeare's plays are frequently performed in theaters, too, and several young playwrights recently wrote works based on his sonnets.

9. Hamlet, perhaps Shakespeare's most famous character, laments "Alas, poor Yorick! I knew him, Horatio, a fellow of infinite jest, of most excellent fancy."

10. Othello, one of Shakespeare's most complex characters, laments that he "loved not wisely, but too well."

Exercise 16.1 Answers (page 60)

1. Correct

2. "[A]ll men are . . . endowed by their creator with certain inalienable rights, . . . among these are life, liberty, and the pursuit of happiness."

3. "Thomas Jefferson wanted the Declaration of Independence to say that men were 'created independent' . . . ."

4. Elizabeth Cady Stanton's "Declaration of Sentiments" announces, "[W]e anticipate no small amount of misconception, misrepresentation, and ridicule. . . ."

5. "Stanton's 'Declaration of Sentiments' was based . . . on the language Jefferson had used in the Declaration of Independence."

6. Correct

7. "Allusions to the language of familiar literature . . . can lend authority to a text that uses them well."

8. Lincoln went on, "Fondly do we hope . . . that this mighty scourge of war may speedily pass away."

9. Martin Luther King Jr. expressed the wish that his children would be judged "by the content of their character."

10. "Repetition of structure can be an effective rhetorical device."

Exercise 17.1 Answers (page 61)

1. African **chiefs'** stories led a German explorer to the stone ruins in Mashonaland, now in Zimbabwe, in 1871.

2. The explorer, **whose** name was Karl Mauch, tried to find out who had built the once great city.

3. The tribes nearby could not answer **Mauch's** question, but they knew gold had been found there.

4. The **Africans** called the site *Zimbabwe.*

5. Correct

6. He thought perhaps the **city's** builder was the Queen of Sheba.

7. An **archeologist's** findings later demonstrated that the city was about six hundred years old and that it had been built by African natives.

8. The Shona tribe probably built the first walls on the site, but **its** more complex structures were added later by the Rozwi tribe.

9. The Rozwi probably erected the temple, which was inhabited by Rozwi ruler-priests until their empire's end in the **1830s.**

10. The legends about the origins of the city persisted for a long time, perhaps because of white South **Africans'** and Europeans' resistance to the idea that black Africans had built the impressive structures.

Exercise 18.1 Answers (page 62)

1. Bad movies (some of which are quite enjoyable to watch) often have a cult following.
2. Some films routinely make every critic's list of worst films (usually, these movies are so bad they are funny).
3. A few filmmakers (like Ed Wood) and movie companies (like American International Pictures) have acquired fame among fans of bad movies.
4. Roger Corman's American International Pictures (AIP) churned out innumerable inexpensive, quickly made films.
5. One Corman film, *Little Shop of Horrors* (1960), was filmed in less than three days.
6. But the director Edward D. Wood Jr. (1924–1978) has a special place in the world of bad movies.
7. Wood gained new fame with Tim Burton's film biography, *Ed Wood* (1994).
8. Like Corman's movies, Wood's were made very quickly, but Wood (unlike Corman) thought he was making great films.
9. Wood's "masterpiece," *Plan 9 from Outer Space* (Bela Lugosi's last film), is a science fiction and horror film with bad acting, dreadful writing, and laughable special effects.
10. Wood said that "*Plan 9* [was his] pride and joy."

Exercise 19.1 Possible Answers (page 63)

1. Songbirds are a part of our national heritage — each state has its own official bird.
2. Some states have official birds unique to the region.
3. The nene — Hawaii's state bird — is a goose found only on those islands.
4. In Salt Lake City, a statue of a seagull, which is Utah's state bird, honors the birds that ate a huge swarm of locusts — without the birds, most crops would have been eaten by the insects.
5. Other states share popular state birds — the cardinal, the meadowlark, and the mockingbird are all official birds in at least five states.
6. When Americans think of spring, they often think of songbirds chirping in the trees.
7. For many years, the Audubon Society — an organization devoted to nature study — has studied populations of songbirds.
8. Birdwatchers — mainly trained volunteers — count birds in small local areas during the year-end holiday season.
9. The numbers of some songbirds — though fortunately not all — have declined alarmingly.
10. Although most people appreciate the sights and sounds of songbirds, they may not realize how modern human habits interfere with many birds' lives.

Exercise 20.1 Answers (page 64)

1. At the turn of a new century and a new **millennium**, many people reflected on historical changes that had taken place in the previous hundred years.
2. In the late 1990s, Americans began making lists reflecting their choices of the greatest **events**, **literature**, people, and **films** of the century.

3. Most Americans would agree that the two **world wars** shaped the twentieth century and this country's role in it.

4. List makers might, however, dispute the importance of *Ulysses* or *Gone with the **Wind**.*

5. Between the beginning and the end of the twentieth century, the United States changed from a minor player in global politics into the single undisputed **world power**.

6. Technology also advanced dramatically in the century of television, the *Apollo* space missions, and personal computers.

7. Of course, technology was sometimes used for evil purposes, as the **Holocaust** and nuclear weapons proved.

8. Some people would even argue that a significant development of the century was an increasing concern for the environment—**in** the United States, in Europe, and in parts of the **former** Soviet Union, among other places.

9. The trend toward urbanization saw people moving from rural areas to cities, with the result in this country that the **Great Plains** grew emptier while the **coasts**' population increased.

10. Only historical distance will reveal whether the twentieth century was "**the** best of times" or "**the** worst of times."

Exercise 21.1 Answers (page 65)

1. When disasters strike, victims count on international organizations like the Red Cross and Doctors without Borders.

2. A **doctor's** help is often the most desperately needed form of aid.

3. People often offer canned goods and blankets, while major **corporations** receive tax benefits for donations of drugs and other medical supplies.

4. When Hurricane Mitch devastated Honduras, many U.S. **citizens** were quick to help.

5. A **registered nurse** who is willing to travel to the disaster area can provide needed services.

6. For several years, volunteer doctors have tried to alleviate the AIDS crisis in Africa.

7. In some situations, **such as** during outbreaks of deadly diseases or in war-torn areas, medical personnel risk their own lives.

8. Doctors from the Centers for Disease Control **(CDC) in Atlanta, Georgia**, travel the globe to isolate and study dangerous viruses.

9. The CDC doctors do not provide medical assistance in war zones, but other **organizations** do.

10. In the aftermath of bloody fighting, a U.N. peacekeeping force may arrive to find **international** doctors already at work.

Exercise 22.1 Answers (page 66)

1. John Lennon, Paul McCartney, George Harrison, and Ringo Starr were **four** young men from Liverpool, England, who formed what would become the most popular rock band of all time.

2. On January **25**, 1964, the Beatles' first hit entered the U.S. charts.

3. The song "I Want to Hold Your Hand" spent seven weeks at number one and **fourteen** weeks in the top **forty**.

4. Almost immediately, the Beatles began to attract **thousands** of screaming fans everywhere they went.

5. Throughout the **1960s**, the Beatles were the world's most popular group.

6. During the eight years of the Beatles' reign on the charts, they had more than forty **3**-minute pop hits.

7. By the **second** half of the decade, the Beatles had stopped touring.

8. They performed live together for the last time on the roof of **3** Savile Row, the headquarters of their doomed record company, Apple.

9. **One hundred fifty** employees worked for Apple, which eventually went bankrupt.

10. By no means did each Beatle earn **25** percent of the group's profits, for Lennon and McCartney wrote more than **90** percent of the songs.

Exercise 23.1 Answers (page 67)

1. Americans today get their information from *60 Minutes*, the *New York Times*, electronic sources, and thousands of other places.

2. Once, choices were limited: to find out about raising a child, for example, parents consulted Dr. Spock's book *Baby and Child Care*.

3. Now, magazines like *Parenting* compete with the new edition of Dr. Spock and dozens of other titles.

4. Obscure information is more accessible than ever, so a fan of the song "Telstar" can find *The Joe Meek Story*, a full-length biography of its producer.

5. A student wanting to learn about the dead language called Old English could consult Web sites like the one maintained by Georgetown University.

6. It may no longer be possible for a single person to know all about, for example, biology.

7. Once, the term *Renaissance man* or *Renaissance woman* referred to a person well educated and talented in many subjects.

8. Leonardo da Vinci, the original Renaissance man, not only painted the *Mona Lisa* but also wrote botanical treatises and devised remarkable engineering plans.

9. Today, we do not expect the builder of the ocean liner *Queen Elizabeth II* to know other subjects.

10. A lifetime of study may lie behind a single article in the *New England Journal of Medicine*.

Exercise 24.1 Answers (page 68)

1. Does buying lottery tickets and entering sweepstakes make a person self-employed?

2. The odds of winning a major lottery prize are often over a million to one.

3. Yet many people, including desperately poor ones who cannot afford the tickets, buy large numbers of them when the jackpot is high and the odds are worst.

4. A sensible approach to such sky-high odds would be not to enter the lottery at all.

5. Sweepstakes are well known to anyone with a mailbox.

6. Unlike lotteries, apparently free sweepstakes do not require any cash investment other than the price of a stamp.

7. Yet many sweepstakes imply that buying a magazine subscription or a product improves the chances of winning.

8. Some sweepstakes companies have been accused of trying to dupe customers who do not read the fine print.

9. Some elderly people have thrown away their great-grandchildren's inheritance, buying hundreds of products they don't need from sweepstakes advertisers.

10. The idea of getting rich with minimal work or investment is so strikingly attractive that many people put logic aside and come up with the money.

Exercise 25.1 Answers (page 69)

Focus groups consist of people selected to express **their** opinions about products **ranging** from sneakers and gum to movies. **Sometimes** people who are supposed to be experts on a subject are selected. When **companies** test a new product, they choose people who might **realistically** be expected to **buy** it. If marketers are **trying** out a new soft drink, for example, they might ask **teenagers** for their **advice**. A company **making** a luxury car would be more inclined to seek the **views** of upper-middle-class buyers. On other **occasions**, a focus group is picked at **random**. To find out how much **consumers** like a new TV show, a network might ask shoppers at a mall to watch an episode and discuss it with other **participants**. The network could **then** learn not only what viewers like and dislike about the show, but also which groups are most **likely** to watch it. This information helps the network determine what changes to make in the show and what **sponsors** to approach. Of course, **since** many people **prefer** the familiar, focus groups sometimes **ensure** that **tried** and true formulas **occur** again and again at the expense of new ideas.

Exercise 26.1 Answers (page 70)

1. The first American land set aside for a national public park was Yellowstone National Park, which was established in 1872 by President Ulysses S. Grant.

2. Yellowstone National Park has not only beautiful scenery but also the strange results of ancient volcanoes.

3. Underground lava left from millions of years ago heats cold groundwater.

4. This heating results in hot springs, geysers, and boiling **mud**.

5. Sequoia National Park, **the** second national park established in the United States, is the home of many giant sequoia trees.

6. To the north of Sequoia National Park is the third oldest national park, Yosemite National Park.

7. Like Sequoia National Park, Yosemite National Park offers **an** area of incredible beauty.

8. **Waterfalls** are found in some of our nation's oldest parks, such as Yosemite National Park and Niagara Reservation State Park.

9. Many other national parks have unusual natural formations; Denali National Park, for example, contains **the** highest mountain in North America.

10. A visitor who takes the time to see America's national parks will have **an** experience he or she will never forget.

Exercise 26.2 Answers (page 71)

1. shrimp
2. cream
3. beds
4. furniture
5. smoke
6. books
7. sand
8. tools
9. equipment
10. mail

Exercise 27.1 Answers (page 72)

1. to play
2. playing
3. took
4. moved
5. had formed
6. began
7. was
8. to play
9. had just turned
10. Correct

Exercise 27.2 Answers (page 73)

1. to work
2. sharing
3. to collaborate
4. plagiarizing
5. cheating
6. to do
7. to judge
8. working
9. asking
10. angering

Exercise 27.3 Answers (page 74)

1. might
2. ought to
3. should
4. would
5. should
6. must
7. would
8. could
9. can
10. might

Exercise 28.1 Answers (page 75)

1. in
2. At
3. at
4. on
5. in
6. in
7. on
8. on
9. at
10. In

Exercise 29.1 Answers (page 76)

1. The first three quilts that I made were not very intricate.
2. Correct
3. Correct
4. The article said that the best memory quilts don't have new fabric in them.
5. To make the squares for my memory quilt, I cut up my son's old shirts and boxer shorts.
6. Correct
7. Assembling a memory quilt from these items was a good opportunity for me to make space in his bureau and to practice my sewing.
8. It was also a good opportunity for me to preserve his childhood memories.
9. Correct
10. He thought the quilt was a wonderful idea, and he now wants me to make a bigger one.

Exercise 30.1 Possible Answers (page 77)

1. Many people once believed that the twentieth century would produce medical miracles that would bring an end to infectious diseases.
2. At the end of the twentieth century, medical research had not made this wish a reality.
3. Vaccines removed some terrible illnesses, such as polio, from the list of childhood diseases.
4. One dangerous disease that completely disappeared in the twentieth century was smallpox.
5. However, a few laboratories can still provide access to samples of the virus to trusted researchers.
6. Ordinary people forgot their fears about smallpox, but other diseases soon took its place.
7. The AIDS epidemic struck many previously healthy young people in the 1980s.
8. AIDS proved that medical science could never declare total victory over disease.
9. In the same decade, other terrifying new viruses whose existence was until recently unknown, such as Ebola, raced through local populations.
10. Medicine today can reveal much more about diseases than people knew during medieval plagues, but this knowledge cannot always save the lives of sick people.

Exercise 30.2 Answers (page 78)

1. Speed limits are not a good idea.
2. Hector does not know the baseball scores.
3. He is not a baseball fan.
4. Olga does not understand the importance of math class.
5. Medical careers are not where math skills make the most difference.
6. Conversation is not acceptable in the library.
7. Morning is not the hardest time for Julia to concentrate.
8. Young hunters cannot shoot safely.
9. Marco never worries about the health of his relatives in Brazil.
10. The high school may not build a new gymnasium.

Appendix

Writing Assessment

The two assessment tests in Appendix A will help you and your instructor determine aspects of your writing that you need to improve. The first test (pp. 107–108) assesses your ability to develop and support ideas about a topic and express them clearly and correctly in an essay. The second test (pp. 108–115) measures your ability to recognize and correct errors in grammar, punctuation, and mechanics.

WRITING ASSESSMENT: WRITING ESSAYS

Choose *either* Essay Assignment A or Essay Assignment B for this writing assessment test. Although the essay assignments are from courses in interpersonal communications and sociology, you do not need any background in these subject areas to write either essay. For whichever option you choose, then, draw from your personal experience for ideas for the essay. Be sure your essay is about the topic you choose and that it states, develops, and supports one main point about your topic. When you have finished drafting your essay, be sure to revise, edit, and proofread it. Your instructor will evaluate your final essay and identify any writing skills that need improvement. With your instructor's feedback, you will then be able to use the Action Plan Checklist (p. 116) to find help with those skills that need improvement.

Essay Assignment A

Suppose you are taking a course in interpersonal communications and have been assigned a two-page essay on one of the following topics. Choose a topic, develop a thesis statement, and support your thesis with evidence.

1. Describe a communication breakdown you have observed or experienced, telling what happened, why it happened, and what could have been done to prevent it.

2. Pretend that you are preparing for a job interview. Describe the communication and leadership skills you would bring to the position of assistant manager at a department store.

3. Recall a conflict, disagreement, or argument you have had with someone. What feelings and emotions did you and the other person express? Explain how you communicated those feelings to each other and how the conflict was (or was not) resolved.

4. Explain how you can tell when a person doesn't mean what he or she says, using people you know as examples.

Essay Assignment B

Suppose you are taking a sociology course and have been assigned a two-page essay on *one* of the following topics. Choose a topic, develop a thesis statement, and support your thesis with evidence.

1. Describe one important function of the family in American life. Explain why it is important and what is expected of family members. Use your own family as an example.

2. Explain one important function of dating in the United States. Support your ideas with your own dating experiences.

3. Examine one major function of the wedding ceremony. Why is this function important? Use weddings that you have attended or been involved in as evidence to support your thesis.

WRITING ASSESSMENT: RECOGNIZING AND CORRECTING SENTENCE ERRORS

Most of the following sentences contain errors; some are correct as written. Look in the <u>underlined</u> part of each sentence for errors in usage, punctuation, grammar, capitalization, or sentence construction. Then choose the one revision that corrects the sentence error(s). If the original sentence contains no errors, select "d. no change." Circle the letter of the item you choose as your answer. An interactive version of this assessment is available in the Writing Guide Software for *Successful College Writing* and online at http://www.bedfordstmartins.com/exercisecentral.

1. <u>Lonnie and Robert should put his ideas together</u> and come up with a plan of action for the class project.
   a. Lonnie and Robert should put his idea together
   b. Lonnie and Robert should put her ideas together
   c. Lonnie and Robert should put their ideas together
   d. no change

2. The school district newsletter informs <u>all parents of beneficial programs for you and your children</u>.
   a. all parents of beneficial programs for your children.
   b. each parent about beneficial programs for you and your children.
   c. you of all beneficial programs for you and your children.
   d. no change

3. Margaret earned an A <u>on her term paper, consequently, she</u> was excused from taking the final exam.
   a. on her term paper; consequently, she
   b. on her term paper, consequently; she
   c. on her term paper consequently, she
   d. no change

4. Some students choose courses <u>without studying degree requirements these students often make</u> unwise choices.
   a. without studying degree requirements, these students often make
   b. without studying degree requirements. These students often make
   c. without studying degree requirements; so these students often make
   d. no change

5. Twenty-five band members <u>picked up their instruments from their chairs which were tuned and began to play</u>.
   a. picked up their tuned instruments from their chairs and began to play.
   b. picked up their instruments from their chairs tuned and began to play.
   c. picked up and began to play their instruments from their chairs which were tuned.
   d. no change

6. I am sure I <u>did good on my midterm exam</u> because it seemed easy to me.
   a. did awful good on my midterm exam
   b. did real good on my midterm exam
   c. did well on my midterm exam
   d. no change

7. In many American families, the financial decisions are made jointly by <u>husband and wife, the wife</u> makes most of the routine household decisions.
   a. husband and wife, in contrast the wife

b. husband and wife the wife
c. husband and wife. The wife
d. no change

8. Professor Simmons <u>pace while he lectures</u>.

    a. pacing while he lectures.
    b. pace while he lecture.
    c. paces while he lectures.
    d. no change

9. When Tara set <u>the cup on the glass-topped table, it broke</u>.

    a. her cup on the glass-topped table, she broke it.
    b. the cup on the table with a glass top; it broke.
    c. it on the glass-topped table, the cup broke.
    d. no change

10. <u>Swimming to shore, my arms got tired</u>.

    a. My arms got tired swimming to shore.
    b. When I was swimming to shore, my arms got tired.
    c. My arms, swimming to shore, got tired.
    d. no change

11. Thousands of fans waited <u>to get into the stadium. Swarmed around the parking lot</u> like angry bees until security opened the gates.

    a. to get into the stadium. Swarming around the parking lot
    b. to get into the stadium; swarmed around the parking lot
    c. to get into the stadium. They swarmed around the parking lot
    d. no change

12. <u>After I left the college library I went</u> to the computer lab.

    a. After I left the college library, I went
    b. After leaving the college library I went
    c. After I left the college library; I went
    d. no change

13. <u>To be honest is better than dishonesty</u>.

    a. Being honest is better than dishonesty.
    b. To be honest is better than being dishonest.
    c. It is better to be honest than dishonest.
    d. no change

14. The amount of time <u>students spend researching a topic depends on his familiarity</u> with the topic.

    a. students spend researching a topic depends on his or her familiarity
    b. students spend researching a topic depends on their familiarity

c. a student spends researching a topic depends on their familiarity
d. no change

15. After Carlos completed <u>his term paper, he seems</u> less tense.

   a. his term paper, he seemed
   b. his term paper, he will seem
   c. his term paper, he is seeming
   d. no change

16. <u>When Maria tried to sign up for those courses in the fall, but they were full.</u>

   a. When Maria tried to sign up for those courses in the fall; however, they were full.
   b. Although Maria tried to sign up for those courses in the fall, but they were full.
   c. Maria tried to sign up for those courses in the fall, but they were full.
   d. no change

17. A course in nutrition <u>may be useful; it may help you make</u> wise food choices.

   a. may be useful, it may help you make
   b. may be useful it may help you make
   c. may be useful; because it may help you make
   d. no change

18. According to the reporter, <u>many pets are run over by automobiles roaming around untended.</u>

   a. many pets are run over roaming around untended by automobiles..
   b. many pets roaming around untended are run over by automobiles.
   c. many pets who are run over by automobiles roaming around untended.
   d. no change

19. You need to take <u>life more serious if you hope to do well</u> in school.

   a. life more serious if you hope to do good
   b. life more seriously if you hope to do well
   c. life seriouser if you hope to do well
   d. no change

20. Leon has already taken <u>three social sciences courses, Introduction to Psychology,</u> Sociology 201, and Anthropology 103.

   a. three social sciences courses; Introduction to Psychology,
   b. three social sciences courses: Introduction to Psychology,
   c. three social sciences courses. Introduction to Psychology,
   d. no change

21. <u>There's several people who can</u> advise you about the engineering program.

   a. There are several people who can

    b. There is several people who can
    c. There's two people who can
    d. no change

22. <u>In Chapter 6 of your book it describes</u> the causes of mental illness.
    a. In Chapter 6 of your book, they describe
    b. Chapter 6 of your book describes
    c. In Chapter 6 of the book, it describes
    d. no change

23. <u>Flood damage was visible crossing the river.</u>
    a. Flood damage was visible, crossing the river.
    b. Crossing the river, the flood damage was visible.
    c. Flood damage was visible as we crossed the river.
    d. no change

24. She had to leave the <u>van in the driveway. The heavy, wet snow halfway up</u> the garage door.
    a. van in the driveway. The heavy, wet snow had piled halfway up
    b. van in the driveway. Because of the heavy, wet snow halfway up
    c. van in the driveway; the heavy, wet snow halfway up
    d. no change

25. Mail <u>carriers who have been bitten by dogs are</u> wary of them.
    a. carriers, who have been bitten by dogs, are
    b. carriers who have been bitten, by dogs, are
    c. carriers who, having been bitten by dogs, are
    d. no change

26. Alfonso <u>need to practice</u> his clarinet every day.
    a. needing to practice
    b. needes to practice
    c. needs to practice
    d. no change

27. <u>Everyone should be sure to bring their notebook</u> to class on Wednesday.
    a. Everyone should be sure to bring their notebooks
    b. Everyone should be sure to bring his or her notebook
    c. Everyone should be sure to bring his notebook
    d. no change

28. <u>The television program ended Janelle read a book</u> to her son.
    a. When the television program ended, Janelle read a book
    b. The television program ended and Janelle read a book
    c. The television program ended, Janelle read a book
    d. no change

29. Georgia <u>replied "The way to a man's heart is through his stomach."</u>
    a. replied "The way to a man's heart is through his stomach".
    b. replied; "The way to a man's heart is through his stomach."
    c. replied, "The way to a man's heart is through his stomach."
    d. no change

30. The <u>plan to travel to three cities in two days seem</u> overly ambitious.
    a. plan to travel to three cities in two days are
    b. plan to travel to three cities in two days seems
    c. plan to travel to three cities in two days do seem
    d. no change

31. <u>You discover that your concentration improves</u> with practice, so now I can study more in less time.
    a. I discovered that my concentration improves
    b. You discover that concentration improves
    c. You discovered that your concentration improves
    d. no change

32. I couldn't watch the <u>rest of the football game. Because there was no chance that we could win</u> now. We were behind by three touchdowns.
    a. rest of the football game and there was no chance that we could win
    b. rest of the football game because there was no chance that we could win
    c. rest of the football game; because there was no chance that we could win
    d. no change

33. <u>"Shopping" Barbara explained "is</u> a form of relaxation for me."
    a. "Shopping" Barbara explained, "is
    b. "Shopping," Barbara explained "is
    c. "Shopping," Barbara explained, "is
    d. no change

34. <u>A balanced diet, exercising regularly, and to get enough sleep</u> are essential to good health.
    a. Eating a balanced diet, exercising regularly, and to get enough sleep
    b. A balanced diet, regular exercise, and enough sleep
    c. To eat a balanced diet, exercising regularly, and to get enough sleep
    d. no change

35. <u>The use of air bags was designed</u> to increase driver and passenger safety.
    a. Air bags were designed
    b. The use of air bags were designed
    c. Increased use of air bags was designed
    d. no change

36. The <u>articles and the book contains</u> the information I need.
    a. book and the articles contains
    b. articles and the book contain
    c. articles and the book has contained
    d. no change

37. Top firms are always <u>looking for skilled managers. People who can adapt</u> to changing times and rise to new challenges.
    a. looking for skilled managers; people who can adapt
    b. looking for skilled managers. People, who can adapt
    c. looking for skilled managers who can adapt
    d. no change

38. <u>Individuals and community groups can assist students in financial need, and</u> help them secure a good education.
    a. Individuals and community groups, can assist students in financial need and
    b. Individuals, and community groups can assist students in financial need, and
    c. Individuals and community groups can assist students in financial need and
    d. no change

39. <u>Someone left their briefcase</u> under the table.
    a. Everyone left their briefcase
    b. Someone left their briefcases
    c. Someone left his or her briefcase
    d. no change

40. Mustard is a versatile <u>seasoning and it can be</u> used to enhance the flavor of many dishes.
    a. seasoning; and it can be
    b. seasoning, and it can be
    c. seasoning, therefore it can be
    d. no change

41. We spent our most happiest days in the little cottage on the lake.
    a. spent our happiest days
    b. spent our more happiest days
    c. spent our more happy days
    d. no change

42. Swimming is an <u>excellent form of exercise, it produces</u> a good aerobic workout.
    a. excellent form of exercise it produces
    b. excellent form of exercise and it produces

c. excellent form of exercise because it produces

d. no change

For a guide to scoring your assessment, turn to p. 117.

ACTION PLAN CHECKLIST

The Action Plan Checklist (p. 116) will help you find the appropriate resources for improving the writing skills that you and your instructor have identified as problem areas.

Resources

1. **Part 7: Handbook: Writing Problems and How to Correct Them.** The Handbook section of *Successful College Writing* contains a systematic review of the rules that correspond to most of the topics listed under "Sentence Skills" in the Action Plan Checklist, as well as exercises to help you understand and apply the rules.

2. **Exercise Central and Additional Exercises for *Successful College Writing*.** The exercises in the workbook and online at http://www.bedfordstmartins.com/ exercisecentral offer you practice in applying the principles presented in Part 7. The workbook and Exercise Central contain additional exercises for all the topics listed in the Action Plan Checklist as well as other topics you may wish to review. These resources are designed so that you can check your answers immediately after completing an exercise. As you work through each exercise, be sure to take the time to discover why you answered any items incorrectly and, if you are still uncertain, to check with a classmate or your instructor.

3. **Writing Guide Software for *Successful College Writing*.** This interactive computer program provides a comprehensive review of many of the topics included in the Action Plan Checklist as well as other key topics. The software includes a tutorial for most of the problem areas identified under "Sentence Skills."

ACTION PLAN CHECKLIST

Directions: Place a check mark next to each skill that you or your instructor has identified as a problem area. An interactive version of this checklist is available in the Writing Guide Software for *Successful College Writing.*

Skills That Need Improvement		Resources That Will Help You			
Paragraph Skills	✔	*Text/ Handbook**	*Workbook*	*Exercise Central*	*Writing Guide Software*
Details—Relevant		Ch. 5	Exercise P-2		Tutorial 1
Details—Specific		Ch. 5	Exercise P-3		Tutorial 2
Topic Sentences		Ch. 5	Exercise P-1		Tutorial 4
Topic Sentences		Ch. 5	Exercise P-4		Tutorial 5
Sentence Skills					
Adjective and Adverb Usage		H9	Exercise 9.1	Ch. 9, #91	Tutorial 6
Capitalization		H20	Exercise 20.1	Ch. 20, #103	
Colon Usage		H14	Exercise 14.1	Ch. 14, #97	
Comma Splices		H4	Exercise 4.1	Ch. 4, #83	Tutorial 7
Comma Usage		H12	Exercise 12.1, 12.2	Ch. 12, #s 94, 95	Tutorial 8
Dangling Modifiers		H10	Exercise 10.1	Ch. 10, #92	Tutorial 9
Sentence Fragments		H3	Exercise 3.1	Ch. 3, #82	Tutorial 10
Misplaced Modifiers		H10	Exercise 10.1	Ch. 10, #92	Tutorial 9
Mixed Constructions		H8	Exercise 8.2	Ch. 8, #90	Tutorial 11
Parallelism		Ch. 7	Exercise E.4	Ch. 34, #116	Tutorial 12
Pronoun-Antecedent Agreement		H7	Exercise 7.2	Ch. 7, #87	Tutorial 13
Pronoun Reference		H7	Exercise 7.1	Ch. 7, #86	Tutorial 14
Punctuation of Quotations		H15	Exercise 15.1	Ch. 15, #98	
Run-on Sentences		H4	Exercise 4.1	Ch. 4, #83	Tutorial 15
Semicolon Usage		H13	Exercise 13.1	Ch. 13, #96	Tutorial 16
Shifts		H8	Exercise 8.1	Ch. 8, #89	Tutorial 17
Subject-Verb Agreement		H5	Exercise 5.1	Ch. 5, #84	Tutorial 18
Spelling		H25	Exercise 25.1	Ch. 25, #108	Tutorial 19
Verb Forms		H6	Exercise 6.1	Ch. 6, #85	Tutorial 20

*Handbook sections are preceded by the letter *H* in this chart.

Working through Your Action Plan

Once you have filled in the check marks in your Action Plan Checklist, use the following suggestions to achieve maximum success with using it to improve your writing skills.

1. Begin by reading the appropriate section(s) in Chapters 5 and 7 and in Part 7 and studying the examples. You may have to read the material several times to grasp it fully.

2. Test your understanding of a particular rule or explanation by looking away from the text and writing the rule or principle in your own words in your journal. If you cannot do so, you do not fully understand the rule. Try discussing it with a classmate and your instructor and recording what you learn from them in your own words. When you can explain the principle or rule in your own words, you are more apt to understand and remember the material.

3. Once you are confident that you understand a rule or explanation for a sentence skill or problem, complete the corresponding exercise in the Handbook, the workbook, or online at http://www.bedfordstmartins.com/exercisecentral.

4. Set a deadline by which you will understand the rules and complete the exercises for all of your problem areas. Try to complete everything within the next two to three weeks. The sooner you understand this essential material, the sooner you will be fully prepared to write clear, effective essays.

SCORING AND INTERPRETING YOUR GRAMMAR ASSESSMENT

Score your assessment by using the answer key that follows. Each question assesses your ability to recognize and correct a particular sentence problem. In the answer key, circle the number of each item you answered incorrectly.

Answer Key: Error Correction Self-Assessment

Answer	Sentence Skill or Problem
1. c	Pronoun-Antecedent Agreement
2. c	Shift in Person
3. a	Comma Splice
4. b	Run-on Sentence
5. a	Misplaced Modifier
6. c	Adverb and Adjective Usage
7. c	Comma Splice
8. c	Subject-Verb Agreement
9. c	Pronoun Reference
10. b	Dangling Modifier
11. c	Sentence Fragment
12. a	Comma Usage
13. c	Parallelism
14. b	Pronoun-Antecedent Agreement
15. a	Shift in Tense
16. c	Mixed Construction
17. d	Semicolon Usage
18. b	Misplaced Modifier

19. b	Adverb and Adjective Usage
20. b	Colon Usage
21. a	Subject-Verb Agreement
22. b	Pronoun Reference
23. c	Dangling Modifier
24. a	Sentence Fragment
25. d	Comma Usage
26. c	Verb Form
27. b	Pronoun-Antecedent Agreement
28. a	Run-on Sentence
29. c	Punctuation of Quotation
30. b	Subject-Verb Agreement
31. a	Shift in Point of View
32. b	Sentence Fragment
33. c	Comma Usage
34. b	Parallelism
35. a	Mixed Construction
36. b	Subject-Verb Agreement
37. c	Sentence Fragment
38. c	Comma Usage
39. c	Pronoun-Antecedent Agreement
40. b	Comma Usage
41. a	Adverb and Adjective Usage
42. c	Comma Splice

2nd Edition

CHINESE MADE EASY

CHINESE MADE EASY

1

Workbook

Simplified Characters Version

轻松学汉语（练习册）

Yamin Ma
Xinying Li

Joint Publishing (H.K.) Co., Ltd.
三联书店（香港）有限公司

02

Chinese Made Easy *(Workbook 1)*

Yamin Ma, Xinying Li

Editor	Chen Cuiling, Luo Fang
Art design	Arthur Y. Wang, Yamin Ma, Xinying Li
Cover design	Arthur Y. Wang, Amanda Wu
Graphic design	Amanda Wu
Typeset	Lin Minxia, Zhou Min

Published by
JOINT PUBLISHING (H.K.) CO., LTD.
Rm. 1304, 1065 King's Road, Quarry Bay, Hong Kong

Distributed in Hong Kong by
SUP PUBLISHING LOGISTICS (HK) LTD.
3/F., 36 Ting Lai Road, Tai Po, N.T., Hong Kong

Distributed in Taiwan by
SINO UNITED PUBLISHING LIMITED
4F., No. 542-3, Jhongjheng Rd., Sindian City, Taipei County 231, Taiwan

First published July 2001
Second edition, first impression, August 2006
Second edition, third impression, August 2007

Copyright ©2001, 2006 Joint Publishing (H.K.) Co., Ltd.

You can contact us via the following:
Tel: (852) 2525 0102, (86) 755 8343 2532
Fax: (852) 2845 5249, (86) 755 8343 2527
Email: publish@jointpublishing.com
http://www.jointpublishing.com/cheasy/

轻 松 学 汉 语 (练习册一)

编　著　马亚敏　李欣颖

责任编辑	陈翠玲　罗　芳
美术策划	王　宇　马亚敏　李欣颖
封面设计	王　宇　吴冠曼
版式设计	吴冠曼
排　　版	林敏霞　周　敏

出　　版	三联书店（香港）有限公司
	香港鲗鱼涌英皇道1065号1304室
香港发行	香港联合书刊物流有限公司
	香港新界大埔汀丽路36号3字楼
台湾发行	联合出版有限公司
	台北县新店市中正路542-3号4楼
印　　刷	深圳市德信美印刷有限公司
	深圳市福田区八卦三路522栋2楼
版　　次	2001年7月香港第一版第一次印刷
	2006年8月香港第二版第一次印刷
	2007年8月香港第二版第三次印刷
规　　格	大16开 (210 x 280mm) 200面
国际书号	ISBN 978.962.04.2585.1

©2001，2006 三联书店（香港）有限公司

CONTENTS 目 录

第一单元　你好

第一课　你好

1 Match the Chinese with the English.

(1) 好 _hǎo_ ——— (a) you

(2) 早 _zǎo_ ——— (b) good; well

(3) 你 _nǐ_ (c) you (respectfully)

(4) 再 _zài_ (d) see

(5) 您 _nín_ (e) again

(6) 见 _jiàn_ (f) morning

2 Translation.

(1) 好 _hǎo_ _____good; well_____

(2) 早 _zǎo_ _____

(3) 你 _nǐ_ _____

(4) 您 _nín_ _____

(5) 你好 _nǐ hǎo_ _____

(6) 再见 _zài jiàn_ _____

3 Fill in the bubbles with the captions in the box.

(a) 你好！ _nǐ hǎo_　(b) 您好！ _nín hǎo_　(c) 你早！ _nǐ zǎo_

(d) 您早！ _nín zǎo_　(e) 再见！ _zài jiàn_

❶ 再见！

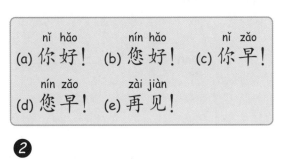

❷

❸

4 Translation.

(1) you ___你___

(2) morning _____

(3) good; well _____

(4) you (respecfully) _____

(5) hello _____

(6) good-bye _____

(7) good morning (respectfully)

_____

(8) again _____

(9) see _____

5 Write the dialogue in Chinese.

Hello, Dan!

Hi, Mary!

Bye!

Good-bye!

Mary: _____

Dan: _____

Mary: _____

Dan: _____

6 Dismantle the characters into parts.

(1) 你^{nǐ} ___亻___ ___尔___

(2) 您^{nín} _____ _____

(3) 早^{zǎo} _____ _____

(4) 好^{hǎo} _____ _____

7 Transcribe the pinyin into Chinese characters.

(1) nǐhǎo ___你好___

(2) nínzǎo _____

(3) zàijiàn _____

2

生 字

		ノ 亻 亻 亻 你 你 你							
nǐ you	你								
		乚 乚 夕 女 女' 奵 好							
hǎo good; well	好								
		ノ 亻 亻 亻 竹 你 你 你 您 您 您							
nín you (respectfully)	您								
		丶 口 口 日 旦 早							
zǎo early; morning	早								
		一 厂 冂 丙 丙 再							
zài again	再								
		丨 冂 贝 见							
jiàn see	见								

偏旁部首(一)

		╱ ╰								
sleeping person	╰									
		╱ 亻								
standing person	亻									
		╱ 人								
stretching person	人									
		╱ ╱ 彳								
two people	彳									
		╱ 八 少 父								
father	父									
		一 二 干 王								
king	王									
		一 十 土								
soil	土									
		一 十 士								
scholar	士									
		丶 屮 山								
mountain	山									

第二课　你好吗

1　Circle the correct pinyin.

(1) 谢　(a) xiè　(b) xèi

(2) 错　(a) cuò　(b) chuò

(3) 很　(a) hěn　(b) hěng

(4) 还　(a) héi　(b) hái

(5) 再　(a) zhài　(b) zài

(6) 您　(a) nín　(b) níng

(7) 也　(a) yě　(b) yiě

(8) 早　(a) zhǎo　(b) zǎo

2　Fill in the blanks with the words in the box.

ma	cuò	hǎo	zǎo	yě	jiàn
吗	错	好	早	也	见

(1) A: 你好 ____吗____ ?
nǐ hǎo

B: 不 _____ 。
bú

(2) A: 你早!
nǐ zǎo

B: 你 _____ !
nǐ

(3) A: 再见!
zài jiàn

B: 再 _____ !
zài

(4) A: 你 _____ 吗?
nǐ　　　　　ma

B: 我很好。你呢?
wǒ hěn hǎo　nǐ ne

A: 我 _____ 很好。
wǒ　　　　hěn hǎo

3　Dismantle the characters into parts.

(1) 你 _____ _____
nǐ

(2) 好 _____ _____
hǎo

(3) 早 _____ _____
zǎo

(4) 错 _____ _____
cuò

(5) 很 _____ _____
hěn

(6) 谢 _____ _____
xiè

(7) 还 _____ _____
hái

(8) 呢 _____ _____
ne

5

4 Finish the dialogues in Chinese.

(1) A: nǐ hǎo
你好!

   B: 你好_____!

(2) A: nǐ zǎo
你早!

   B: _____!

(3) A: zài jiàn
再见!

   B: _____!

(4) A: nǐ hǎo ma
你好吗?

   B: _____。

(5) A: _____?

   B: wǒ hěn hǎo   nǐ ne
我很好。你呢?

(6) A: nǐ hǎo ma
你好吗?

   B: bú cuò
不错。_____?

   A: hái kě yǐ
还可以。

(7) A: nín hǎo
您好!

   B: _____!

5 Match the Chinese with the English.

(1) bù hǎo
不好   (a) very early

(2) hěn zǎo
很早   (b) very bad

(3) hěn bù hǎo
很不好   (c) not bad

(4) bù zǎo
不早   (d) not good

(5) hái hǎo
还好   (e) not early

(6) bù hěn hǎo
不很好   (f) not at all

(7) bú xiè
不谢   (g) thank you

(8) xiè xie nǐ
谢谢你   (h) not very good

6 Translation.

(1) Not bad. _____

(2) OK. _____

(3) How are you ? _____

(4) How about you ?_____

(5) I'm also very well. _____

(6) Good-bye ! _____

(7) Thank you. _____

7 Transcribe the pinyin into Chinese characters.

(1) nǐhǎo ma _____

(2) búcuò _____

(3) wǒ hěnhǎo _____

(4) nǐ ne _____

(5) hái kěyǐ _____

(6) wǒ yě hěnhǎo _____

(7) xièxie _____

(8) zàijiàn _____

8 Answer the question.

1: 我很好。_____

nǐ hǎo ma
你好吗?

2: _____

3: _____

9 Correct the mistakes.

(1) 你 〔nǐ〕 你 _____

(2) 甲 〔zǎo〕 _____

(3) 错 〔cuò〕 _____

(4) 很 〔hěn〕 _____

(5) 再贝 〔zài jiàn〕 _____

(6) 您 〔nín〕 _____

(7) 谢 〔xiè〕 _____

10 Find the phrases. Write them out.

也	不	错
您	很	早
你	好	吗

(1) 你好 _____

(2) _____

(3) _____

(4) _____

(5) _____

(6) _____

生字

	丶 丨 口 口 吗 吗									
ma particle	吗									
	一 丆 丆 不									
bù not; no	不									
	丿 丿 上 仨 仨 钅 钅 针 钳 锴 错 错 错									
cuò mistake; bad	错									
	一 丆 丆 不 不 还 还									
hái also; fairly	还									
	一 丆 厂 司 口 可									
kě can; may	可									
	丶 丷 以 以									
yǐ use; take	以									
	丿 一 于 手 我 我 我									
wǒ I; me	我									
	丶 丿 彳 彳 彳 彳 彳 很 很 很									
hěn very; quite	很									
	丶 讠 讠 讠 讠 讷 讷 讷 讷 谢 谢									
xiè thank	谢									
	丶 丨 口 口 吖 吖 呢 呢									
ne particle	呢									
	フ 田 也									
yě also; as well	也									

偏旁部首(二)

		丶 丷 忄								
feeling	忄									
		丶 心 心 心								
heart	心									
		丶 丨 冂 口								
mouth	口									
		丶 丷 丷 丷 丷 兰 羊 羊								
sheep	羊									
		丶 丨 冂 口 口 足 足 足 足								
foot	足									
		丶 冫 讠								
speech	讠									
		丿 广 广 卢 钅								
metal	钅									
		丿 广 饣								
food	饣									
		乚 纟 纟								
silk	纟									

第三课　你是我的好朋友

1 Match the numbers in row A with the ones in row B.

Ⓐ

(1) 12 　　(2) 40 　　(3) 54 　　(4) 78 　　(5) 66 　　(6) 98

Ⓑ

wǔ shí sì　　　qī shí bā　　　liù shí liù　　　sì shí　　　jiǔ shí bā　　　shí èr

(a) 五十四　(b) 七十八　(c) 六十六　(d) 四十　(e) 九十八　(f) 十二

2 Count and then write the numbers in Chinese.

Example

五

❶

❷

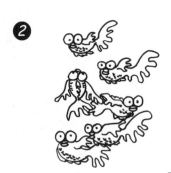
❸

❹

❺

3 Write the numbers in Chinese.

(1) 16   十六

(2) 20   _____

(3) 39   _____

(4) 50   _____

(5) 65   _____

(6) 73   _____

(7) 88   _____

(8) 90   _____

(9) 94   _____

(10) 99   _____

4 Translation.

(1) How are you?

(2) I'm very well. How about you ?

(3) Hello!

(4) Good morning!

(5) Good-bye!

(6) Not bad.

(7) Pretty good.

(8) I am also very well.

(9) Thanks!

(10) You are my friend.

5 Translate the telephone numbers into Chinese.

Telephone Number   Telephone Number

(1) 2476 3804   二四七六 三八〇四

(2) 2845 6672

(3) 2907 2548

(4) 2595 7976

(5) 2987 8452

生字

		⟍ 丨 口 日 日 旦 早 旱 昃 是										
shì be	是											
		⟍ 亻 白 白 白 白 的 的										
de of; 's	的											
		丿 刀 月 月 刖 朋 朋 朋										
péng friend	朋											
		一 ナ 方 友										
yǒu friend	友											
		丨 冂 冂 四 四										
sì four	四											
		一 厂 五 五										
wǔ five	五											
		⟍ 一 六 六										
liù six	六											
		一 七										
qī seven	七											
		丿 八										
bā eight	八											
		丿 九										
jiǔ nine	九											
		一 十										
shí ten	十											

偏旁部首(三)

	丨 冂 月 日										
sun	日										
	丿 亻 白 白 白										
white	白										
	丨 冂 月 月 目										
eye	目										
	丿 刀 月 月										
flesh	月										
	丨 冂 日 甲 田										
field	田										
	丶 丶丶 氵										
water	氵										
	丶 丷 灬 灬										
fire	灬										
	一 厂 戶 雨 雨 雨 雨 雨										
rain	雨										
	丿 夕 夕										
sunset	夕										

第四课 今天是几月几号

1 Write the numbers in Chinese.

(1) 7 _____   (6) 41 _____

(2) 10 _____   (7) 53 _____

(3) 12 _____   (8) 69 _____

(4) 24 _____   (9) 78 _____

(5) 35 _____   (10) 99 _____

2 Match the Chinese with the English.

(1) bā yuè sān hào
八月三号   (a) July 12

(2) xīng qī rì
星期日   (b) Wednesday

(3) qī yuè shí èr hào
七月十二号   (c) Sunday

(4) xīng qī sān
星期三   (d) August 3

(5) shí èr yuè shí hào
十二月十号   (e) December 10

3 Write the following dates in Chinese.

 Example

二月二十八号，

星期一

 ①

_____

 ③

_____

 ②

_____

 ④

_____

14

4 Write the missing dates in Chinese. Finish the dialogues.

二〇〇一年　一月

星期日	星期一	星期二	星期三	星期四	星期五	星期六
	一		三	四		
七		今天	十			
	十五					二十
二十一					二十六	
	二十九		三十一			

(1) A: jīn tiān shì jǐ yuè jǐ hào 今天是几月几号？

B: jīn tiān shì 今天是一月九号。

(2) A: zuó tiān shì jǐ yuè jǐ hào 昨天是几月几号？

B: _____

(3) A: míng tiān shì jǐ yuè jǐ hào 明天是几月几号？

B: _____

(4) A: jīn tiān xīng qī jǐ 今天星期几？

B: _____

5 Write the dates in Chinese.

(1) New Year's Day
一月一号
_____

(2) your mother's birthday
_____

(3) the name of this month
_____

(4) today's date
_____

(5) Which months have 30 days ?
_____

(6) Which month has 28 / 29 days ?
_____

(7) What day follows Thursday ?
_____

(8) What day will it be tomorrow ?
_____

(9) If today is February 3, what date was yesterday ?
_____

生 字

	ノ	人	今	今							
jīn today	今										
	一	二	于	天							
tiān today	天										
	ノ	几									
jǐ how many	几										
	ノ	刀	月	月							
yuè the moon; month	月										
	丶	口	口	므	号						
hào number; date	号										
	丶	口	口	日	尸	昆	是	星	星		
xīng star	星										
	一	十	廿	共	甘	其	其	期	期	期	期
qī a period of time	期										
	丨	门	日	日	日'	旷	昕	昨	昨		
zuó yesterday	昨										
	丨	门	月	日							
rì sun; day	日										
	丨	门	月	日	旳	明	明	明			
míng bright; clear	明										

偏旁部首(四)

	一 厂									
cliff	厂									
	丶 亠 广									
shelter	广									
	丿 丆 丹 丹 舟 舟									
boat	舟									
	乛 马 马									
horse	马									
	乛 力									
strength	力									
	一 扌 扌									
hand	扌									
	丨 刂									
knife	刂									
	乛 了 子									
son	子									
	乛 乛 弓									
bow	弓									

1 Finish the dialogues with the sentences given.

nǐ hǎo ma
(1) A: 你好吗？

B: ___我很好。___ nǐ ne 你呢？

A: _____

nǐ jiào shén me míng zi
(3) A: 你叫什么名字？

B: _____ nǐ ne 你呢？

A: _____ zài jiàn 再见！

B: _____

nǐ xìng shén me
(2) A: 你姓什么？

B: _____ nǐ ne 你呢？

A: _____

zài jiàn	wǒ xìng lǐ
再见！	我姓李。
wǒ hěn hǎo	wǒ yě hěn hǎo
我很好。	我也很好。
wǒ jiào lǐ shān	wǒ jiào wáng yuè
我叫李山。	我叫王月。
wǒ xìng wáng	
我姓王。	

2 Find the missing word.

zì	nǐ	hǎo	jiàn	xiè
字	你	好	见	谢
me	bù	kě yǐ	péng	zǎo
么	不	可以	朋	早

shén
(1) 什 __么__

míng
(2) 名 _____

nǐ
(3) 你 _____

xiè
(4) 谢 _____

cuò
(5) _____错

nǐ
(6) 你 _____

zài
(7) 再 _____

hái
(8) 还 _____

ne
(9) _____呢

you
(10) _____友

3 Translation.

nǐ jiào shén me míng zi
(1) 你叫什么名字？

tā xìng shén me
(2) 他姓什么？

tā de míng zi jiào wáng yuè
(3) 她的名字叫王月。

tā xìng mǎ   wǒ yě xìng mǎ
(4) 他姓马。我也姓马。

lǐ shān shì wǒ de hǎo péng you
(5) 李山是我的好朋友。

zuó tiān shì xīng qī wǔ
(6) 昨天是星期五。

jīn tiān shì bā yuè jiǔ hào
(7) 今天是八月九号。

4 Dismantle the characters into parts.

ma
(1) 吗 ___ ___

hěn
(7) 很 ___ ___

péng
(2) 朋 ___ ___

nín
(8) 您 ___ ___ ___

tā
(3) 她 ___ ___

xiè
(9) 谢 ___ ___ ___

tā
(4) 他 ___ ___

xìng
(10) 姓 ___ ___

zì
(5) 字 ___ ___

shén
(11) 什 ___ ___

cuò
(6) 错 ___ ___

lǐ
(12) 李 ___ ___

5 Translation.

(1) How are you ?

(2) What is your surname ?

(3) What is your name ?

(4) Not bad.

(5) OK.

(6) He is my friend.

(7) Thanks.

(8) Good-bye !

6 Finish the dialogues in Chinese.

nǐ hǎo ma
(1) A: 你好吗?

B: _____。你呢?

A: _____。

(2) A: _____?

wǒ xìng mǎ
B: 我姓马。

(3) A: _____?

tā jiào wáng yuè
B: 她叫王月。

(4) A: _____?

wǒ xìng lǐ
B: 我姓李。_____?

wǒ yě xìng lǐ
A: 我也姓李。

7 Answer the following questions.

nǐ hǎo ma
(1) 你好吗?

nǐ xìng shén me
(2) 你姓什么?

nǐ jiàoshén me míng zi
(3) 你叫什么名字?

jīn tiān shì jǐ yuè jǐ hào
(4) 今天是几月几号?

jīn tiānxīng qī jǐ
(5) 今天星期几?

zuó tiān shì jǐ yuè jǐ hào
(6) 昨天是几月几号?

míng tiān xīng qī jǐ
(7) 明天星期几?

8   Ask a question for each answer.

(1) A: <u>今天是几月几号</u>？

jīn tiān shì shí yī yuè shí hào
B: 今天是十一月十号。

(2) A: _____?

jīn tiān xīng qī wǔ
B: 今天星期五。

(3) A: _____?

zuó tiān xīng qī sì
B: 昨天星期四。

(4) A: _____?

míng tiān xīng qī liù
B: 明天星期六。

9   Write the pinyin for the following numbers.

(1) 一 <u>yī</u>   (2) 二 ____   (3) 三 ____   (4) 四 ____   (5) 五 ____

(6) 六 ____   (7) 七 ____   (8) 八 ____   (9) 九 ____   (10) 十 ____

10   Fill in the missing numbers.

shí yī   shí èr   shí sì
(1) 十一、十二、_____、十四

shí wǔ   shí liù   shí qī
(2) 十五、十六、十七、_____

sān shí   sān shí yī
(3) 三十、三十一、_____

sì shí jiǔ   wǔ shí yī
(4) 四十九、_____、五十一

bā shí èr   bā shí sì
(5) 八十二、_____、八十四

bā shí jiǔ   jiǔ shí yī
(6) 八十九、_____、九十一

liù shí bā   liù shí jiǔ
(7) 六十八、六十九、_____

11   Transcribe the pinyin into Chinese characters.

(1) péngyou _____

(2) wǒ de _____

(3) xìng _____

(4) shénme _____

(5) míngzi _____

(6) lǐ shān _____

(7) wáng yuè _____

(8) mǎ _____

生 字

		㇐ 丨 ㇂ 口 叫 叫								
jiào call	叫									
		㇒ 亻 仁 什								
shén what	什									
		㇒ ㄥ 么								
me	么									
		㇒ ㇆ 夕 夕 名 名								
míng name	名									
		丶 ⺍ 宀 宀 宁 字								
zì character; word	字									
		㇗ ㇙ 女 如 如 她								
tā she; her	她									
		㇗ ㇙ 女 女 如 妒 姓 姓								
xìng surname	姓									
		㇕ 马 马								
mǎ horse; surname	马									
		㇒ 亻 仂 仲 他								
tā he; him	他									
		㇐ 十 才 木 本 李 李								
lǐ plum; surname	李									

偏旁部首(五)

		一 十 才 木								
tree; wood	木									
		´ 二 千 禾 禾								
crops	禾									
		一 十 艹								
grass	艹									
		ノ 广 卜 竹 竹 竹								
bamboo	竹									
		一 ナ 大								
big	大									
		亅 刂 小								
small	小									
		、 宀 之								
movement	之									
		了 阝								
ear	阝									
		、 二 广 立 立								
stand	立									

第六课　他住在哪儿

1 Finish the dialogues in Chinese.

(1) A: nǐ shì nǎ guó rén
你是哪国人？（中国人 zhōng guó rén）

B: 我是中国人。

(2) A: tā shì nǎ guó rén
他是哪国人？（日本人 rì běn rén）

B: ＿＿＿＿＿＿＿＿＿＿＿＿＿＿。

(3) A: tā zhù zài nǎr
她住在哪儿？（西安 xī ān）

B: ＿＿＿＿＿＿＿＿＿＿＿＿＿＿。

(4) A: tā zhù zài nǎr
他住在哪儿？（北京 běi jīng）

B: ＿＿＿＿＿＿＿＿＿＿＿＿＿＿。

(5) A: nǐ péngyou shì nǎ guó rén
你朋友是哪国人？（中国人 zhōng guó rén）

B: ＿＿＿＿＿＿＿＿＿＿＿＿＿＿。

(6) A: nǐ péngyou zhù zài nǎr
你朋友住在哪儿？（香港 xiāng gǎng）

B: ＿＿＿＿＿＿＿＿＿＿＿＿＿＿。

(7) A: tā péngyou zhù zài nǎr
她朋友住在哪儿？（上海 shàng hǎi）

B: ＿＿＿＿＿＿＿＿＿＿＿＿＿＿。

2 Write a few sentences based on the information given.

Example

他叫李海。
他住在西安。
他是中国人。

lǐ hǎi　tā
李海（他）
xī ān
西安
zhōng guó rén
中国人

1

wáng yuè　　tā
王月（她）
shàng hǎi
上海
zhōng guó rén
中国人

2

wáng ān　　tā
王安（他）
xiāng gǎng
香港
zhōng guó rén
中国人

3 Give the meanings of the radicals. Find a word for each radical.

(1) 口 _____mouth_____ 吗   (6) 月 _____ _____

(2) 氵 _____ _____   (7) 夕 _____ _____

(3) 辶 _____ _____   (8) 木 _____ _____

(4) 白 _____ _____   (9) 讠 _____ _____

(5) 亻 _____ _____   (10) 钅 _____ _____

4 Translation.

(1) How are you ?

(2) I am very well.

(3) Not bad.

(4) What is your surname ?

(5) What is your name ?

(6) She is my friend.

(7) Where do you live ?

(8) What is your nationality ?

(9) What day is today ?

5 Answer the questions according to the calendar.

十 月

日	一	二	三	四	五	六
今天	1	2	3	4	5	6
7	8	9	10	11	12	13
14	15	16	17	18	19	20
21	22	23	24	25	26	27
28	29	30	31			

jīn tiān jǐ yuè jǐ hào
(1) 今天几月几号? _____ 。

jīn tiān xīng qī jǐ
(2) 今天星期几? _____ 。

zuó tiān jǐ hào
(3) 昨天几号? _____ 。

zuó tiān xīng qī jǐ
(4) 昨天星期几? _____ 。

míng tiān jǐ hào
(5) 明天几号? _____ 。

míng tiān xīng qī jǐ
(6) 明天星期几? _____ 。

6 Fill in the blanks with the words in the box.

shén me	jǐ	nǎr	ma	nǎ
什么	几	哪儿	吗	哪

(1) 你叫 _____ 名字？ nǐ jiào / míng zi

(2) 你是 ____ 国人？ nǐ shì / guó rén

(3) 你住在 _____？ nǐ zhù zài

(4) 今天星期 _____？ jīn tiān xīng qī

(5) 你姓 _____？ nǐ xìng

(6) 你好 _____？ nǐ hǎo

(7) 明天星期 _____？ míng tiān xīng qī

7 Transcribe the pinyin into Chinese characters.

(1) zhù _____
(2) zài _____
(3) běijīng _____
(4) xiānggǎng _____
(5) nǎr _____
(6) shénme _____
(7) xīngqī _____

8 Fill in the blanks in Chinese.

zuó tiān 昨天　jīn tiān 今天　_____

_____　xīng qī wǔ 星期五　_____

_____　shí yuè liù rì 十月六日　_____

9 Match the Chinese with the English.

(1) 他很友好。 tā hěn yǒu hǎo — (a) He is a good person.
(2) 他是好人。 tā shì hǎo rén — (b) Shanghai is in China.
(3) 他是北京人。 tā shì běi jīng rén — (c) Good morning!
(4) 上海在中国。 shàng hǎi zài zhōng guó — (d) He is very friendly.
(5) 早上好！ zǎo shang hǎo — (e) He is from Beijing.

10 Study the following pairs of phrases.

(1) 好友 hǎo yǒu good friend / 友好 yǒu hǎo friendly
(2) 国王 guó wáng king / 王国 wáng guó kingdom
(3) 上海 shàng hǎi Shanghai / 海上 hǎi shang at the sea
(4) 人名 rén míng name / 名人 míng rén celebrity

11 Match the Chinese with the English.

guówáng
(1) 国王   (a) friendly

yǒu hǎo
(2) 友好   (b) kingdom

wángguó
(3) 王国   (c) good morning

zǎo ān
(4) 早安   (d) King

xìng míng
(5) 姓名   (e) early morning

zǎo shang
(6) 早上   (f) full name

hǎi gǎng
(7) 海港   (g) friend

hǎo yǒu
(8) 好友   (h) harbour

míng rén
(9) 名人   (i) good friend

yǒu rén
(10) 友人   (j) a huge crowd

hǎo rén
(11) 好人   (k) celebrity

rén hǎi
(12) 人海   (l) good person

hǎi mǎ
(13) 海马   (m) sea horse

12 Finish the sentences.

nǐ shì
(1) 你是____哪国人____？ (what nationality)

tā zhù zài
(2) 她住在_____。 (Beijing)

tā yě shì
(3) 他也是_____。 (Japanese)

wǒ shì
(4) 我是_____。(Chinese)

tā zhù zài
(5) 她住在_____？ (where)

wǒ zhù zài
(6) 我住在_____。 (Hong Kong)

nǐ péngyou shì
(7) 你朋友是_____？ (what nationality)

tā jiào
(8) 他叫_____。 (Li Shan)

tā péngyou zhù zài
(9) 他朋友住在_____。 (Shanghai)

tā shì
(10) 他是_____。 (Beijing person)

nǐ xìng
(11) 你姓_____？ (what)

tā jiào
(12) 他叫_____？ (what name)

wǒ yě
(13) 我也_____。 (very well)

tā shì wǒ de
(14) 她是我的_____。 (good friend)

nǐ péngyou zhù zài
(15) 你朋友住在_____？ (where)

生 字

		ノ　亻　彳　仁　住　住　住								
zhù live; reside	住									
		一　ナ　才　左　在　在								
zài in; on	在									
		丶　ロ　ロ　叮　叨　吲　明　哪　哪								
nǎ which; what	哪									
		ノ　儿								
ér child; son; suffix	儿									
		丶　ロ　ロ　中								
zhōng middle; centre	中									
		一　门　门　月　用　国　国　国								
guó country; kingdom	国									
		ノ　人								
rén person; people	人									
		一　十　才　才　北								
běi north	北									
		丶　一　六　古　古　宁　京　京								
jīng capital	京									
		一　卜　上								
shàng up; previous; attend	上									
		丶　氵　氵　氵　汇　汇　海　海　海　海								
hǎi sea	海									

生 字

		一 丆 丙 丙 西 西								
xī west	西									
		、 丷 宀 宀 安 安								
ān safe	安									
		一 十 才 木 本								
běn root; origin	本									
		丿 二 千 チ 禾 禾 香 香 香								
xiāng fragrant	香									
		、 冫 氵 汀 汼 泄 洪 洪 洪 港 港								
gǎng habour	港									

偏旁部首(六)

	フ ㄡ									
again	ㄡ									
	ノ ㄅ ㄅ 欠									
owe	欠									
	丶 亠 亍 方									
square	方									
	ㄑ ㄩ 女									
female	女									
	丶 冖									
roof without chimney	冖									
	丶 丷 宀									
roof with chimney	宀									
	丨 冂									
border	冂									
	丶 冂 门									
door	门									
	丨 冂 口									
enclosure	口									

生词

第一课　　你好　　您好　　你早　　您早　　再见

nǐ hǎo　　nín hǎo　　nǐ zǎo　　nín zǎo　　zài jiàn

一　亻　入　彳　父　王　土　士　山

第二课　　你好吗　　不错　　还可以　　我　　很好　　谢谢　　你呢　　也

nǐ hǎo ma　　bú cuò　　hái kě yǐ　　wǒ　　hěn hǎo　　xiè xie　　nǐ ne　　yě

忄　心　口　羊　⻊　讠　钅　饣　纟

第三课　　是　　我的　　朋友　　一　二　三　四　五　六　七　八　九　十

shì　　wǒ de　　péngyou　　yī　èr　sān　sì　wǔ　liù　qī　bā　jiǔ　shí

日　白　目　月　田　三　灬　雨　夕

第四课　　今天　　几月　　十月　　几号　　八号　　星期一

jīn tiān　　jǐ yuè　　shí yuè　　jǐ hào　　bā hào　　xīng qī yī

星期几　　昨天　　星期日／天　　明天

xīng qī jǐ　　zuó tiān　　xīng qī rì　tiān　　míng tiān

厂　广　角　马　力　才　刂　孑　弓

第五课　　叫　　什么　　名字　　她　　姓　　马　　他　　李　　王　　山

jiào　　shén me　　míng zi　　tā　　xìng　　mǎ　　tā　　lǐ　　wáng　　shān

木　禾　艹　竹　大　小　辶　阝　立

第六课　　住　在　哪儿　　中国人　　北京　　上海　　西安　　日本人

zhù　zài　nǎr　　zhōng guó rén　　běi jīng　　shàng hǎi　　xī ān　　rì běn rén

香港　　哪国人

xiāng gǎng　　nǎ guó rén

又　欠　方　女　冖　宀　门　门　口

总复习

1. Greetings

nǐ hǎo
你好!

nín hǎo
您好!

nǐ ne
你呢?

nǐ zǎo
你早!

zài jiàn
再见!

nǐ hǎo ma
你好吗?

wǒ hěn hǎo
我很好。

xiè xie
谢谢!

bú cuò
不错。

hái kě yǐ
还可以。

wǒ yě hěn hǎo
我也很好。

2. Numbers

yī　èr　sān　sì　wǔ　liù　qī　bā　jiǔ　shí
一　二　三　四　五　六　七　八　九　十

shí yī　shí èr　èr shí　èr shí wǔ　sān shí
十一　十二　二十　二十五　三十

sì shí　liù shí jiǔ　bā shí qī　jiǔ shí jiǔ
四十　六十九　八十七　九十九

3. Places

zhōng guó　shàng hǎi　xiāng gǎng　xī ān　běi jīng　rì běn
中国　上海　香港　西安　北京　日本

4. People

nǐ　wǒ　tā　tā　péng you
你　我　他　她　朋友

5. Surnames and names

mǎ　lǐ shān　wáng yuè　lǐ hǎi　wáng ān yī　shān běn　rì běn xìng
马　李山　王月　李海　王安一　山本（日本姓）

6. Question words and particals

ne　ma　shén me　jǐ　nǎr　nǎ
呢　吗　什么　几　哪儿　哪

7. Radicals

亠　亻　入　彳　父　王　土　士　山

忄　心　口　羊　足　讠　钅　饣　纟

日　白　目　月　田　氵　灬　雨　夕

厂　广　角　马　力　扌　刂　孑　弓

木　禾　艹　竹　大　小　辶　阝　立

又　欠　方　女　一　宀　冂　门　口

8. Dates

xīng qī yī	xīng qī èr	xīng qī sān	xīng qī sì	xīng qī wǔ	xīng qī liù
星期一	星期二	星期三	星期四	星期五	星期六

xīng qī rì　tiān
星期日（天）

yī yuè	èr yuè	sān yuè	sì yuè	wǔ yuè	liù yuè
一月	二月	三月	四月	五月	六月

qī yuè	bā yuè	jiǔ yuè	shí yuè	shí yī yuè	shí èr yuè
七月	八月	九月	十月	十一月	十二月

zuó tiān	jīn tiān	míngtiān	sān yuè jiǔ hào　rì
昨天	今天	明天	三月九号（日）

9. Phonetics

Vowels:　　　　a　o　e　i　u　ü

Consonants:　　b　p　m　f　d　t　n　l

　　　　　　　g　k　h　j　q　x

　　　　　　　zh　ch　sh　r　z　c　s

　　　　　　　y　w

32

10. Questions and answers

(1) nǐ hǎo ma
你好吗？ 　 wǒ hěn hǎo　bú cuò　hái kě yǐ
我很好。（不错。／还可以。）

(2) nǐ shì zhōng guó rén ma
你是中国人吗？ 　 shì　bú shì
是。（不是。）

(3) nǐ xìng shén me
你姓什么？ 　 wǒ xìng wáng
我姓王。

(4) nǐ jiào shén me míng zi
你叫什么名字？ 　 wǒ jiào wáng yuè
我叫王月。

(5) nǐ shì nǎ guó rén
你是哪国人？ 　 wǒ shì zhōng guó rén
我是中国人。

(6) nǐ zhù zài nǎr
你住在哪儿？ 　 wǒ zhù zài shàng hǎi
我住在上海。

(7) jīn tiān shì jǐ yuè jǐ hào
今天（是）几月几号？ 　 shí yī yuè shí hào
十一月十号。

(8) jīn tiān xīng qī jǐ
今天星期几？ 　 jīn tiān xīng qī wǔ
今天星期五。

(9) míng tiān shì xīng qī èr ma
明天是星期二吗？ 　 bú shì
不是。

(10) zuó tiān xīng qī jǐ
昨天星期几？ 　 xīng qī tiān rì
星期天（日）。

33

测验

1 Match the Chinese with the pinyin.

(1) 什么   (a) xǐ ān

(2) 再见   (b) zàijiàn

(3) 还可以   (c) shénme

(4) 不错   (d) hái kěyǐ

(5) 中国   (e) nǎr

(6) 哪儿   (f) zhōngguó

(7) 西安   (g) búcuò

(8) 星期   (h) zuótiān

(9) 昨天   (i) xīngqī

2 Fill in the blanks with the words in the box.

呢	吗	什么
哪	几	哪儿

(1) 你好_____?

(2) 你叫_____名字?

(3) 你是_____国人?

(4) 你住在_____?

(5) 我很好，你_____?

(6) 今天星期_____?

3 Write the numbers in Chinese.

Example

13 → 十三

_____

(1) 29

(2) 37

(3) 69

(4) 78

(5) 54

(6) 81

4 Give the meanings of the following radicals.

(1) 亻 _____   (6) 心 _____

(2) 讠 _____   (7) 宀 _____

(3) 钅 _____   (8) 禾 _____

(4) 自 _____   (9) 人 _____

(5) 辶 _____   (10) 夕 _____

5 Answer the following questions.

(1) 你姓什么？

(2) 你叫什么名字？

(3) 你住在哪儿？

(4) 你是日本人吗？

(5) 你是哪国人？

(6) 今天星期几？

(7) 今天是几月几号？

(8) 明天是星期四吗？

6 Circle the correct pinyin.

(1) 谢谢　(a) xièxie　(b) shièshie

(2) 七　(a) chī　(b) qī

(3) 九　(a) jiǔ　(b) zhiǔ

(4) 名字　(a) míngzhi　(b) míngzi

(5) 住　(a) zù　(b) zhù

(6) 香港　(a) xiānggǎn　(b) xiānggǎng

(7) 姓　(a) xìn　(b) xìng

(8) 日本　(a) rèběn　(b) rìběn

7 Translation.

(1) How are you?

(2) I am fine, thanks. And you?

(3) He is also Chinese.

(4) What is your name?

(5) Is she from Hong Kong?

(6) Where do you live?

(7) What day is today?

(8) What is the date today?

第二单元 一家人

第七课 这是我的一家

1 Categorize the following phrases into two groups: male and female.

bà ba	mā ma	gē ge
爸爸	妈妈	哥哥
dì di	mèi mei	jiě jie
弟弟	妹妹	姐姐

Male: 爸爸 _____

Female: _____

2 Dismantle the characters into parts.

hǎo
(1) 好 ____ ____

men
(2) 们 ____ ____

mā
(3) 妈 ____ ____

bà
(4) 爸 ____ ____

jiě
(5) 姐 ____ ____

mèi
(6) 妹 ____ ____

xīng
(7) 星 ____ ____

nǐ
(8) 你 ____ ____

zhè
(9) 这 ____ ____

xìng
(10) 姓 ____ ____

míng
(11) 名 ____ ____

tā
(12) 他 ____ ____

3 Match the Chinese with the pinyin.

(1) 哥哥   (a) shuí

(2) 弟弟   (b) dìdi

(3) 姐姐   (c) yìjiārén

(4) 谁   (d) tāmen

(5) 妹妹   (e) gēge

(6) 一家人   (f) jiějie

(7) 他们   (g) mèimei

4 Translation.

(1) one family

(2) elder brother

(3) younger sister

(4) younger brother

(5) elder sister

(6) China

(7) who

5 Find the phrases. Write them out.

呢	朋	很	好	不	错
我	们	友	一	家	人
什	你	们	还	可	以
么	再	见	名	字	的

(1) _____   (5) _____

(2) _____   (6) _____

(3) _____   (7) _____

(4) _____   (8) _____

6 Give the meanings of the following radicals.

(1) 足 ___foot___   (10) 力 _____

(2) 方 _____   (11) 欠 _____

(3) 又 _____   (12) 广 _____

(4) 饣 _____   (13) 扌 _____

(5) 朩 _____   (14) 白 _____

(6) 禾 _____   (15) 弓 _____

(7) 钅 _____   (16) 亠 _____

(8) 纟 _____   (17) 土 _____

(9) 刂 _____   (18) 士 _____

7 Write the pinyin for the following words.

(1) 家 ___jiā___   (7) 他们 _____

(2) 爸爸 _____   (8) 住 _____

(3) 哥哥 _____   (9) 哪儿 _____

(4) 弟弟 _____   (10) 姓 _____

(5) 妹妹 _____   (11) 名字 _____

(6) 姐姐 _____   (12) 昨天 _____

8 Answer the following questions.

(1) nǐ xìng shén me
你姓什么？

(2) nǐ jiào shén me míng zi
你叫什么名字？

(3) nǐ shì nǎ guó rén
你是哪国人？

(4) jīn tiān shì jǐ yuè jǐ hào
今天是几月几号？

(5) jīn tiān xīng qī jǐ
今天星期几？

(6) míng tiān xīng qī jǐ
明天星期几？

9 Form as many questions as you can. Write them out.

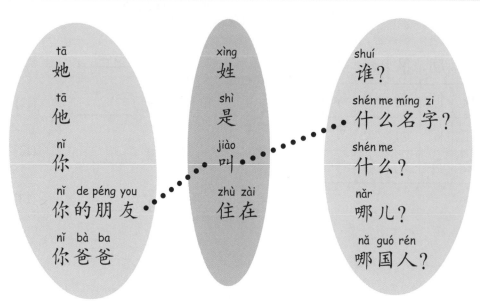

(1) 你的朋友叫什么名字?

(2) _____

(3) _____

(4) _____

(5) _____

(6) _____

10 Fill in the blanks with the words in the box.

jǐ	shén me	shuí	nǎr	nǎ	ma	ne
几	什么	谁	哪儿	哪	吗	呢

nǐ jiào　　　　　　míng zi
(1) 你叫 _____ 名字?

jīn tiān xīng qī
(2) 今天星期 _____?

nǐ bà ba hǎo
(3) 你爸爸好 _____?

wǒ hěn hǎo　　nǐ
(4) 我很好，你 _____?

nǐ shì　　　　guó rén
(5) 你是 _____ 国人?

tā zhù zài
(6) 他住在 _____?

tā shì
(7) 她是 _____?

zuó tiān shì　　　　yuè　　　　hào
(8) 昨天是 _____ 月 _____ 号?

nǐ péng you zhù zài
(9) 你朋友住在 _____?

wáng yuè shì
(10) 王月是 _____?

nǐ men shì zhōng guó rén
(11) 你们是中国人 _____?

nǐ men yě zhù zài xiāng gǎng
(12) 你们也住在香港 _____?

38

11 Match the Chinese with the English.

nǐ jiā
(1) 你家   (a) at home

guó jiā
(2) 国家   (b) your family

zài jiā
(3) 在家   (c) country

rì qī
(4) 日期   (d) whose

shuí de
(5) 谁的   (e) people

rén men
(6) 人们   (f) family members

jiā rén
(7) 家人   (g) date

jiā jiā
(8) 家家   (h) every family

12 Put the words / phrases into sentences.

Example

wǒ dì di shì zhè
我弟弟 是 这。

zhè shì wǒ dì di
→ 这是我弟弟。

shì zhè wǒ bà ba
(1) 是 这 我爸爸。

shén me xìng tā
(2) 什么 姓 她?

míng zi tā shén me jiào
(3) 名字 他 什么 叫?

nǎr tā zhù zài
(4) 哪儿 他 住在?

wǒ de yì jiā shì zhè
(5) 我的一家 是 这。

13 Translation.

(1) What day was yesterday?

(2) What is your surname?

(3) What is your name?

(4) Where do you live?

(5) What is your nationality?

(6) This is my family.

(7) They are my friends.

(8) Who is she?

14 Write a paragraph to introduce your family.

生字

		丶	亠	讠	文	文	议	这			
zhè this	这										
		丶	宀	宀	宀	宁	宇	家	家	家	
jiā family; home	家										
		丿	亻	亻	们	们					
men plural suffix	们										
		乚	女	女	妁	妈	妈				
mā mum; mother	妈										
		乚	女	女	女	奼	奼	妹	妹		
mèi younger sister	妹										
		丶	⺍	⺌	当	肖	弟	弟			
dì younger brother	弟										
		丶	八	父	父	爷	爷	爸	爸		
bà dad; father	爸										
		乚	女	女	奵	如	姐	姐	姐		
jiě elder sister	姐										
		一	丆	哥	哥	可	哥	哥	哥	哥	哥
gē elder brother	哥										
		丶	讠	计	讠	讠	访	诈	谁	谁	谁
shuí who	谁										

识字 (一)

		一 ナ 大								
dà big	大									
		丶 丨 冂 口								
kǒu measure word; mouth	口									
		丿 ク 夕 夗 多 多								
duō more; many	多									
		丶 一 亠 方								
fāng square; direction; surname	方									
		丶 一 亠 三 言 言 言								
yán speech; say	言									
		一 厂 厉 历								
lì experience; calendar	历									
		丶 丨 口 口 史 史								
shǐ history; surname	史									
		丿 ㇒ 七 长 长								
cháng long	长									

1 Match the pinyin with the Chinese and English.

(1) rénkǒu   中国   dialect

(2) zhōngguó   人口 ——— population

(3) fāngyán   方言   history

(4) lìshǐ   历史   China

2 Match the Chinese with the pinyin and English.

(1) 长   duō   many

(2) 大   cháng   big

(3) 多   fāng   long

(4) 方   dà   square

3 Match the Chinese with the English.

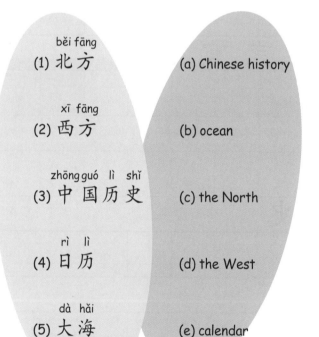

běi fāng
(1) 北方

xī fāng
(2) 西方

zhōng guó lì shǐ
(3) 中国历史

rì lì
(4) 日历

dà hǎi
(5) 大海

(a) Chinese history

(b) ocean

(c) the North

(d) the West

(e) calendar

4 Give the meanings of each word.

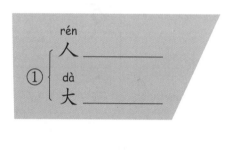

rén
① 人 _____
dà
大 _____

zhōng
② 中 _____
shǐ
史 _____

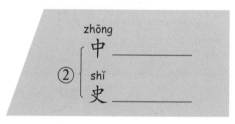

fāng
③ 方 _____
lì
历 _____

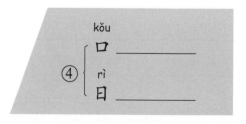

kǒu
④ 口 _____
rì
日 _____

第八课　他家有七口人

1 Write in Chinese.

1 I 我

2 we _____

3 they _____

4 you _____

5 he _____

6 she _____

2 Match the Chinese with the pictures.

mā ma
(1) 妈妈

dì di
(2) 弟弟

gē ge
(3) 哥哥

jiě jie
(4) 姐姐

bà ba
(5) 爸爸

mèi mei
(6) 妹妹

3 Ask questions by using the question words given.

wǒ jiào wáng yuè　　shén me
(1) 我叫王月。(什么)

→ 你叫什么名字？

wǒ yǒu sì ge mèi mei　　jǐ ge
(2) 我有四个妹妹。(几个)

→ _____?

wǒ jiā yǒu liù kǒu rén　　jǐ kǒu rén
(3) 我家有六口人。(几口人)

→ _____?

tā shì wǒ jiě jie　　shuí
(4) 她是我姐姐。(谁)

→ _____?

wǒ jiā yǒu bà ba　　mā ma hé wǒ　　shuí
(5) 我家有爸爸、妈妈和我。(谁)

→ _____?

4 Answer questions according to the pictures.

5 Give the meanings of the radicals. Find a word for each radical.

(1) 女 _____ _____

(2) 父 _____ _____

(3) 艹 _____ _____

(4) 讠 _____ _____

(5) 夕 _____ _____

(6) 月 _____ _____

(7) 禾 _____ _____

(8) 口 _____ _____

(9) 氵 _____ _____

(10) 宀 _____ _____

6 Match the Chinese with the English.

yǒu rén
(1) 有人

yǒu míng
(2) 有名

yǒu de
(3) 有的

dà hào
(4) 大号

dà jiā
(5) 大家

dà rén
(6) 大人

liǎng jiě mèi
(7) 两姐妹

zhōng hào
(8) 中号

liǎng xiōng dì
(9) 两兄弟

(a) medium size

(b) everybody

(c) there is somebody

(d) two sisters

(e) adult

(f) large size

(g) famous

(h) two brothers

(i) some

7 Ask questions in another way.

Example

nǐ yǒu gē ge ma
你有哥哥吗？ → 你有没有哥哥？

_____

zhè shì nǐ bà ba ma
(1) 这是你爸爸吗？

nǐ yǒu xiōng dì jiě mèi ma
(2) 你有兄弟姐妹吗？

tā shì nǐ mā ma ma
(3) 她是你妈妈吗？

nǐ yǒu dì di ma
(4) 你有弟弟吗？

nǐ shì yīng guó rén ma
(5) 你是英国人吗？

nǐ yǒu mèi mei ma
(6) 你有妹妹吗？

45

8 Match the question with the answer.

nǐ yǒu mèi mei ma
(1) 你有妹妹吗？

nǐ jiā yǒu jǐ kǒu rén
(2) 你家有几口人？

nǐ yǒu jǐ ge jiě jie
(3) 你有几个姐姐？

nǐ men yì jiā rén zhù zài nǎr
(4) 你们一家人住在哪儿？

nǐ jiào shén me míng zi
(5) 你叫什么名字？

nǐ de péng you xìng shén me
(6) 你的朋友姓什么？

nà ge rén shì shuí
(7) 那个人是谁？

nǐ mā ma shì nǎ guó rén
(8) 你妈妈是哪国人？

wǒ jiào wáng yuè
(a) 我叫王月。

wǒ men yì jiā rén zhù zài xiāng gǎng
(b) 我们一家人住在香港。

wǒ jiā yǒu sān kǒu rén
(c) 我家有三口人。

wǒ yǒu mèi mei
(d) 我有妹妹。

wǒ mā ma shì yīng guó rén
(e) 我妈妈是英国人。

wǒ yǒu liǎng ge jiě jie
(f) 我有两个姐姐。

tā shì wǒ bà ba
(g) 他是我爸爸。

wǒ de péng you xìng lǐ
(h) 我的朋友姓李。

9 Change the following sentences into "吗" questions.

Example

tā shì wǒ mèi mei
她是我妹妹。

→ 她是你妹妹吗？

zhè shì wǒ bà ba
(1) 这是我爸爸。

wǒ zhù zài yīng guó
(2) 我住在英国。

wǒ de péng you shì rì běn rén
(3) 我的朋友是日本人。

tā jiào lǐ shān
(4) 他叫李山。

wǒ yǒu gē ge
(5) 我有哥哥。

10 Answer the following questions.

nǐ shì nǎ guó rén
(1) 你是哪国人？

nǐ jiā yǒu jǐ kǒu rén
(2) 你家有几口人？

nǐ yǒu jǐ ge xiōng dì jiě mèi
(3) 你有几个兄弟姐妹？

nǐ yǒu méi yǒu gē ge
(4) 你有没有哥哥？

jīn tiān shì jǐ yuè jǐ hào
(5) 今天是几月几号？

jīn tiān xīng qī jǐ
(6) 今天星期几？

míng tiān xīng qī jǐ
(7) 明天星期几？

11 Reading comprehension.

bà ba
爸爸

mā ma
妈妈

xiǎo míng
小明

xiǎo fāng
小方

zhè shì wǒ de yì jiā   wǒ jiā yǒu sì kǒu
这是我的一家。我家有四口
rén   bà ba   mā ma   mèi mei hé wǒ   wǒ
人：爸爸、妈妈、妹妹和我。我
mèi mei jiào xiǎo fāng   wǒ jiào xiǎo míng   wǒ bà
妹妹叫小方，我叫小明。我爸
ba shì yīng guó rén   wǒ mā ma shì zhōng guó rén
爸是英国人，我妈妈是中国人。
wǒ men yì jiā rén zhù zài yīng guó
我们一家人住在英国。

Answer the questions.

xiǎo míng yì jiā yǒu jǐ kǒu rén
(1) 小明一家有几口人？

xiǎo míng yǒu xiōng dì jiě mèi ma
(2) 小明有兄弟姐妹吗？

xiǎo míng yǒu gē ge ma
(3) 小明有哥哥吗？

xiǎo míng yǒu jǐ gè mèi mei
(4) 小明有几个妹妹？

tā mèi mei jiào shén me míng zi
(5) 他妹妹叫什么名字？

tā bà ba shì nǎ guó rén
(6) 他爸爸是哪国人？

tā mā ma shì yīng guó rén ma
(7) 他妈妈是英国人吗？

tā men yì jiā rén zhù zài nǎr
(8) 他们一家人住在哪儿？

12 Match the Chinese with the English.

wǒ jiā méi yǒu rén
(1) 我家没有人。

nà ge rén shì wǒ dì di
(2) 那个人是我弟弟。

tā mā ma hěn yǒu míng
(3) 她妈妈很有名。

yǒu de rén hěn yǒu hǎo
(4) 有的人很友好。

zhè ge rén bú shì wǒ de péng you
(5) 这个人不是我的朋友。

tā men shì liǎng xiōng dì
(6) 他们是两兄弟。

(a) This person is not my friend.

(b) Her mother is very famous.

(c) That person is my younger brother.

(d) There is nobody at home.

(e) Some people are friendly.

(f) They are brothers.

13 Reading comprehension.

fāng jīng
方京

fāng jīng jiā yǒu qī kǒu rén   bà ba
方京家有七口人：爸爸、

mā ma   yí ge gē ge   yí ge jiě jie
妈妈、一个哥哥、一个姐姐、

liǎng ge mèi mei hé tā   fāng jīng de bà ba
两个妹妹和她。方京的爸爸

shì yīng guó rén   tā mā ma shì rì běn
是英国人，她妈妈是日本

rén   tā men yì jiā rén zhù zài shàng hǎi
人。他们一家人住在上海。

Answer the questions.

fāng jīng jiā yǒu jǐ kǒu rén
(1) 方京家有几口人？

tā jiā yǒu shuí
(2) 她家有谁？

tā yǒu méi yǒu dì di
(3) 她有没有弟弟？

tā bà ba shì nǎ guó rén
(4) 她爸爸是哪国人？

tā mā ma shì nǎ guó rén
(5) 她妈妈是哪国人？

tā men yì jiā rén zhù zài nǎr
(6) 他们一家人住在哪儿？

14 Write the pinyin for the following words.

(1) 中国 _____   (5) 也 _____

(2) 和 _____   (6) 没有 _____

(3) 哥哥 _____   (7) 英国 _____

(4) 不错 _____   (8) 谁 _____

15 Ask questions about the underlined parts.

Example

wǒ xìng wáng   shén me
我姓王。（什么）

→ 你姓什么？

wǒ shì yīng guó rén   nǎ guó rén
(1) 我是英国人。（哪国人）
→

wǒ jiā yǒu sì kǒu rén   jǐ kǒu rén
(2) 我家有四口人。（几口人）
→

wǒ yǒu liǎng ge jiě jie   jǐ ge
(3) 我有两个姐姐。（几个）
→

xiǎo shān jiā zhù zài xiāng gǎng   nǎr
(4) 小山家住在香港。（哪儿）
→

jīn tiān liù yuè qī hào   jǐ
(5) 今天六月七号。（几）
→

tā shì wǒ mā ma   shuí
(6) 她是我妈妈。（谁）
→

48

16 Translation.

(1) His last name is Ma.

(2) His name is Ma Benshan.

(3) There are six people in his family.

(4) He has three brothers and sisters.

(5) She does not have any younger brothers.

(6) His parents are English.

(7) They live in Beijing.

(8) My family consists of mother, father and me.

17 This is a family photo. Write a passage in Chinese.

mā ma yīng guó rén
妈妈（英国人）

bà ba yīng guó rén
爸爸（英国人）

gē ge
哥哥

jiě jie
姐姐

dì di
弟弟

mǎ běnshān
马本山

他叫马本山。_____

_____

_____

_____

生 词

	一	广	才	冇	有	有				
yǒu have; there is	有									
	亅	小	小							
xiǎo small; little	小									
	刀	刁	刍	尹	那	那				
nà that	那									
	丿	人	个							
gè measure word (general)	个									
	一	厂	厅	丙	丙	两	两			
liǎng two	两									
	丿	二	千	禾	禾	和	和			
hé and	和									
	一	十	艹	艹	艻	苂	英	英		
yīng hero	英									
	丶	丷	口	口	尸	兄				
xiōng elder brother	兄									
	丶	冫	氵	沪	沪	汐	没			
méi no	没									

识字 (二)

		一 厂 丌 丌 丌 耳 耳							
ěr ear	耳								
		ノ 二 三 手							
shǒu hand	手								
		、 一 亠 文 齐 齐							
qí in order; together; surname	齐								
		丿 冂 月 月 用							
yòng use	用								
		丿 人 人 今 全 全							
quán whole	全								
		′ 亻 竹 白 身 身							
shēn body	身								
		、 心 心 心							
xīn heart	心								
		、 ″ ″ ″ 兴 学 学 学							
xué study	学								
		、 一 亠 文							
wén word; literature	文								

1 Match the pictures with the characters.

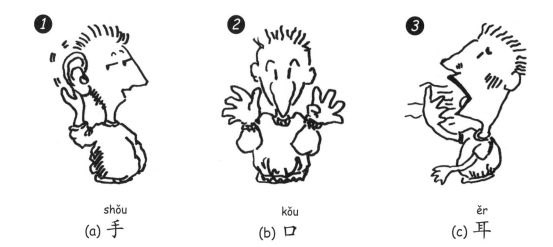

shǒu
(a) 手

kǒu
(b) 口

ěr
(c) 耳

2 Give the meanings of each word.

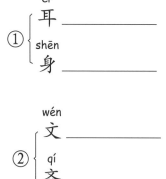

① ⎰ ěr
　 耳 _____
　 ⎱ shēn
　 身 _____

② ⎰ wén
　 文 _____
　 ⎱ qí
　 齐 _____

3 Write the pinyin for the following words.

(1) 齐 _____　(5) 心 _____

(2) 全 _____　(6) 文 _____

(3) 身 _____　(7) 耳 _____

(4) 用 _____　(8) 手 _____

4 Give the meanings of the following phrases.

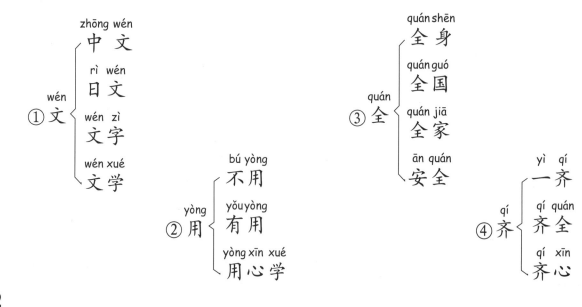

① 文
wén

　zhōng wén
　中 文

　rì wén
　日 文

　wén zì
　文 字

　wén xué
　文 学

② 用
yòng

　bú yòng
　不用

　yǒu yòng
　有用

　yòng xīn xué
　用心学

③ 全
quán

　quán shēn
　全 身

　quán guó
　全 国

　quán jiā
　全 家

　ān quán
　安 全

④ 齐
qí

　yì qí
　一 齐

　qí quán
　齐 全

　qí xīn
　齐 心

52

第九课　我爸爸工作，我妈妈也工作

1 Give the meanings of the following phrases.

gōng zuò
(1) 工作 _____

duō dà le
(4) 多大了 _____

méi yǒu
(7) 没有 _____

zhōng xué shēng
(2) 中学生 _____

xiōng dì jiě mèi
(5) 兄弟姐妹 _____

bú shì
(8) 不是 _____

jǐ suì le
(3) 几岁了 _____

wǔ kǒu rén
(6) 五口人 _____

xiǎo xué shēng
(9) 小学生 _____

2 Form as many questions as you can. Write them out.

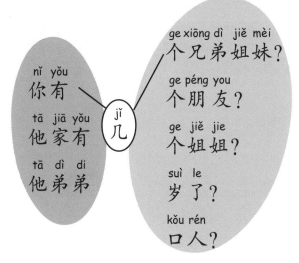

(1) 你有几个兄弟姐妹？

(2) _____

(3) _____

(4) _____

3 Put the words / phrases into sentences.

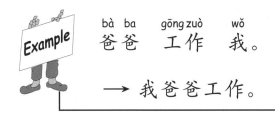

bà ba　　gōng zuò　　wǒ
爸爸　　工作　　我。

→ 我爸爸工作。

shí jiǔ suì　　wǒ gē ge
(1) 十九岁　我哥哥。

xiǎo xué shēng　　tā mèi mei　　shì
(2) 小学生　她妹妹　是。

zhù zài　　běi jīng　　tā men
(3) 住在　北京　他们。

tā　　mèi mei　　yí ge　　yǒu
(4) 他　妹妹　一个　有。

yǒu　　wǔ kǒu rén　　tā jiā
(5) 有　五口人　他家。

yǒu　　tā　　xiōng dì jiě mèi　　sì ge
(6) 有　她　兄弟姐妹　四个。

shì　　zhè　　tā bà ba
(7) 是　这　他爸爸。

4 Transcribe the pinyin into Chinese characters.

(1) qīsuì _____   (3) gōngzuò _____   (5) míngzi _____

(2) xuésheng _____   (4) méiyǒu _____   (6) zàijiàn _____

5 Ask questions according to the information given.

Example

她几岁了?

她是小学生吗?

wǔ suì
五岁,
xiǎo xué shēng
小学生

❶
shí wǔ suì
十五岁,
zhōng xué shēng
中学生

❷ sān shí èr suì
三十二岁,
gōng zuò
工作

❸ èr shí èr suì
二十二岁,
dà xué shēng
大学生

❹ shí èr suì
十二岁,
zhōng guó rén
中国人

❺ qī suì
七岁,
xiǎo xué shēng
小学生

❻ èr shí bā suì
二十八岁,
gōng zuò
工作

6 Form as many questions as you can. Write them out.

nǐ jiào
你叫
nǐ jiā yǒu
你家有
nǐ jiā zhù zài
你家住在
nǐ shì
你是
tā shì
他是

jǐ
几
shuí
谁？
shén me
什么
nǎr
哪儿？
nǎ
哪

guó rén
国人？
míng zi
名字？
kǒu rén
口人？

(1) _____

(4) _____

(2) _____

(5) _____

(3) _____

(6) _____

7 Find the phrases. Write them out.

西	很	好	我	们	妈	妈
上	安	工	人	爸	爸	兄
海	北	京	作	日	没	弟
名	大	学	生	本	有	姐
还	字	中	英	星	期	妹
可	你	不	国	再	香	港
以	好	小	错	见	不	是

(1) _____ (8) _____

(2) _____ (9) _____

(3) _____ (10) _____

(4) _____ (11) _____

(5) _____ (12) _____

(6) _____ (13) _____

(7) _____ (14) _____

8 Dismantle the characters into parts.

zuò
(1) 作＿＿ ＿＿

méi
(6) 没＿＿ ＿＿

xué
(2) 学＿＿ ＿＿

hé
(7) 和＿＿ ＿＿

duō
(3) 多＿＿ ＿＿

suì
(8) 岁＿＿ ＿＿

yīng
(4) 英＿＿ ＿＿

shuí
(9) 谁＿＿ ＿＿ ＿＿

nà
(5) 那＿＿ ＿＿

bà
(10) 爸＿＿ ＿＿

9 Fill in the blanks with the words in the box.

shuí	shén me	nǎr	jǐ
谁	什么	哪儿	几
ma	ne	nǎ	
吗	呢	哪	

nǐ shì   guó rén
(1) 你是 ＿＿＿＿ 国人？

nǐ jiào   míng zi
(2) 你叫 ＿＿＿＿ 名字？

nǐ jiā yǒu   kǒu rén
(3) 你家有 ＿＿＿＿ 口人？

nǐ jiā yǒu
(4) 你家有 ＿＿＿＿？

nǐ yǒu   ge xiōng dì jiě mèi
(5) 你有 ＿＿＿＿ 个兄弟姐妹？

wǒ hěn hǎo   nǐ
(6) 我很好，你 ＿＿＿＿？

nǐ shì zhōng xué shēng
(7) 你是中学生 ＿＿＿＿？

nǐ men yì jiā rén zhù zài
(8) 你们一家人住在 ＿＿＿＿？

10 Ask a question for each answer.

(1) A: ＿＿＿＿＿＿＿＿＿？

wǒ xìng lǐ
B: 我姓李。

(2) A: ＿＿＿＿＿＿＿＿＿？

wǒ jiào lǐ shān
B: 我叫李山。

(3) A: ＿＿＿＿＿＿＿＿＿？

tā shì zhōng xué shēng
B: 他是中学生。

(4) A: ＿＿＿＿＿＿＿＿＿？

tā jiā yǒu wǔ kǒu rén
B: 她家有五口人。

(5) A: ＿＿＿＿＿＿＿＿＿？

wǒ jiā yǒu bà ba   mā ma hé wǒ
B: 我家有爸爸、妈妈和我。

(6) A: ＿＿＿＿＿＿＿＿＿？

xiǎo yīng yǒu xiōng dì jiě mèi
B: 小英有兄弟姐妹。

(7) A: ＿＿＿＿＿＿＿＿＿？

wǒ bà ba gōngzuò
B: 我爸爸工作。

(8) A: ＿＿＿＿＿＿＿＿＿？

tā zhù zài běi jīng
B: 他住在北京。

11 Translation.

(1) wǒ bà ba gōng zuò　wǒ mā ma yě gōng zuò
我爸爸工作，我妈妈也工作。

(2) wǒ shì zhōng xué shēng　wǒ mèi mei yě shì zhōng xué shēng
我是中学生，我妹妹也是中学生。

(3) wǒ jiě jie zhù zài yīng guó　wǒ bú zhù zài yīng guó
我姐姐住在英国，我不住在英国。

(4) wǒ yǒu gē ge　tā méi yǒu gē ge
我有哥哥，她没有哥哥。

(5) tā xìng mǎ　wǒ yě xìng mǎ
他姓马，我也姓马。

(6) tā shì zhōng guó rén　wǒ yě shì zhōng guó rén
她是中国人，我也是中国人。

(7) tā jiā yǒu wǔ kǒu rén　wǒ jiā yě yǒu wǔ kǒu rén
他家有五口人，我家也有五口人。

(8) tā mèi mei sì suì　wǒ mèi mei yě sì suì
他妹妹四岁，我妹妹也四岁。

12 Match the Chinese with the English.

(1) gōng rén 工人　(a) children

(2) xiǎo péng you 小朋友　(b) big country

(3) hěn duō 很多　(c) this month

(4) dà guó 大国　(d) worker

(5) zhè ge yuè 这个月　(e) birthday

(6) xiǎo jie 小姐　(f) many; much

(7) shēng ri 生日　(g) university

(8) dà xué 大学　(h) last month

(9) shàng ge yuè 上个月　(i) eldest sister

(10) dà jiě 大姐　(j) Miss

13 Reading comprehension.

xiǎo shān jiā yǒu sì kǒu rén　bà ba
小山家有四口人：爸爸、
mā ma　gē ge hé tā　xiǎo shān de gē
妈妈、哥哥和他。小山的哥
ge shí jiǔ suì　shì dà xué shēng　xiǎo
哥十九岁，是大学生。小
shān shí wǔ suì　shì zhōng xué shēng　tā
山十五岁，是中学生。他
bà ba gōng zuò　tā mā ma bù gōng zuò
爸爸工作，他妈妈不工作。

Answer the questions.

(1) xiǎo shān yǒu xiōng dì jiě mèi ma
小山有兄弟姐妹吗？

(2) xiǎo shān yǒu jǐ ge gē ge
小山有几个哥哥？

(3) tā gē ge duō dà le
他哥哥多大了？

(4) xiǎo shān shì dà xué shēng ma
小山是大学生吗？

(5) xiǎo shān de bà ba gōng zuò ma
小山的爸爸工作吗？

14 Write the pinyin for the following words.

(1) 工作 _____   (7) 不是 _____

(2) 学生 _____   (8) 谁 _____

(3) 岁 _____   (9) 住 _____

(4) 多 _____   (10) 家 _____

(5) 没有 _____   (11) 名字 _____

(6) 这 _____   (12) 姓 _____

15 Translation.

(1) How many people are there in your family?

(2) How many brothers and sisters do you have?

(3) How old are you?

(4) Are you a secondary school student?

(5) Does your father work?

16 Give the meanings of the radicals. Find a word for each radical.

(1) 日 _____ _____   (5) 艹 _____ _____

(2) 亻 _____ _____   (6) 口 _____ _____

(3) 夕 _____ _____   (7) 讠 _____ _____

(4) 禾 _____ _____   (8) 女 _____ _____

17 Translation.

wǒ gē ge shí bā suì le
(1) 我哥哥十八岁了。

wǒ men bú shì zhōng guó rén   wǒ men
(2) 我们不是中国人，我们
shì rì běn rén
是日本人。

wǒ de péng you shì zhōng xué shēng
(3) 我的朋友是中学生。

nà ge rén shì shuí
(4) 那个人是谁？

tā mèi mei shì xiǎo xué shēng
(5) 她妹妹是小学生。

tā jiě jie zhù zài yīng guó
(6) 她姐姐住在英国。

wǒ bà ba gōng zuò   wǒ mā ma yě gōng zuò
(7) 我爸爸工作，我妈妈也工作。

tā gē ge bú shì zhōng xué shēng   shì dà xué shēng
(8) 他哥哥不是中学生，是大学生。

tā méi yǒu xiōng dì jiě mèi
(9) 他没有兄弟姐妹。

18 Correct the mistakes.

(1) ^{zhù} 任 _____   (3) ^{xiè} 谢 _____   (5) ^{zì} 字 _____   (7) ^{zuò} 作 _____   (9) ^{nǎ} 哪 _____

(2) ^{guó} 国 _____   (4) ^{de} 旳 _____   (6) ^{zhè} 这 _____   (8) ^{shēng} 生 _____   (10) ^{hé} 和 _____

19 Answer the questions according to the calendar.

(1) ^{jīn tiān shì jǐ yuè jǐ hào} 今天是几月几号？ _____

(2) ^{zuó tiān shì jǐ yuè jǐ hào} 昨天是几月几号？ _____

(3) ^{míng tiān shì jǐ yuè jǐ hào} 明天是几月几号？ _____

(4) ^{jīn tiān xīng qī jǐ} 今天星期几？ _____

(5) ^{míng tiān xīng qī jǐ} 明天星期几？ _____

20 Read the passage below. Write a paragraph about your family.

^{wǒ jiào wáng míng} 我叫王明。^{wǒ shì zhōng guó rén} 我是中国人。
^{wǒ jiā yǒu sì kǒu rén} 我家有四口人：^{bà ba} 爸爸、^{mā ma} 妈妈、
^{jiě jie hé wǒ} 姐姐和我。^{wǒ jiě jie shí liù suì shì} 我姐姐十六岁，是
^{zhōng xué shēng} 中学生。^{wǒ jiǔ suì shì xiǎo xué shēng} 我九岁，是小学生。
^{wǒ bà ba gōng zuò} 我爸爸工作，^{wǒ mā ma yě gōng zuò} 我妈妈也工作。
^{wǒ men zhù zài xiāng gǎng} 我们住在香港。

妈妈 (mā ma) 爸爸 (bà ba) 我 (wǒ) 姐姐 (jiě jie)

生 字

	一 丁 工								
gōng work	工								
	ノ イ 仁 仵 作 作 作								
zuò do; work	作								
	ᐟ 山 屵 屵 岁 岁								
suì year of age	岁								
	ノ ヒ 一 牛 生								
shēng bear; grow	生								
	了 了								
le particle	了								

识字 (三)

		亅 氺 水 水								
shuǐ water	水									
		丶 丷 少 火								
huǒ fire	火									
		一 十 土								
tǔ soil	土									
		丨 冂 冂 用 田								
tián field; surname	田									
		丨 冂 冂 日 旦 申 里								
lǐ inside	里									
		一 十 才 木								
mù tree; wood	木									
		一 二 云 云								
yún cloud	云									

1 | Match the words with the pictures.

shuǐ
(1) 水

huǒ
(2) 火

tǔ
(3) 土

rì
(4) 日

yuè
(5) 月

tián
(6) 田

shān
(7) 山

mù
(8) 木

yún
(9) 云

tiān
(10) 天

a

f

b

g

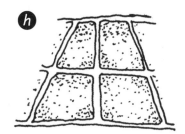
c

d

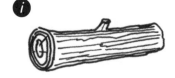
h

e

j

i

2 Give the meanings of the following phrases.

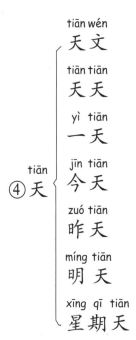

① shuǐ 水
xiāng shuǐ 香水
kǒu shuǐ 口水
hǎi shuǐ 海水
shān shuǐ 山水
shuǐ shǒu 水手
shuǐ tián 水田

③ rì 日
rì běn 日本
rì lì 日历
rì qī 日期
shēng rì 生日
xīng qī rì 星期日

④ tiān 天
tiān wén 天文
tiān tiān 天天
yì tiān 一天
jīn tiān 今天
zuó tiān 昨天
míng tiān 明天
xīng qī tiān 星期天

② huǒ 火
dà huǒ 大火
shān huǒ 山火
huǒ shān 火山

⑤ mù 木
mù mǎ 木马
mù ěr 木耳

3 Match the Chinese with the English.

(1) duō 多 (a) long
(2) fāng 方 (b) square
(3) cháng 长 (c) more
(4) yán 言 (d) whole
(5) yòng 用 (e) speech
(6) quán 全 (f) inside
(7) qí 齐 (g) in order
(8) lǐ 里 (h) use

4 Give the meanings of the radicals. Find a word for each radical.

(1) 口 _____ _____
(2) 人 _____ _____
(3) 厂 _____ _____
(4) 夕 _____ _____
(5) 刀 _____ _____
(6) 讠 _____ _____
(7) 阝 _____ _____

第十课　我上五年级

1 Circle the correct pinyin.

(1) 年级　(a) niángjí　(b) niánjí

(2) 岁　(a) shuì　(b) suì

(3) 都　(a) dōu　(b) duō

(4) 多　(a) duō　(b) dōu

(5) 工作　(a) gōngzuò　(b) gōngzhuò

(6) 今年　(a) jīnnián　(b) jīngnián

2 Give the meanings of the radicals. Find a word for each radical.

(1) 阝 _____ _____

(2) 山 _____ _____

(3) 辶 _____ _____

(4) 钅 _____ _____

(5) 纟 _____ _____

(6) 禾 _____ _____

3 Use "也" to express "also". Finish the following sentences.

tā bà ba gōng zuò　　wǒ bà ba
(1) 他爸爸工作，我爸爸<u>也工作</u>。

tā mā ma gōng zuò　　wǒ mā ma
(2) 她妈妈工作，我妈妈_____。

tā shí èr suì　　wǒ
(3) 他十二岁，我_____。

xiǎo míng shì xiǎo xué shēng　　wǒ mèi mei
(4) 小明是小学生，我妹妹_____。

xiǎo tiān shàng jiǔ nián jí　　wǒ gē ge
(5) 小天上九年级，我哥哥_____。

4 Use "都" to combine two sentences.

tā shì zhōng xué shēng　　wǒ yě shì zhōng xué shēng
(1) 他是中学生，我也是中学生。→我们都是中学生。

xiǎo tiān shì zhōng guó rén　　wǒ yě shì zhōng guó rén
(2) 小天是中国人，我也是中国人。→

xiǎo míng jīn nián shí èr suì　　wǒ yě shí èr suì
(3) 小明今年十二岁，我也十二岁。→

wáng yuè shàng shí nián jí　　wǒ yě shàng shí nián jí
(4) 王月上十年级，我也上十年级。→

5 Separate the two stories.

xiǎo yún shí liù suì　shàng shí yī nián jí
小云十六岁，上十一年级。

xiǎo tiān èr shí yī suì　shàng dà xué sì nián jí
小天二十一岁，上大学四年级。

xiǎo yún zhù zài xiāng gǎng
小云住在香港。

xiǎo tiān zhù zài yīng guó
小天住在英国。

xiǎo tiān méi yǒu xiōng dì jiě mèi
小天没有兄弟姐妹。

xiǎo yún yǒu yí ge dì di　tā jīn nián jiǔ suì
小云有一个弟弟，他今年九岁。

xiǎo yún de bà ba　mā ma dōu gōng zuò
小云的爸爸、妈妈都工作。

xiǎo tiān de bà ba gōng zuò　mā ma bù gōng zuò
小天的爸爸工作，妈妈不工作。

xiǎo yún
小云

xiǎo tiān
小天

小云十六岁，　　　小天二十一岁，

_____　　_____

_____　　_____

_____　　_____

6 Find the phrases and then write them out with English meanings.

姐	哥	香	英	国	年
兄	姐	弟	港	不	级
上	那	工	作	错	谢
学	生	人	再	见	没
还	可	以	很	多	有
我	们	名	字	中	国

(1) _____ _____

(2) _____ _____

(3) _____ _____

(4) _____ _____

(5) _____ _____

(6) _____ _____

(7) _____ _____

(8) _____ _____

(9) _____ _____

(10) _____ _____

7 Ask questions about the underlined parts.

(1) wǒ jiào xiǎo shān
我叫<u>小山</u>。（什么） shén me → 你叫什么名字？

(2) xiǎo shān jiā yǒu sì kǒu rén
小山家有<u>四</u>口人。（几） jǐ →

(3) tā yǒu liǎng ge dì di
他有<u>两</u>个弟弟。（几） jǐ →

(4) tā bà ba wǔ shí suì
她爸爸<u>五十岁</u>。（多大） duō dà →

(5) wǒ gē ge shàng shí nián jí
我哥哥上<u>十</u>年级。（几） jǐ →

(6) lǐ yīng zhù zài běi jīng
李英住在<u>北京</u>。（哪儿） nǎr →

(7) tā shì rì běn rén
她是<u>日本人</u>。（哪国人） nǎ guó rén →

(8) wǒ jiā yǒu bà ba mā ma yí ge gē ge hé wǒ
我家有<u>爸爸、妈妈、一个哥哥和我</u>。（谁） shuí →

8 Find the missing words.

jí	shēng	jiě	xué	zì	bà	suì	ér	zuò
级	生	姐	学	字	爸	岁	儿	作

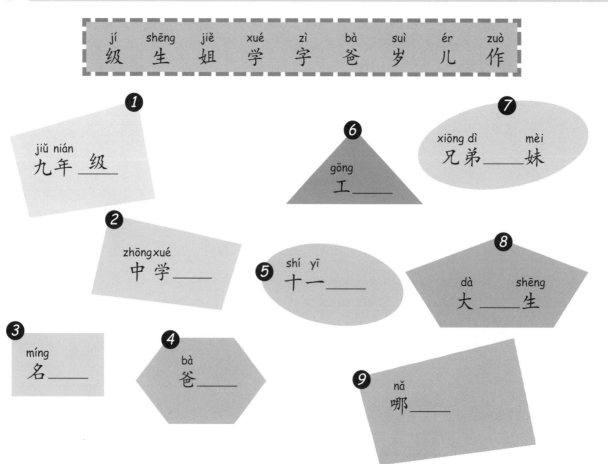

❶ jiǔ nián
九年＿级

❻ gōng
工＿

❼ xiōng dì   mèi
兄弟＿妹

❷ zhōng xué
中学＿

❺ shí yī
十一＿

❽ dà   shēng
大＿生

❸ míng
名＿

❹ bà
爸＿

❾ nǎ
哪＿

66

9 Write the telephone numbers in Chinese.

(1) 8647 3091 _____

(2) 2566 4480 _____

(3) 5424 7602 _____

(4) 9474 8551 _____

(5) 2524 7135 _____

(6) 5483 6209 _____

(7) 6247 3201 _____

(8) 5689 2033 _____

10 Match the Chinese with the English.

shàng ge yuè
(1) 上个月   (a) every year

míng nián
(2) 明年   (b) last month

gōng rén
(3) 工人   (c) intermediate level

wǔ nián
(4) 五年   (d) worker

nián nián
(5) 年年   (e) middle-aged person

zhōng nián rén
(6) 中年人   (f) this month

zhè ge yuè
(7) 这个月   (g) next year

zhōng jí
(8) 中级   (h) school term

xué nián
(9) 学年   (i) five years

xué qī
(10) 学期   (j) school year

11 Put the parts together to form characters.

身 宀
父 女 十 寸
口 之 讠 日 巴
生 亻 子 马
不 也

(1) 爸 _____   (6) _____

(2) _____   (7) _____

(3) _____   (8) _____

(4) _____   (9) _____

(5) _____   (10) _____

12 Fill in the blanks with the words in the box.

jǐ	shuí	duō dà
几	谁	多大
nǎr	nǎ	shén me
哪儿	哪	什么

(1)
nǐ jiào   míng zi
A: 你叫 _____ 名字？

wǒ jiào wáng yīng
B: 我叫王英。

(2)
nǐ jiā yǒu   kǒu rén
A: 你家有 _____ 口人？

wǒ jiā yǒu wǔ kǒu rén
B: 我家有五口人。

(3)
nǐ jiā yǒu
A: 你家有 _____ ？

wǒ jiā yǒu bà ba   mā ma   yí ge
B: 我家有爸爸、妈妈、一个

jiě jie   liǎng ge dì di hé wǒ
姐姐、两个弟弟和我。

(4)
nǐ dì di   suì le
A: 你弟弟 _____ 岁了？

tā jiǔ suì le
B: 他九岁了。

(5)
nǐ jīn nián   le
A: 你今年 _____ 了？

wǒ shí sì suì
B: 我十四岁。

(6)
nǐ jīn nián shàng   nián jí
A: 你今年上 _____ 年级？

wǒ jīn nián shàng shí nián jí
B: 我今年上十年级。

(7)
nǐ men yì jiā rén zhù zài
A: 你们一家人住在 _____ ？

wǒ men yì jiā rén zhù zài běi jīng
B: 我们一家人住在北京。

13 Write the following dates in Chinese.

(1) September

(2) November

(3) 8th August

(4) 26th April

(5) Monday, 13th March

(6) Tuesday, 17th July

(7) Friday, 23rd June, 2001

(8) Sunday, 30th December, 2001

14 Write the pinyin for the following words.

(1) 我们 _____   (8) 多大 _____

(2) 没有 _____   (9) 几岁 _____

(3) 年级 _____   (10) 日本 _____

(4) 工作 _____   (11) 姐姐 _____

(5) 都 _____   (12) 谁 _____

(6) 大学生 _____

(7) 一家人 _____

15 Fill in the blanks with the words in the box.

dōu	yě	bú	méi	hé
都	也	不	没	和

(1)
tā　　　shì wǒ gē ge
他＿＿＿是我哥哥。

(2)
wǒ bà ba　　mā ma　　　gōng zuò
我爸爸、妈妈＿＿＿工作。

(3)
tā dì di shì xiǎo xué shēng　　wǒ dì di
她弟弟是小学生，我弟弟

shì xiǎo xué shēng
＿＿＿是小学生。

(4)
wǒ gē ge　　　jiě jie dōu shì dà xué shēng
我哥哥＿＿＿姐姐都是大学生。

(5)
xiǎo yīng　　yǒu dì di　　tā yǒu yí ge
小英＿＿＿有弟弟，她有一个

gē ge
哥哥。

16 Translation.

(1) Are you a secondary school student?

(2) Which grade are you in?

(3) Do both of your parents work?

(4) Are you Chinese?

(5) This is my friend.

(6) That is my elder sister.

(7) We all live in Beijing.

17 Write a paragraph about this family. You might need the following words in the box.

yì jiā	zhù zài běi jīng	méi yǒu	liǎng ge	gōng zuò	shàng	nián jí
一家	住在北京	（没)有	两个	工作	上……年级
xué sheng	hé	dōu	xiōng dì jiě mèi	yīng guó rén		
学生	和	都	兄弟姐妹	英国人		

xiǎo tián
小田

小田一家有……

18 Reading comprehension.

<table>
<tr><td>wáng xīng
王 星</td><td>bà ba
爸爸</td><td>mā ma
妈妈</td><td>mèi mei
妹妹</td></tr>
</table>

zhè shì wǒ de yì jiā　wǒ jiā yǒu sì kǒu
这是我的一家。我家有四口
rén　tā men shì bà ba　mā ma　mèi mei hé
人，他们是爸爸、妈妈、妹妹和
wǒ　wǒ mèi mei jiǔ suì　shàng sì nián jí　wǒ
我。我妹妹九岁，上四年级。我
shí yī suì　shàng liù nián jí　wǒ men dōu shì xiǎo
十一岁，上六年级。我们都是小
xué shēng　wǒ bà ba　mā ma dōu gōng zuò　wǒ
学生。我爸爸、妈妈都工作。我
men shì zhōng guó rén　wǒ men zhù zài běi jīng
们是中国人。我们住在北京。

Answer the questions.

wáng xīng jiā yǒu jǐ kǒu rén
(1) 王 星家有几口人？

tā yǒu xiōng dì jiě mèi ma
(2) 他有兄弟姐妹吗？

tā yǒu méi yǒu mèi mei
(3) 他有没有妹妹？

tā mèi mei jǐ suì le
(4) 他妹妹几岁了？

wáng xīng duō dà le
(5) 王 星多大了？

tā shàng jǐ nián jí
(6) 他上几年级？

wáng xīng shì zhōng xué shēng ma
(7) 王 星是中学生吗？

tā men shì nǎ guó rén
(8) 他们是哪国人？

tā men zhù zài nǎr
(9) 他们住在哪儿？

19 Ask questions according to the calendar below.

<table>
<tr><td colspan="7">八月</td></tr>
<tr><td>日</td><td>一</td><td>二</td><td>三</td><td>四</td><td>五</td><td>六</td></tr>
<tr><td></td><td>今天</td><td></td><td>1</td><td>2</td><td>3</td><td>4</td></tr>
<tr><td>5</td><td>6</td><td>7</td><td>8</td><td>9</td><td>10</td><td>11</td></tr>
<tr><td>12</td><td>13</td><td>14</td><td>15</td><td>16</td><td>17</td><td>18</td></tr>
<tr><td>19</td><td>20</td><td>21</td><td>22</td><td>23</td><td>24</td><td>25</td></tr>
<tr><td>26</td><td>27</td><td>28</td><td>29</td><td>30</td><td>31</td><td></td></tr>
</table>

(1) 今天是几月几号？

(2) _____

(3) _____

(4) _____

(5) _____

(6) _____

生字

		丿 亠 乍 乍 乍 年								
nián year	年									
		纟 纟 纟 纟 级 级								
jí grade	级									
		一 十 土 耂 耂 者 者 者 都 都								
dōu all; both	都									

生词

第七课	zhè 这	yì jiā rén 一家人	tā men 他们	wǒ men 我们	mā ma 妈妈	mèi mei 妹妹	dì di 弟弟	bà ba 爸爸
	shuí 谁	jiě jie 姐姐	gē ge 哥哥					

	dà 大	rén kǒu 人口	duō 多	fāng yán 方言	lì shǐ 历史	cháng 长

第八课	yǒu 有	qī kǒu rén 七口人	dà dì di 大弟弟	xiǎo dì di 小弟弟	nà 那	yí ge gē ge 一个哥哥	liǎng ge dì di 两个弟弟
	hé 和	yīng guó rén 英国人	jǐ kǒu rén 几口人	xiōng dì jiě mèi 兄弟姐妹	méi yǒu 没有		

	ěr 耳	shǒu 手	yì qí 一齐	yòng 用	quán 全	shēn xīn 身心	xué 学	zhōngwén 中文

第九课	gōng zuò 工作	shí èr suì 十二岁	zhōng xué shēng 中学生	xiǎo xué shēng 小学生	le 了	jǐ suì 几岁	duō dà 多大

	shuǐ 水	huǒ 火	tǔ 土	tián 田	lǐ 里	mù 木	yún 云

第十课	jīn nián 今年	shàng wǔ nián jí 上五年级	dà gē 大哥	dà xué shēng 大学生	èr gē 二哥	dōu 都

总复习

1. People

nǐ men	wǒ men	tā men	tā men	xué shēng men
你们	我们	他们	她们	学生（们）

dà xué shēng	zhōng xué shēng	xiǎo xué shēng
大学生	中学生	小学生

2. Family members

bà ba	mā ma	gē ge	jiě jie	dì di	mèi mei
爸爸	妈妈	哥哥	姐姐	弟弟	妹妹

xiōng dì jiě mèi	jiā rén
兄弟姐妹	家人

3. Question words and phrases

shuí	jǐ suì	duō dà	jǐ kǒu ge rén	jǐ nián jí	jǐ ge xiōng dì jiě mèi
谁	几岁	多大	几口(个)人	几年级	几个兄弟姐妹

4. Measure words

gè	kǒu
个	口

5. Adjectives and adverbs

dà	xiǎo	duō	cháng	qí	quán	dōu
大	小	多	长	齐	全	都

6. Verbs

(méi) yǒu　　gōng zuò　　shàng xué　　xué　　yòng
（没）有　　工　作　　上　学　　学　　用

7. Parts of the body

ěr　　kǒu　　shǒu　　shēn　　xīn
耳　　口　　手　　身　　心

8. Surnames

fāng　　shǐ　　qí　　tián
方　　史　　齐　　田

9. Nature

rì　　yuè　　shuǐ　　tǔ　　huǒ　　mù　　yún　　tiān　　tián　　shān
日　　月　　水　　土　　火　　木　　云　　天　　田　　山

10. Phonetics

Diphthongs:　　ai　　ei　　ui　　ao　　ou　　iu

ie　　üe　　er　　an　　en　　in

un　　ün　　ang　　eng　　ing　　ong

11. Questions and answers

tā shì shuí
(1) 他是谁？

tā shì wǒ bà ba
他是我爸爸。

zhè shì shuí
(2) 这是谁？

zhè shì wǒ mā ma
这是我妈妈。

nà shì shuí
(3) 那是谁？

nà shì wǒ mèi mei
那是我妹妹。

(4) nǐ jiā yǒu jǐ kǒu rén
你家有几口人？

wǒ jiā yǒu sì kǒu rén
我家有四口人。

(5) nǐ jiā yǒu shuí
你家有谁？

wǒ jiā yǒu bà ba　mā ma　liǎng ge gē ge hé wǒ
我家有爸爸、妈妈、两个哥哥和我。

(6) nǐ yǒu méi yǒu xiōng dì jiě mèi
你有没有兄弟姐妹？

yǒu
有。

(7) nǐ yǒu jǐ ge xiōng dì jiě mèi
你有几个兄弟姐妹？

sān ge
三个。

(8) nǐ bà ba gōng zuò ma
你爸爸工作吗？

gōng zuò
工作。

(9) nǐ bà ba duō dà le
你爸爸多大了？

sān shí jiǔ suì
三十九岁。

(10) nǐ dì di jǐ suì le
你弟弟几岁了？

tā liù suì le
他六岁了。

(11) nǐ shì zhōng xué shēng ma
你是中学生吗？

shì
是。

(12) nǐ shì bú shì yīng guó rén
你是不是英国人？

bú shì
不是。

(13) nǐ shàng jǐ nián jí
你上几年级？

qī nián jí
七年级。

测验

1 Write the pinyin and give the meanings of the following words.

(1) 日 _____ _____

(2) 水 _____ _____

(3) 月 _____ _____

(4) 火 _____ _____

(5) 土 _____ _____

(6) 木 _____ _____

(7) 云 _____ _____

(8) 天 _____ _____

(9) 田 _____ _____

(10) 山 _____ _____

2 Match the Chinese with the English.

(1) 耳   (a) heart

(2) 身   (b) hand

(3) 口   (c) body

(4) 手   (d) mouth

(5) 心   (e) ear

3 Fill in the blanks with the words in the box.

谁　几口人　几岁　几个
多大　几年级

(1) 你家有_____?

(2) 你有_____兄弟姐妹?

(3) 你弟弟_____了?

　　（他六岁了。）

(4) 你爸爸_____了?

　　（他四十岁了。）

(5) 你姐姐上_____?

　　（七年级）

(6) 他是_____?

76

4 Translation.

(1) one elder brother

(2) two elder sisters

(3) four younger brothers

(4) five middle school students

(5) six family members

(6) seven university students

(7) eight Chinese people

(8) eleven friends

5 Put the words / phrases into sentences.

有　我家　六口人。

→ 我家有六口人。

(1) 谁　是　他？

(2) 兄弟姐妹　没有　她。

(3) 是　那个人　我哥哥。

(4) 是　大学生　他姐姐。

(5) 我　二年级　上。

6 Write the following dates in Chinese.

(1) Tuesday

(2) Sunday

(3) 20th April

(4) 8th June

(5) 29th August

(6) 10th December, 2000

(7) 25th November, 1998

7 Circle the correct pinyin.

(1) 兄　(a) xiōng　(b) xōng

(2) 姐　(a) jě　(b) jiě

(3) 都　(a) dōu　(b) duō

(4) 上　(a) sàng　(b) shàng

(5) 工作　(a) gōngzhuò　(b) gōngzuò

(6) 岁　(a) suì　(b) shuì

(7) 年　(a) nián　(b) lián

8   Answer the following questions.

(1) 你家有几口人？

(2) 你家有谁？

(3) 你有兄弟姐妹吗？

(4) 你有几个兄弟姐妹？

(5) 你有没有哥哥？

(6) 你有没有妹妹？

(7) 你今年多大了？

(8) 你是不是中学生？

(9) 你上几年级？

(10) 你爸爸、妈妈都工作吗？

9   Reading comprehension.

方云家有五口人：爸爸、妈妈、哥哥、妹妹和她。她爸爸是中国人，她妈妈是英国人。她今年七岁，上小学二年级。她哥哥今年九岁，上小学四年级。妹妹今年四岁，她还没有上学。她爸爸、妈妈都工作。他们一家人住在英国。

Answer the questions.

(1) 方云家有几口人？

(2) 方云有几个兄弟姐妹？

(3) 方云有没有姐姐？

(4) 方云的爸爸是哪国人？

(5) 方云的妈妈工作吗？

(6) 他们一家住在哪儿？

第三单元　国家、语言

第十一课　中国在亚洲

1 Write the pinyin for the following places.

(1) 法国 _____

(2) 英国 _____

(3) 德国 _____

(4) 欧洲 _____

(5) 加拿大 _____

(6) 南非 _____

(7) 马来西亚 _____

(8) 澳大利亚 _____

2 Give the meanings of the following phrases.

(1) xiōng dì 兄弟 _____ 　(7) fāng yán 方言 _____

(2) jiě mèi 姐妹 _____ 　(8) qù guo 去过 _____

(3) nián jí 年级 _____ 　(9) guó jiā 国家 _____

(4) kě shì 可是 _____ 　(10) xīng qī 星期 _____

(5) lì shǐ 历史 _____ 　(11) xìng míng 姓名 _____

(6) rén kǒu 人口 _____ 　(12) xué sheng 学生 _____

3 Dismantle the characters into parts.

(1) xiè 谢 讠 身 寸　(8) yīng 英 ____ ____

(2) lì 利 ____ ____　(9) cuò 错 ____ ____

(3) fǎ 法 ____ ____　(10) hái 还 ____ ____

(4) yáng 洋 ____ ____　(11) nà 那 ____ ____

(5) ōu 欧 ____ ____　(12) xìng 姓 ____ ____

(6) xīng 星 ____ ____　(13) ān 安 ____ ____

(7) zhōu 洲 ____ ____　(14) xiāng 香 ____ ____

4 Put the words / phrases into sentences.

Example
qù guo　tā　jiā ná dà
去过　他　加拿大。

→ 他去过加拿大。

(1) tā　hěn duō　qù guo　guó jiā
她　很多　去过　国家。

(2) dōu　wǒ bà ba　mā ma　gōng zuò
都　我爸爸、妈妈　工作。

(3) ma　qù guo　nǐ　dé guó
吗　去过　你　德国？

(4) ōu zhōu　yīng guó　zài
欧洲　英国　在。

(5) zhù zài　tā gē ge　yīng guó
住在　他哥哥　英国。

79

5 Circle the correct pinyin.

(1) 欧洲   (a) ōuzhōu   (b) ōujōu

(2) 加拿大   (a) jiānádà   (b) zhiānádà

(3) 去过   (a) qùguo   (b) qùguò

(4) 南非   (a) nánfāi   (b) nánfēi

(5) 澳大利亚   (a) àodàlíyà   (b) àodàlìyà

(6) 马来西亚   (a) mǎléisīyà   (b) mǎláixīyà

(7) 大洋洲   (a) dàyángzhōu   (b) dàyángzōu

(8) 国家   (a) guōjiā   (b) guójiā

6 True or false?

( )(1) 澳大利亚在大洋洲。

ào dà lì yà zài dà yáng zhōu

( )(2) 英国在南非。

yīng guó zài nán fēi

( )(3) 加拿大在北美洲。

jiā ná dà zài běi měi zhōu

( )(4) 马来西亚在非洲。

mǎ lái xī yà zài fēi zhōu

( )(5) 美国在亚洲。

měi guó zài yà zhōu

( )(6) 法国和德国都在欧洲。

fǎ guó hé dé guó dōu zài ōu zhōu

( )(7) 香港在亚洲。

xiānggǎng zài yà zhōu

7 Give the meanings of the radicals.
Find a word for each radical.

(1) 禾 _____ _____

(2) 艹 _____ _____

(3) 氵 _____

(4) 力 _____

(5) 阝 _____

(6) 讠 _____

(7) 辶 _____

(8) 白 _____

(9) 夕 _____

8 Correct the mistakes.

(1) 澳 _____

ào

(2) 美 _____

měi

(3) 洋 _____

yáng

(4) 非 _____

fēi

(5) 南 _____

nán

(6) 欧 _____

ōu

(7) 西 _____

xī

(8) 加 _____

jiā

(9) 德 _____

dé

(10) 亚 _____

yà

9 Reading comprehension.

wáng fēi jīn nián bā suì   tā jiā yǒu sì
王非今年八岁。她家有四

kǒu rén   bà ba   mā ma   jiě jie hé
口人：爸爸、妈妈、姐姐和

tā   tā bà ba shì zhōng guó rén   tā mā
她。她爸爸是中国人，她妈

ma shì yīng guó rén   wáng fēi de jiě jie jīn
妈是英国人。王非的姐姐今

nián shí èr suì   shàng shí nián jí   wáng fēi shàng
年十二岁，上十年级。王非上

xiǎo xué sān nián jí   tā bà ba   mā ma dōu
小学三年级。她爸爸、妈妈都

gōng zuò   tā men yì jiā rén qù guo hǎo duō
工作。他们一家人去过好多

guó jiā   tā men qù guo fǎ guó   yīng guó
国家。他们去过法国、英国、

dé guó   měi guó   jiā ná dà hé rì běn
德国、美国、加拿大和日本。

wáng fēi
王非

True or false?

wáng fēi jīn nián shàng shí nián jí
( )(1) 王非今年上十年级。

wáng fēi de mā ma shì zhōng guó rén
( )(2) 王非的妈妈是中国人。

wáng fēi méi yǒu jiě jie
( )(3) 王非没有姐姐。

wáng fēi méi yǒu qù guo rì běn
( )(4) 王非没有去过日本。

10 Transcribe the pinyin into Chinese characters.

(1) xīngqīliù _____

(2) zuótiān _____

(3) méiyǒu _____

(4) jiānádà _____

(5) àodàlìyà _____

(6) shàngxué _____

11 Answer the questions.

nǐ jīn nián duō dà le
(1) 你今年多大了？

nǐ de shēng ri shì jǐ yuè jǐ hào
(2) 你的生日是几月几号？

nǐ jiā yǒu jǐ kǒu rén
(3) 你家有几口人？

nǐ jiā yǒu shuí
(4) 你家有谁？

nǐ jīn nián shàng jǐ nián jí
(5) 你今年上几年级？

nǐ de hǎo péng you shì shuí
(6) 你的好朋友是谁？

nǐ qù guo shén me guó jiā
(7) 你去过什么国家？

nǐ bà ba   mā ma dōu gōng zuò ma
(8) 你爸爸、妈妈都工作吗？

12 Re-arrange the sentences into the order of the English translation.

lǐ ōu jīn nián shí suì
(1) 李欧今年十岁。

tā zài rì běn gōng zuò
(2) 他在日本工作。

tā shàng xiǎo xué liù nián jí
(3) 他上小学六年级。

lǐ ōu de mā ma shì rì běn rén
(4) 李欧的妈妈是日本人。

tā qù guo zhōng guó   měi guó   jiā ná
(5) 他去过中国、美国、加拿

dà   fǎ guó   yīng guó hé ào dà lì
大、法国、英国和澳大利

yà
亚。

lǐ ōu de bà ba shì měi guó rén
(6) 李欧的爸爸是美国人。

tā qù guo hěn duō guó jiā
(7) 他去过很多国家。

tā men yì jiā rén zhù zài rì běn
(8) 他们一家人住在日本。

Li Ou is ten years old. He is in primary six. He has been to many countries. He has been to China, America, Canada, France, England and Australia. Li Ou's father is American. He works in Japan. Li Ou's mother is Japanese. The family lives in Japan.

13 Find the opposites.

shì	xiǎo	nán	qù	fēi	běi	dà	lái
是	小	南	去	非	北	大	来

(1) _____ 是 → 非 _____

(2) _____ → _____

(3) _____ → _____

(4) _____ → _____

14 Finish the following paragraph about yourself.

wǒ jiào   wǒ jīn nián
我叫_____。我今年

suì   shàng   nián jí
_____岁，上_____年级。

wǒ jiā yǒu   rén   tā men
我家有_____人，他们

shì
是_____。

wǒ bà ba shì   rén   wǒ mā
我爸爸是_____人，我妈

ma shì   rén   wǒ bà ba
妈是_____人。我爸爸

mā ma
_____，妈妈_____(work)。

wǒ qù guo
我去过_____,

kě shì wǒ méi yǒu qù guo
可是我没有去过_____。

wǒ men
我们_____(live)。

生 字

	一 丁 丌 邒 亜 亚									
yà second; Asia	亚									
	丶 丶 氵 氵 汐 沙 洲 洲 洲									
zhōu continent	洲									
	丁 力 加 加 加									
jiā add	加									
	丿 人 人 仌 仝 合 會 會 盒 拿									
ná take	拿									
	丶 丷 丷 丷 半 羊 美 美									
měi beautiful	美									
	丆 丁 叮 叮 巴									
bā hope earnestly	巴									
	一 十 卄 南 南 南 南 南 南									
nán south	南									
	丶 丶 氵 氵 汇 汁 注 法 法									
fǎ law; method	法									
	丿 彳 彳 彳 彳 徃 徔 德 德 德 德 德 德 德									
dé morals; virtue	德									
	丨 丆 非 扌 非 非 非 非									
fēi wrong; not; no	非									
	一 丆 又 区 区 欧 欧 欧									
ōu Europe; surname	欧									

83

生字

		一 一 丁 不 平 来 来										
lái come	来										
		丶 丶 氵 氵 氵 氵 洋 洋 洋									
yáng ocean	洋										
		丶 丶 氵 氵 氵 氵 沪 沪 澍 澍 澎 澳 澳									
ào inlet of the sea; bay	澳										
		一 十 土 去 去									
qù go	去										
		一 寸 寸 寸 过 过									
guò pass; cross over; particle	过										

84

识字 (四)

	乛 了 子									
zǐ son	子									
	丶 冂 口 呈 另 吴 吴									
wú surname	吴									
	乛 ㄱ 弓									
gōng bow	弓									
	乛 ㄱ 弓 弓' 引 张 张									
zhāng surname; measure word	张									
	一 十 十 古 古									
gǔ ancient	古									
	一 十 十 古 古 刮 胡 胡 胡									
hú surname	胡									

1 Separate the surnames from the first names.

mǎ	yún	wú	lǐ	míng	hú
马	云	吴	李	明	胡
zhāng	gǔ	shǐ	fāng	wáng	qí
张	古	史	方	王	齐
quán	shān	tiān	zhōng		
全	山	天	中		

xìng
姓

míng
名

(1) ___马___   (a) ___云___

(2) _____   (b) _____

(3) _____   (c) _____

(4) _____   (d) _____

(5) _____   (e) _____

(6) _____   (f) _____

2 Match the pinyin with the Chinese.

(1) yán   (a) 古

(2) shuǐ   (b) 言

(3) gǔ   (c) 胡

(4) hú   (d) 子

(5) wú   (e) 水

(6) gōng   (f) 长

(7) cháng   (g) 云

(8) mù   (h) 弓

(9) zǐ   (i) 木

(10) yún   (j) 吴

3 Give the meanings of each word.

wén
① 文 _____
   qí
   齐 _____
   zhè
   这 _____

② 里 _____
   zǎo
   早 _____
   gǔ
   古 _____

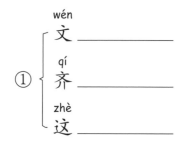

4 Give the meanings of the following phrases.

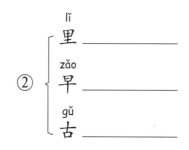

① 月
   shàng ge yuè
   上 个 月
   zhè ge yuè
   这 个 月
   yuè lì
   月 历

② 胡
   hú zi
   胡 子
   èr hú
   二 胡

③ 古
   gǔ rén
   古 人
   gǔ wén
   古 文

第十二课　他去过很多国家

1 Write the pinyin for the following phrases.

(1) 笔友 _____　(5) 现在 _____

(2) 地方 _____　(6) 非洲 _____

(3) 但是 _____　(7) 哪儿 _____

(4) 出生 _____　(8) 名字 _____

2 Write the following dates in Chinese.

(1) New Years's Day _____

(2) Christmas Day _____

(3) April Fool's Day _____

(4) Valentine's Day _____

(5) Halloween _____

(6) your birthday _____

3 Give the meanings of the radicals. Group the characters according to their radicals.

(1) 土 _____ _____

(2) 欠 _____ _____

(3) 竹 _____ _____

(4) 彳 _____ _____

(5) 亻 _____ _____

(6) 氵 _____ _____

dàn	ōu	dé	zuò	dì
但	欧	德	作	地
děng	míng	bǐ	xiàn	ào
等	明	笔	现	澳
shì	zhōu	lì		
是	洲	利		

4 Match the Chinese with the English.

chū qu
(1) 出去　　　　　　(a) sunrise

chū kǒu
(2) 出口　　　　　　(b) land

rì chū
(3) 日出　　　　　　(c) go out

chū guó
(4) 出国　　　　　　(d) export; exit

chū míng
(5) 出名　　　　　　(e) local people

tǔ dì
(6) 土地　　　　　　(f) famous

tián dì
(7) 田地　　　　　　(g) go abroad

běn dì rén
(8) 本地人　　　　　(h) farmland

dì lǐ
(9) 地理　　　　　　(i) geography

5 Complete the form about yourself.

xìng míng 姓名：	chū shēng rì qī 出生日期：	chū shēng dì 出生地：
nán nǚ 男／女：	duō dà le 多大了：	nián jí 年级：
nǎ guó rén 哪国人：	zhù zài nǎr 住在哪儿：	
bà ba de xìng míng 爸爸的姓名：		mā ma de xìng míng 妈妈的姓名：

6 Reading comprehension.

wǒ jiào shǐ xiǎo yún, jīn nián shí qī
我叫史小云，今年十七
suì shì zhōng xué shēng wǒ jīn nián shàng shí
岁，是中学生。我今年上十
èr nián jí wǒ chū shēng zài zhōng guó dàn
二年级。我出生在中国，但
shì wǒ shì měi guó rén wǒ qù guo ōu zhōu
是我是美国人。我去过欧洲、
yà zhōu hé dà yáng zhōu dàn shì wǒ méi yǒu
亚洲和大洋洲，但是我没有
qù guo fēi zhōu wǒ xiàn zài zhù zài měi guó
去过非洲。我现在住在美国。

True or false?

shǐ xiǎo yún jīn nián shàng shí yī nián jí
( )(1) 史小云今年上十一年级。
tā shì zhōng guó rén
( )(2) 她是中国人。
tā chū shēng zài měi guó
( )(3) 她出生在美国。
tā méi yǒu qù guo fēi zhōu
( )(4) 她没有去过非洲。

7 Translation.

wáng ān xiàn zài zhù zài shàng hǎi
(1) 王安现在住在上海。
wǒ de bǐ yǒu xìng wú
(2) 我的笔友姓吴。
tā bà ba qù guo hěn duō dì fang
(3) 他爸爸去过很多地方。
wǒ mèi mei de shēng ri shì qī yuè bā rì
(4) 我妹妹的生日是七月八日。
nǐ qù guo shén me guó jiā
(5) 你去过什么国家？
tā chū shēng zài běi jīng dàn shì tā shì
(6) 她出生在北京，但是她是
rì běn rén
日本人。
wǒ qù guo yīng guó dàn shì wǒ méi yǒu
(7) 我去过英国，但是我没有
qù guo dé guó hé fǎ guó
去过德国和法国。
wǒ bà ba yě xué zhōng wén
(8) 我爸爸也学中文。
tā bà ba gōng zuò dàn shì tā mā ma
(9) 她爸爸工作，但是她妈妈
bù gōng zuò
不工作。

8   Match the Chinese with the English.

wǒ bà ba qù guo běi jīng
(1) 我爸爸去过北京。

(a) Xiao Ming has learned French before.

xiǎo míng xué guo fǎ wén
(2) 小明学过法文。

(b) Wang Yue used to have a Japanese friend.

wáng yuè yǒu guo yí ge rì běn péng you
(3) 王月有过一个日本朋友。

(c) My father has been to Beijing.

tā mā ma zài shàng hǎi zhù guo
(4) 她妈妈在上海住过。

(d) He has studied at university.

tā shàng guo dà xué
(5) 他上过大学。

(e) Her mother used to live in Shanghai.

9   Reading comprehension.

lǐ ān yǒu yí ge bǐ yǒu jiào fāng dà nián fāng dà nián jīn nián
李安有一个笔友，叫方大年。方大年今年
shí sān suì shàng jiǔ nián jí tā xiàn zài zhù zài běi jīng tā jiā
十三岁，上九年级。他现在住在北京。他家
yǒu sān kǒu rén tā bà ba mā ma hé tā tā qù guo hěn duō dì
有三口人：他爸爸、妈妈和他。他去过很多地
fang tā qù guo yīng guó fǎ guó ào dà lì yà měi guó jiā
方，他去过英国、法国、澳大利亚、美国、加
ná dà děng guó jiā tā bà ba shì zhōng guó rén tā mā ma shì měi
拿大等国家。他爸爸是中国人，他妈妈是美
guó rén tā bà ba gōng zuò tā mā ma yě gōng zuò
国人。他爸爸工作，他妈妈也工作。

fāng dà nián
方大年

Answer the questions.

fāng dà nián jīn nián duō dà le
(1) 方大年今年多大了？

tā qù guo shén me dì fang
(4) 他去过什么地方？

tā shàng jǐ nián jí
(2) 他上几年级？

tā bà ba shì nǎ guó rén
(5) 他爸爸是哪国人？

tā qù guo hěn duō dì fang ma
(3) 他去过很多地方吗？

tā bà ba mā ma dōu gōng zuò ma
(6) 他爸爸、妈妈都工作吗？

10 Write the country / city names in Chinese.

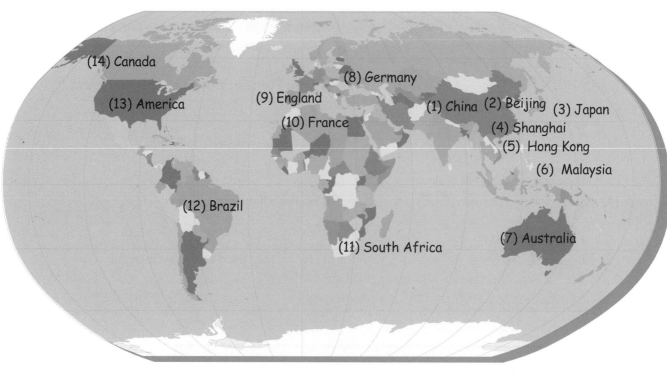

(14) Canada

(13) America

(8) Germany

(9) England

(10) France

(1) China (2) Beijing (3) Japan

(4) Shanghai

(5) Hong Kong

(6) Malaysia

(12) Brazil

(11) South Africa

(7) Australia

(1) ___中国___ (2) _____ (3) _____ (4) _____

(5) _____ (6) _____ (7) _____ (8) _____

(9) _____ (10) _____ (11) _____ (12) _____

(13) _____ (14) _____

11 Group the characters according to their radicals.

(1) 讠 __谢、___ (5) 宀 _____

(2) 辶 _____ (6) 女 _____

(3) 亻 _____ (7) 艹 _____

(4) 氵 _____ (8) 竹 _____

mā 妈	ān 安	zhù 住	yīng 英	zhè 这
tā 他	shuí 谁	zuò 作	zhōu 洲	xiè 谢
gǎng 港	men 们	jiā 家	dàn 但	jiě 姐
nǐ 你	yáng 洋	guò 过	hǎi 海	hái 还
hǎo 好	děng 等	mèi 妹	bǐ 笔	xìng 姓

12 Match the Chinese with the English.

     tā shì ge yǒu míng de zuò jiā
(1) 他是个有名的作家。

     xiǎo wáng xiàn zài zhù zài měi guó
(2) 小王现在住在美国。

     shàng hǎi bú shì wǒ de chū shēng dì
(3) 上海不是我的出生地。

     zhè xué qī hěn cháng   yǒu wǔ ge yuè
(4) 这学期很长, 有五个月。

     děng deng wǒ
(5) 等等我。

     wǒ de bǐ you xìng wáng
(6) 我的笔友姓王。

(a) Shanghai is not my birthplace.

(b) He is a well-known writer.

(c) This term is long, five months.

(d) My penpal's surname is Wang.

(e) Xiao Wang is now living in America.

(f) Wait for me.

13 Put the following information into a paragraph.

xìng míng   lǐ xiāng xiang
姓名: 李香香

chū shēng dì   shàng hǎi
出生地: 上海

chū shēng nián yuè rì   nián yuè rì
出生年月日: 1986 年 7 月 28 日

nián jí   shí nián jí
年级: 十年级

bà ba   zhōng guó rén
爸爸: 中国人

mā ma   jiā ná dà rén
妈妈: 加拿大人

qù guo de guó jiā   rì běn měi guó hé
去过的国家: 日本、美国和

          jiā ná dà
          加拿大

14 Fill in the blanks in Chinese.

    nǐ jiào   míng zi
(1) 你叫_____ 名字?

    nǐ shì nǎ   rén
(2) 你是哪 _____ 人?

    nǐ jīn nián   dà le
(3) 你今年_____ 大了?

    nǐ jīn nián shàng   nián jí
(4) 你今年上 _____ 年级?

    nǐ jiā yǒu   kǒu rén
(5) 你家有 _____ 口人?

    nǐ yǒu méi   xiōng dì jiě mèi
(6) 你有没 _____ 兄弟姐妹?

    jīn tiān shì jǐ   jǐ hào
(7) 今天是几 _____ 几号?

    jīn tiān   qī jǐ
(8) 今天 _____ 期几?

Example

nán fēi zài năr
A: 南非在哪儿？

nán fēi zài fēi zhōu
B: 南非在非洲。

dà yáng zhōu
大洋洲

(1)	nán fēi 南非	(9)	ào dà lì yà 澳大利亚
(2)	bā xī 巴西	(10)	zhōng guó 中国
(3)	dé guó 德国	(11)	fǎ guó 法国
(4)	jiā ná dà 加拿大	(12)	yìn dù 印度
(5)	měi guó 美国	(13)	yìn dù ní xī yà 印度尼西亚
(6)	yīng guó 英国	(14)	xīn jiā pō 新加坡
(7)	yì dà lì 意大利	(15)	xī bān yá 西班牙
(8)	mǎ lái xī yà 马来西亚	(16)	rì běn 日本

fēi zhōu
非洲

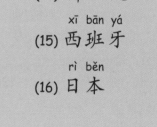

ōu zhōu
欧洲

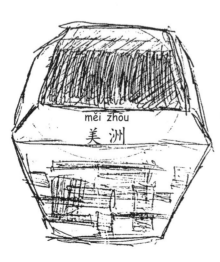

měi zhōu
美洲

yà zhōu
亚洲

生字

		ノ ト た ゲ 竹 ゲ 竺 竺 竺 笔									
bǐ pen	笔										
		一 十 土 北 地 地									
dì earth; fields; ground	地										
		ノ ト た ゲ 竹 ゲ ゲ 竺 竺 笙 等 等									
děng etc.; rank; wait	等										
		ノ イ 亻 们 但 但									
dàn but	但										
		ㄴ 凵 屮 出 出									
chū out; exit	出										
		一 二 干 王 扫 现 现 现									
xiàn present	现										

识字 (五)

		人 女 女									
nǔ female	女										
		フ カ									
lì power; strength	力										
		ノ 口 曰 田 田 甼 男									
nán male	男										
		丶 亓 门									
mén door	门										
		丶 亓 门 门 问 问									
wèn ask	问										
		丨 ˙l丶 小 少 少 尖									
jiān tip; pointed; sharp	尖										

1 Match the pictures with the words in the box.

wáng zǐ
(1) 王子 **e**

nán rén
(2) 男人

guó wáng
(3) 国王

nǚ wáng
(4) 女王

nǚ rén
(5) 女人

2 Give the meanings of the following phrases.

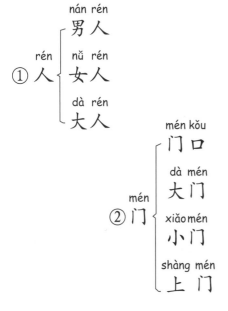

rén
① 人
┌ nán rén
│ 男人
│ nǚ rén
┤ 女人
│ dà rén
└ 大人

mén
② 门
┌ mén kǒu
│ 门口
│ dà mén
│ 大门
┤ xiǎo mén
│ 小门
│ shàng mén
└ 上门

lì
③ 力
┌ lì xué
│ 力学
│ shuǐ lì
┤ 水力
│ rén lì
└ 人力

nǚ
④ 女
┌ zǐ nǚ
│ 子女
│ ér nǚ
│ 儿女
│ nǚ ér
┤ 女儿
│ nǚ zǐ
│ 女子
│ nǚ wáng
└ 女王

1 Finish the following sentences by using the words in the box.

fǎ guó rén shuō
(1) 法国人说 ＿＿＿＿＿＿。

dé guó rén shuō
(2) 德国人说 ＿＿＿＿＿＿。

jiā ná dà rén shuō
(3) 加拿大人说 ＿＿＿＿＿＿。

yīng guó rén shuō
(4) 英国人说 ＿＿＿＿＿＿。

měi guó rén shuō
(5) 美国人说 ＿＿＿＿＿＿。

rì běn rén shuō
(6) 日本人说 ＿＿＿＿＿＿。

nán fēi rén shuō
(7) 南非人说 ＿＿＿＿＿＿。

xiāng gǎng rén shuō
(8) 香港人说 ＿＿＿＿＿＿。

mǎ lái xī yà rén shuō
(9) 马来西亚人说 ＿＿＿＿＿＿。

yīng yǔ
(a) 英语

mǎ lái yǔ
(b) 马来语

fǎ yǔ
(c) 法语

rì yǔ
(d) 日语

guǎng dōng huà
(e) 广东话

pǔ tōng huà
(f) 普通话

dé yǔ
(g) 德语

hàn yǔ
(h) 汉语

2 True or false?

二〇〇一年				一月		
日	一	二	三	四	五	六
今天 1	1	2	3	4	5	6
7	8	9	10	11	12	13
14	15	16	17	18	19	20
21	22	23	24	25	26	27
28	29	30	31	二月 1	2	3

zhè ge yuè shì yī yuè
( )(1) 这个月是一月。

shàng ge yuè shì èr yuè
( )(2) 上个月是二月。

jīn nián shì èr líng líng yī nián
( )(3) 今年是二〇〇一年。

jīn tiān shì yī yuè shí hào
( )(4) 今天是一月十号。

jīn tiān xīng qī sān
( )(5) 今天星期三。

zuó tiān xīng qī sì
( )(6) 昨天星期四。

míng tiān xīng qī èr
( )(7) 明天星期二。

yī yuè èr shí èr rì shì xīng qī yī
( )(8) 一月二十二日是星期一。

3 Write the pinyin for the following phrases.

(1) 普通话 _____

(2) 广东话 _____

(3) 现在 _____

(4) 地方 _____

(5) 出生 _____

(6) 但是 _____

(7) 笔友 _____

(8) 德语 _____

4 Give the meanings of the following phrases.

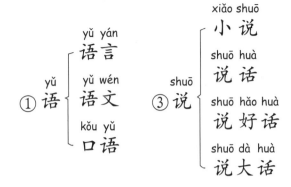

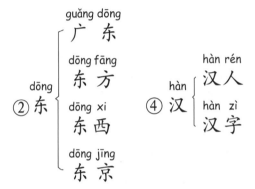

5 True or false?

( )(1) yīng guó rén shuō yīng yǔ 英国人说英语。

( )(2) měi guó rén shuō fǎ yǔ 美国人说法语。

( )(3) jiā ná dà rén dōu shuō yīng yǔ hé 加拿大人都说英语和 fǎ yǔ 法语。

( )(4) mǎ lái xī yà rén shuō mǎ lái yǔ 马来西亚人说马来语。

( )(5) nán fēi rén shuō yīng yǔ 南非人说英语。

( )(6) xiāng gǎng rén shuō yīng yǔ hé guǎng 香港人说英语和广 dōng huà 东话。

( )(7) rì běn rén shuō rì yǔ hé yīng yǔ 日本人说日语和英语。

6 Match the Chinese with the English.

(1) děng rén 等人 (a) last year

(2) děng jí 等级 (b) third class

(3) sān děng 三等 (c) wait for someone

(4) qù nián 去年 (d) pen name

(5) chū qu 出去 (e) date of birth

(6) chū shēng rì qī 出生日期 (f) go out

(7) shàng ge yuè 上个月 (g) grade; rank

(8) bǐ míng 笔名 (h) last month

97

7

Give the meanings of the following radicals.

(1) 刂 _____ (6) 欠 _____

(2) 辶 _____ (7) 饣 _____

(3) 氵 _____ (8) 力 _____

(4) 竹 _____ (9) 钅 _____

(5) 夕 _____ (10) 人 _____

8

Correct the mistakes.

shuō hàn yǔ
(1) 说 汉语 _____

pǔ tōng huà
(2) 晋 通 话 _____

guǎng dōng huà
(3) 广 车 话 _____

děng
(4) 筹 _____

xiàn zài
(5) 现 在 _____

9

Fill in the blanks with the words in the box.

shuí	shén me	jǐ	nǎr
谁	什么	几	哪儿

nǎ　duō dà
哪　多大

nǐ jiào　　　　míng zi
(1) 你 叫 _____ 名字？

nǐ jiā yǒu
(2) 你 家 有 _____？

nǐ yǒu　　　　ge xiōng dì jiě mèi
(3) 你 有 _____ 个 兄弟 姐妹？

nǐ shì　　　　guó rén
(4) 你 是 _____ 国人？

nǐ men yì jiā rén xiàn zài zhù zài
(5) 你们 一 家 人 现在 住在 _____？

nǐ jīn nián　　　　le
(6) 你 今年 _____ 了？

nǐ jīn nián shàng　　　　nián jí
(7) 你 今年 上 _____ 年级？

nǐ qù guo　　　　dì fang
(8) 你 去过 _____ 地方？

10

Translation.

dé guó zài ōu zhōu
(1) 德国 在 欧洲。

ào dà lì yà zài dà yáng zhōu
(2) 澳大利亚 在 大洋 洲。

nán fēi zài fēi zhōu
(3) 南非 在 非洲。

měi guó zài běi měi zhōu
(4) 美国 在 北 美洲。

jiā ná dà rén shuō yīng yǔ hé fǎ yǔ
(5) 加拿大人 说 英语 和 法语。

xiāng gǎng rén shuō guǎng dōng huà hé yīng yǔ
(6) 香 港 人 说 广 东 话 和 英语。

xiǎo míng chū shēng zài mǎ lái xī yà
(7) 小 明 出 生 在 马来 西亚。

wáng lì qù guo hěn duō dì fang
(8) 王 力 去过 很 多 地方。

lǐ xiāng yǒu liǎng ge bǐ yǒu
(9) 李 香 有 两 个 笔友。

11 Give the meanings of the following words.

(1) 田 tián _____

(2) 力 lì _____

(3) 男 nán _____

(4) 尖 jiān _____

(5) 问 wèn _____

(6) 长 cháng _____

(7) 子 zǐ _____

(8) 古 gǔ _____

(9) 月 yuè _____

(10) 弓 gōng _____

(11) 天 tiān _____

(12) 早 zǎo _____

12 Translation.

(1) I have one penpal. He is Japanese.

(2) She has been to many places.

(3) He has not been to Germany.

(4) I speak Cantonese, Putonghua and English.

(5) My younger sister was born on July 15th, 1972.

(6) My father works, but my mother does not work.

(7) Canada is in North America.

(8) French people speak French.

13 Reading comprehension. Then write a similar passage about yourself.

wǒ jiào wén
我 叫 文
fāng   wǒ shì zhōng
方，我 是 中
guó rén   dàn shì
国人，但 是
wǒ chū shēng zài yīng
我 出 生 在 英
guó   wǒ hé bà ba   mā ma xiàn zài zhù
国。我 和 爸 爸、妈 妈 现 在 住
zài xiāng gǎng   wǒ bà ba zài běi jīng gōng
在 香 港。我 爸 爸 在 北 京 工
zuò   wǒ mā ma zài xiāng gǎng gōng zuò   wǒ
作。我 妈 妈 在 香 港 工 作。我
qù guo hěn duō dì fang   wǒ qù guo dà yáng
去 过 很 多 地 方，我 去 过 大 洋
zhōu de ào dà lì yà   běi měi zhōu de měi
洲 的 澳 大 利 亚，北 美 洲 的 美
guó hé jiā ná dà   ōu zhōu de dé guó
国 和 加 拿 大，欧 洲 的 德 国、
fǎ guó hé yīng guó   yà zhōu de rì běn hé
法 国 和 英 国，亚 洲 的 日 本 和
mǎ lái xī yà   dàn shì wǒ méi yǒu qù guo
马 来 西 亚，但 是 我 没 有 去 过
fēi zhōu
非 洲。

Answer the questions.

wén fāng chū shēng zài nǎr
(1) 文 方 出 生 在 哪 儿？

tā xiàn zài zhù zài nǎr
(2) 她 现 在 住 在 哪 儿？

tā qù guo jǐ ge guó jiā
(3) 她 去 过 几 个 国 家？

tā yǒu méi yǒu qù guo nán fēi
(4) 她 有 没 有 去 过 南 非？

生字

shuō speak; talk; say	说	`	讠	讠	讠	讠	讠	讠	讠	说	
hàn the Han nationality	汉	`	丶	氵	汈	汉					
yǔ language	语	`	讠	讠	讠	讠	语	语	语	语	
guǎng broad	广	`	亠	广							
dōng east	东	一	七	左	夯	东					
huà word; talk	话	`	讠	讠	讠	话	话	话	话		
pǔ general; universal	普	`	丷	丷	䒑	并	并	並	普	普	普
tōng open; through	通	⁷	マ	マ	丙	甬	甬	甬	诵	诵	通

识字(六)

		一 十 土 耂 耂 老								
lǎo old	老									
		丨 小 小 少								
shào young	少									
		丶 二 六 方 立 立 辛 辛 亲								
qīn parent; relative	亲									

1 Choose the words in the box to describe the people.

nán	nǚ	lǎo	shào
男	女	老	少

男、老 ❶

❷

❸

❹

❺ ❻ ❼

2 Give the meanings of the following phrases.

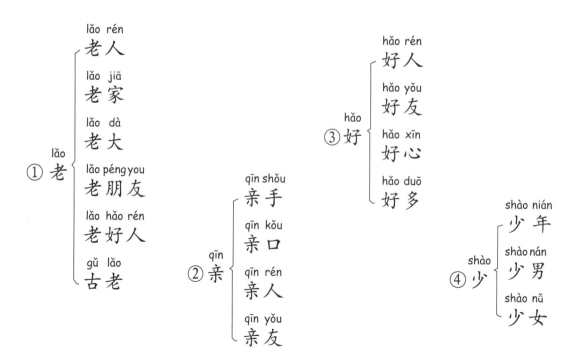

lǎo rén
老人

lǎo jiā
老家

lǎo dà
老大

① lǎo
老

lǎo péng you
老朋友

lǎo hǎo rén
老好人

gǔ lǎo
古老

qīn shǒu
亲手

qīn kǒu
亲口

② qīn
亲

qīn rén
亲人

qīn yǒu
亲友

hǎo rén
好人

hǎo yǒu
好友

③ hǎo
好

hǎo xīn
好心

hǎo duō
好多

shào nián
少年

shào nán
少男

④ shào
少

shào nǚ
少女

第十四课　她会说好几种语言

1 Circle the correct pinyin.

(1) 汉语　(a) hànyǔ　(b) hàngyǔ

(2) 昨天　(a) zhuótiān　(b) zuótiān

(3) 世界　(a) shìjiè　(b) sìjiè

(4) 想　(a) xiǎng　(b) xiān

(5) 种　(a) zǒng　(b) zhǒng

(6) 会　(a) huì　(b) hìu

(7) 普通　(a) pǔtōng　(b) pǒtōng

(8) 广东　(a) guǎndōng　(b) guǎngdōng

2 Find the radical. Give the meanings of each word.

xiǎng
(1) 想 心 ___ think; want to; would like to

huì
(2) 会 _____

yé
(3) 爷 _____

nǎi
(4) 奶 _____

děng
(5) 等 _____

dōu
(6) 都 _____

jí
(7) 级 _____

suì
(8) 岁 _____

3 Find the missing word.

duō	shì	yǔ	jiè
多	是	语	界
yán	shēng	huà	zuò
言	生	话	作
zài	yǒu	nián	zhǒng
在	友	年	种
guò	jiā	wén	fāng
过	家	文	方

guǎng dōng
(1) 广 东 话 ___

hàn
(2) 汉 _____

xiàn
(3) 现 _____

jīn
(4) 今 _____

zhōng
(5) 中 _____

shì
(6) 世 _____

chū
(7) 出 _____

dàn
(8) 但 _____

gōng
(9) 工 _____

hǎo jǐ
(10) 好 几 _____

yǔ
(11) 语 _____

guó
(12) 国 _____

dì
(13) 地 _____

bǐ
(14) 笔 _____

4 Fill in the blanks with the words in the box.

jǐ	duō dà	nǎr	nǎ	shén me
几	多大	哪儿	哪	什么

nǐ mèi mei jīn nián　　　　 suì le
(1) 你妹妹今年_____岁了？

tā jīn nián wǔ suì le
她今年五岁了。

nǐ shì　　guó rén　　 wǒ shì zhōng guó rén
(2) 你是___国人？我是中国人。

xiǎo wén xiàn zài zhù zài
(3) 小文现在住在_____？

tā xiàn zài zhù zài běi jīng
她现在住在北京。

xiǎo wáng huì shuō　　 zhǒng yǔ yán
(4) 小王会说_____种语言？

tā huì shuō sān zhǒng yǔ yán
他会说三种语言。

lǐ lì huì shuō　　 yǔ yán
(5) 李力会说_____语言？

tā huì shuō yīng yǔ　　 fǎ yǔ hé hàn yǔ
他会说英语、法语和汉语。

nǐ gē ge jīn nián　　　 le
(6) 你哥哥今年_____了？

tā jīn nián èr shí wǔ suì le
他今年二十五岁了。

nǐ jīn nián shàng　　 nián jí
(7) 你今年上_____年级？

wǒ jīn nián shàng bā nián jí
我今年上八年级。

nǐ xìng　　 wǒ xìng mǎ
(8) 你姓_____？我姓马。

nǐ jiào　　 míng zi
(9) 你叫_____名字？

wǒ jiào wáng yuè
我叫王月。

nǐ jiā yǒu　　 kǒu rén
(10) 你家有_____口人？

wǒ jiā yǒu wǔ kǒu rén
我家有五口人。

5 Transcribe the pinyin into Chinese characters.

(1) yéye _____　(6) yǔyán _____

(2) nǎinai _____　(7) guǎngdōng _____

(3) shìjiè _____　(8) pǔtōng _____

(4) huì _____　(9) déyǔ _____

(5) xiǎng _____　(10) hànyǔ _____

6 Correct the mistakes.

huì
(1) 会 _____

yán
(2) 言 _____

yé
(3) 爺 _____

nǎi
(4) 妳 _____

zhǒng
(5) 种 _____

jiè
(6) 累 _____

de
(7) 旳 _____

zhù
(8) 佳 _____

nǎ
(9) 哪 _____

qīn
(10) 亲 _____

104

7 Match the question with the answer.

xiǎo míng huì shuō jǐ zhǒng yǔ yán
(1) 小明会说几种语言？

zhāng lì qù guo shén me guó jiā
(2) 张力去过什么国家？

lǐ yún jīn nián duō dà le
(3) 李云今年多大了？

tián lì jīn nián shàng jǐ nián jí
(4) 田力今年上几年级？

mǎ yīng shì nǎ guó rén
(5) 马英是哪国人？

nǐ yé ye nǎi nai xiàn zài zhù zài nǎr
(6) 你爷爷、奶奶现在住在哪儿？

nǐ gē ge xiǎng xué shén me yǔ yán
(7) 你哥哥想学什么语言？

shǐ yán de bà ba zài nǎr gōng zuò
(8) 史言的爸爸在哪儿工作？

lǐ yún jīn nián shí wǔ suì
(a) 李云今年十五岁。

xiǎo míng huì shuō sì zhǒng yǔ yán
(b) 小明会说四种语言。

zhāng lì qù guo fǎ guó yīng guó hé dé guó
(c) 张力去过法国、英国和德国。

mǎ yīng shì zhōng guó rén
(d) 马英是中国人。

tián lì jīn nián shàng shí nián jí
(e) 田力今年上十年级。

wǒ gē ge xiǎng xué hàn yǔ
(f) 我哥哥想学汉语。

wǒ yé ye nǎi nai xiàn zài zhù zài shàng hǎi
(g) 我爷爷、奶奶现在住在上海。

shǐ yán de bà ba zài měi guó gōng zuò
(h) 史言的爸爸在美国工作。

8 Form as many questions as you can. Write them out.

wáng dà lì
王大力

wú xiǎo míng
吴小明

hú yuè
胡月

lǐ ān
李安

chū shēng zài
出生在

xiǎng xué
想学

qù guo
去过

huì shuō
会说

zhù zài
住在

yǒu
有

jǐ zhǒng yǔ yán
几种语言？

shén me yǔ yán
什么语言？

shén me dì fang
什么地方？

nǎr
哪儿？

jǐ ge dì di
几个弟弟？

(1) _____

(2) _____

(3) _____

(4) _____

(5) _____

(6) _____

9 Translation.

(1) He has several Japanese friends.

(2) She can speak several languages.

(3) My grandparents are now living in Beijing.

(4) I want to learn German.

(5) My father has been to many countries in the world.

(6) What languages can you speak ?

(7) How many languages can she speak ?

(8) Where was he born ?

10 Answer the following questions.

(1) nǐ jiā yǒu jǐ kǒu rén   yǒu shuí
你家有几口人？有谁？

(2) nǐ shì nǎ guó rén
你是哪国人？

(3) nǐ chū shēng zài nǎr
你出生在哪儿？

(4) nǐ men yì jiā rén xiàn zài zhù zài nǎr
你们一家人现在住在哪儿？

(5) nǐ jīn nián duō dà le   shàng jǐ nián jí
你今年多大了？上几年级？

(6) nǐ bà ba   mā ma dōu gōng zuò ma
你爸爸、妈妈都工作吗？

(7) nǐ huì shuō jǐ zhǒng yǔ yán
你会说几种语言？

(8) nǐ huì shuō shén me yǔ yán
你会说什么语言？

(9) nǐ xiǎng xué shén me yǔ yán
你想学什么语言？

(10) nǐ qù guo shì jiè shang shén me guó jiā
你去过世界上什么国家？

11 Put the following information into a paragraph.

mǎ xiǎo lì
－马小力

shí èr suì
－十二岁

chū shēng zài rì běn
－出生在日本

zhù zài xiāng gǎng
－住在香港

yì jiā wǔ kǒu rén   bà ba   mā ma   liǎng ge gē ge hé tā
－一家五口人：爸爸、妈妈、两个哥哥和他

liǎng ge gē ge dōu shì dà xué shēng
－两个哥哥都是大学生

bà ba hé mā ma dōu gōng zuò
－爸爸和妈妈都工作

huì shuō yīng yǔ   fǎ yǔ   hàn yǔ
－会说英语、法语、汉语

mǎ xiǎo lì
马小力

12 Match the Chinese with the English.

yǔ fǎ
(1) 语法   (a) spoken language

kǒu yǔ
(2) 口语   (b) grammar

dà xī yáng
(3) 大西洋   (c) be born

shēng rì huì
(4) 生日会   (d) the whole world

chū shì
(5) 出世   (e) territory

quán shì jiè
(6) 全世界   (f) Southeast Asia

guó tǔ
(7) 国土   (g) the Atlantic (Ocean)

dōng nán yà
(8) 东南亚   (h) birthday party

xiǎng jiā
(9) 想家   (i) homesick

13 Translation.

(1) world _____

(2) now _____

(3) grandfather _____

(4) grandmother _____

(5) language _____

(6) can _____

(7) want; would like to _____

(8) several languages _____

(9) penpal _____

14 Reading comprehension.

wǒ jiào zhāng guó lì　wǒ shì zhōng xué shēng
我叫张国立。我是中学生。
wǒ jiā yǒu sān kǒu rén　bà ba　mā ma hé
我家有三口人：爸爸、妈妈和
wǒ　wǒ méi yǒu xiōng dì jiě mèi　wǒ men yì jiā
我。我没有兄弟姐妹。我们一家
rén zhù zài xiāng gǎng　wǒ qù guo shì jiè shang hǎo
人住在香港。我去过世界上好
jǐ ge guó jiā　yīng guó　fǎ guó　dé
几个国家：英国、法国、德
guó　rì běn　měi guó hé jiā ná dà
国、日本、美国和加拿大。
wǒ huì shuō yīng yǔ　guǎng dōng huà hé
我会说英语、广东话和
pǔ tōng huà
普通话。

Answer the questions.

zhāng guó lì shì zhōng xué shēng ma
(1) 张国立是中学生吗？

tā jiā yǒu shuí
(2) 他家有谁？

tā men yì jiā rén xiàn zài zhù
(3) 他们一家人现在住
zài nǎ
在哪儿？

tā qù guo jǐ ge guó jiā
(4) 他去过几个国家？

tā huì shuō shén me yǔ yán
(5) 他会说什么语言？

15 Match the question with the answer.

(1) nǐ bà ba mā ma dōu gōng zuò ma
你爸爸、妈妈都工作吗?

(2) nǐ qù guo jiā ná dà ma
你去过加拿大吗?

(3) nǐ huì shuō guǎng dōng huà ma
你会说广东话吗?

(4) nǐ yǒu méi yǒu xiōng dì jiě mèi
你有没有兄弟姐妹?

(5) nǐ shì xiǎo xué shēng ma
你是小学生吗?

(6) nǐ xiàn zài zhù zài nǎr
你现在住在哪儿?

(7) nǐ xiǎng xué dé yǔ ma
你想学德语吗?

(a) bú huì shuō
不会说。

(b) tā men dōu gōng zuò
他们都工作。

(c) yǒu
有。

(d) shì
是。

(e) wǒ zhù zài běi jīng
我住在北京。

(f) xiǎng xué
想学。

(g) méi yǒu qù guo
没有去过。

16 Interview two classmates. Prepare a file like the ones below for each classmate.

①
tā jiào wáng xiǎo wén tā
她叫王小文。她
chū shēng zài rì běn dàn shì tā
出生在日本,但是她
shì zhōng guó rén tā jīn nián shí
是中国人。她今年十
èr suì shàng bā nián jí tā
二岁,上八年级。她
qù guo ōu zhōu měi zhōu hé dà
去过欧洲、美洲和大
yáng zhōu tā huì shuō yīng yǔ
洋洲。她会说英语、
rì yǔ hé hàn yǔ
日语和汉语。

③

④

②
tā jiào fāng míng tā chū
他叫方明。他出
shēng zài měi guó tā bà ba shì
生在美国。他爸爸是
zhōng guó rén tā mā ma shì měi
中国人,他妈妈是美
guó rén tā huì shuō hǎo jǐ zhǒng
国人。他会说好几种
yǔ yán tā xiǎng xué dé yǔ hé
语言。他想学德语和
rì yǔ
日语。

108

生 词

		ノ 人 人 今 会 会
huì can; meeting; party	会	
		ノ 几
jǐ a few; several	几	
		ノ ニ 千 禾 禾 利 和 种
zhǒng type; race; seed	种	
		ノ ハ ゾ 父 爷 爷
yé grandfather	爷	
		く 女 女 奶 奶
nǎi milk; grandmother	奶	
		一 十 廿 世 世
shì lifetime; world	世	
		） 口 日 田 田 甲 界 界 界
jiè boundary; scope	界	
		一 十 才 木 机 机 相 相 相 相 想 想 想
xiǎng think; want to; would like to	想	

生词

第十一课　亚洲 yà zhōu　加拿大 jiā ná dà　美国 měi guó　巴西 bā xī　南美洲 nán měi zhōu　北美洲 běi měi zhōu　法国 fǎ guó

德国 dé guó　非洲 fēi zhōu　欧洲 ōu zhōu　南非 nán fēi　马来西亚 mǎ lái xī yà　大洋洲 dà yáng zhōu

澳大利亚 ào dà lì yà　去过 qù guo　很多 hěn duō　国家 guó jiā　可是 kě shì

子 zǐ　吴 wú　弓 gōng　张 zhāng　古 gǔ　胡 hú

第十二课　笔友 bǐ yǒu　地方 dì fang　等 děng　但是 dàn shì　出生 chū shēng　现在 xiàn zài

女 nǚ　力 lì　男 nán　门 mén　问 wèn　尖 jiān

第十三课　说 shuō　汉语 hàn yǔ　英语 yīng yǔ　日语 rì yǔ　法语 fǎ yǔ　德语 dé yǔ　广东话 guǎng dōng huà

普通话 pǔ tōng huà

老 lǎo　少 shào　亲朋好友 qīn péng hǎo yǒu

第十四课　会 huì　好几种 hǎo jǐ zhǒng　语言 yǔ yán　爷爷 yé ye　奶奶 nǎi nai　世界上 shì jiè shang　想 xiǎng

总复习

1. Continents and countries

(1) yà zhōu 亚洲：zhōng guó 中国　rì běn 日本　mǎ lái xī yà 马来西亚

(2) ōu zhōu 欧洲：yīng guó 英国　fǎ guó 法国　dé guó 德国

(3) běi měi zhōu 北美洲：měi guó 美国　jiā ná dà 加拿大

(4) dà yáng zhōu 大洋洲：ào dà lì yà 澳大利亚

(5) fēi zhōu 非洲：nán fēi 南非

(6) nán měi zhōu 南美洲：bā xī 巴西

2. Languages and dialects

yīng yǔ 英语（yīng wén 英文）　hàn yǔ 汉语（zhōng wén 中文）　rì yǔ 日语（rì wén 日文）

fǎ yǔ 法语（fǎ wén 法文）　dé yǔ 德语（dé wén 德文）　pǔ tōng huà 普通话　guǎng dōng huà 广东话

3. Verbs

| qù 去 | lái 来 | qù guo 去过 | chū shēng 出生 | shuō 说 | xiǎng 想 | wèn 问 | huì 会 |

4. Adjectives and adverbs

| měi 美 | lǎo 老 | gǔ 古 | shào 少 | qīn 亲 | jiān 尖 | xiàn zài 现在 | pǔ tōng 普通 | hěn duō 很多 |

5. People

| nán rén 男人 | nǚ rén 女人 | lǎo rén 老人 | yé ye 爷爷 | nǎi nai 奶奶 | bǐ yǒu 笔友 |

6. Surnames

wú   hú   zhāng   gǔ   fāng

吴   胡   张   古   方

7. Grammar: "过"(guò)

wǒ qù guo měi guó
(1) 我去过美国。

tā lái guo xiāng gǎng
(2) 他来过香港。

tā shuō guo tā shì shàng hǎi rén
(3) 他说过他是上海人。

tā yǒu guo yí ge bǐ yǒu
(4) 他有过一个笔友。

nǐ qù guo rì běn ma
(5) 你去过日本吗?

wǒ zài běi jīng zhù guo
(6) 我在北京住过。

wǒ mā ma méi yǒu gōng zuò guo
(7) 我妈妈没有工作过。

tā xué guo fǎ yǔ
(8) 她学过法语。

tā shàng guo dà xué
(9) 他上过大学。

tā méi yǒu qù guo xī ān
(10) 他没有去过西安。

8. Questions and answers

zhōng guó zài nǎr
(1) 中国在哪儿?
zhōng guó zài yà zhōu
中国在亚洲。

nǐ qù guo nǎ ge guó jiā
(2) 你去过哪个国家?
wǒ qù guo   rì běn
(我去过) 日本。

nǐ chū shēng zài nǎr
(3) 你出生在哪儿?
wǒ chū shēng zài   běi jīng
(我出生在) 北京。

nǐ xiàn zài zhù zài nǎr
(4) 你现在住在哪儿?
shàng hǎi
上海。

nǐ jīn nián duō dà le
(5) 你今年多大了?
shí èr suì
十二岁。

nǐ huì shuō shén me yǔ yán
(6) 你会说什么语言?
yīng yǔ hé hàn yǔ
英语和汉语。

nǐ yǒu yé ye   nǎi nai ma
(7) 你有爷爷、奶奶吗?
yǒu
有。

nǐ qù guo fǎ guó ma
(8) 你去过法国吗?
méi   yǒu   qù guo
没 (有) 去过。

测验

1 Match the country with the continent.

(1) 南非   (a) 亚洲

(2) 马来西亚   (b) 欧洲

(3) 加拿大   (c) 非洲

(4) 巴西   (d) 北美洲

(5) 澳大利亚   (e) 大洋洲

(6) 法国   (f) 南美洲

2 Translation.

(1) China   (7) come

(2) Chinese   (8) many

(3) England   (9) male

(4) America   (10) female

(5) go   (11) friend

(6) can   (12) student

3 Match the Chinese with the pinyin.

(1) 少   (a) jiān

(2) 古   (b) qīn

(3) 老   (c) gǔ

(4) 亲   (d) shào

(5) 尖   (e) lǎo

(6) 长   (f) fāng

(7) 美   (g) cháng

(8) 方   (h) měi

4 Fill in the blanks with the words in the box.

哪儿   什么   吗

(1) 你出生在_____？

(2) 你会说_____语言？

(3) 你去过美国_____？

(4) 你有爷爷、奶奶_____？

(5) 你想学_____语言？

(6) 你去过_____地方？

5 Translation.

(1) 今天是我的生日。

(2) 我去年去过日本。

(3) 我今年想去马来西亚。

(4) 我星期五不上学。

(5) 今天我爷爷、奶奶来我家。

(6) 我今年十一岁。

6 True or false?

( )(1) 中国是一个大国。

( )(2) 南非在亚洲。

( )(3) 澳大利亚人说英语。

( )(4) 广东话是一种方言。

( )(5) 一年有十个月。

( )(6) 一个星期有七天。

7 Answer the following questions.

(1) 美国在哪儿?

(2) 南非是不是在非洲?

(3) 你去过法国吗?

(4) 你出生在哪儿?

(5) 你有没有笔友?

(6) 你会说什么语言?

(7) 你想学什么语言?

(8) 你去过什么国家?

(9) 今天是几月几号? 星期几?

8 Put the words / phrases into sentences.

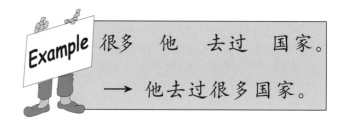
Example 很多 他 去过 国家。
→ 他去过很多国家。

(1) 我 在 出生 日本。
→

(2) 英语 美国人 说。
→

(3) 想 哥哥 法语 学。
→

(4) 吗 会说 广东话 你?
→

(5) 去过 南非 吗 你?
→

114

9 Translation.

(1) China and Japan are both in Asia.

(2) U.S.A. is in North America.

(3) British people speak English.

(4) I want to go to France this year.

(5) I have an English penpal.

(6) I can speak English and Chinese.

(7) My grandparents live in Canada at the moment.

(8) I was born in Germany, but I am living in Beijing now.

10 Reading comprehension.

王海云是中国人。她今年十岁，上小学五年级。她出生在北京，但是她现在住在英国。她爷爷、奶奶也住在英国。她去过世界上很多国家。她去过美国、加拿大、日本、马来西亚等国家，可是她没有去过非洲国家。她会说英语、法语和汉语。

Answer the questions.

(1) 王海云今年多大了？

(2) 她出生在哪儿？

(3) 她现在住在哪儿？

(4) 她爷爷、奶奶住在中国吗？

(5) 她去过加拿大吗？

(6) 她会说什么语言？

第四单元　工作

第十五课　她是医生

1　Circle the correct pinyin.

(1) 医生　(a) yīshēn　(b) yīshēng

(2) 大夫　(a) dàfu　(b) dàifu

(3) 银行　(a) yíngháng　(b) yínháng

(4) 律师　(a) lùshī　(b) lùshī

(5) 护士　(a) hùsi　(b) hùshi

(6) 商人　(a) shāngrén　(b) shānrén

(7) 老师　(a) lǎoshī　(b) lǎosī

2　Give the meanings of the following radicals.

(1) 门　___door___

(2) 弓　_____

(3) 欠　_____

(4) 立　_____

(5) 夕　_____

(6) 方　_____

(7) 舟　_____

(8) 冂　_____

(9) 忄　_____

(10) 雨　_____

(11) 刂　_____

(12) 羊　_____

3　Find phrases in the scarf. Write them out.

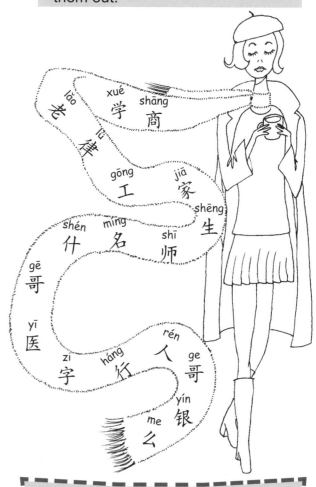

(1) ___工人___　(6) _____

(2) _____　(7) _____

(3) _____　(8) _____

(4) _____　(9) _____

(5) _____　(10) _____

4 Group the characters according to their radicals.

(1) 彳 行 ___ ___ ___

(2) 女 ___ ___ ___

(3) 钅 ___ ___ ___

(4) 氵 ___ ___ ___

(5) 讠 ___ ___ ___

(6) 扌 ___

(7) 木 ___ ___

(8) 广 ___

háng	cuò	lǜ	xiè
行	错	律	谢
shuō	fù	mā	hěn
说	妇	妈	很
gǎng	jī	tíng	hù
港	机	庭	护
nǎi	zhōu	yín	hǎi
奶	洲	银	海

5 Translation.

tā shì wǒ mèi mei de péng you
(1) 她是我妹妹的朋友。

wǒ gē ge de hǎo péng you shì dà xué
(2) 我哥哥的好朋友是大学
shēng
生。

tā shì wǒ mā ma de jiě jie
(3) 她是我妈妈的姐姐。

tā shì bà ba de dì di de lǎo shī
(4) 他是爸爸的弟弟的老师。

tā shì wǒ péng you de lǜ shī
(5) 他是我朋友的律师。

tā shì wǒ nǎi nai de jiā tíng yī shēng
(6) 她是我奶奶的家庭医生。

wǒ hàn yǔ lǎo shī de gē ge shì yín háng
(7) 我汉语老师的哥哥是银行
jiā
家。

xiǎo yún de bà ba shì dī shì sī jī
(8) 小云的爸爸是的士司机。

tiān xīng de mā ma shì jiā tíng zhǔ fù
(9) 天星的妈妈是家庭主妇。

wén jiā de mā ma shì hù shì
(10) 文家的妈妈是护士。

6 Write the pinyin for the following phrases.

(1) 律师 _____

(2) 银行家 _____

(3) 老师 _____

(4) 商人 _____

(5) 工人 _____

(6) 大夫 _____

(7) 家庭主妇 _____

(8) 护士 _____

(9) 司机 _____

(10) 学生 _____

(11) 医生 _____

7 Use "也" to finish the following dialogues.

(1) A: wǒ bà ba shì lǜ shī
我爸爸是律师。

B: <u>她爸爸也是律师</u>。

(2) A: wǒ mā ma shì yín háng jiā
我妈妈是银行家。

B: _____。

(3) A: wǒ shì zhōng xué shēng
我是中学生。

B: _____。

(4) A: wǒ gē ge shì dà xué shēng
我哥哥是大学生。

B: _____。

(5) A: wǒ nǎi nai shì jiā tíng zhǔ fù
我奶奶是家庭主妇。

B: _____。

(6) A: wǒ yé ye shì dài fu
我爷爷是大夫。

B: _____。

(7) A: tā gē ge shì sī jī
他哥哥是司机。

B: _____。

(8) A: wáng yuè de jiě jie shì yín háng jiā
王月的姐姐是银行家。

B: _____。

8 Prepare a personal file for your friend.

1. tā   tā xìng
他 / 她姓 _____。

2. tā   tā jiào
他 / 她叫 _____。

3. tā   tā jīn nián   suì
他 / 她今年 _____ 岁，
shàng   nián jí
上 _____ 年级。

4. tā   tā chū shēng zài
他 / 她出生在 _____。

5. tā   tā qù guo
他 / 她去过 _____

_____。

6. tā   tā huì shuō
他 / 她会说 _____。

tā   tā xiǎng xué
他 / 她想学 _____。

7. tā   tā bà ba
他 / 她爸爸 _____ (work)。

tā   tā mā ma
他 / 她妈妈 _____ (work)。

8. tā   tā men yì jiā rén xiàn zài zhù zài
他 / 她们一家人现在住在

_____。

118

9 Match the question with the answer.

nǐ jiào shén me míng zi
(1) 你叫什么名字？

nǐ shì nǎ guó rén
(2) 你是哪国人？

nǐ jīn nián duō dà le
(3) 你今年多大了？

nǐ zhù zài nǎr
(4) 你住在哪儿？

nǐ yǒu xiōng dì jiě mèi ma
(5) 你有兄弟姐妹吗？

nǐ jiā yǒu jǐ kǒu rén
(6) 你家有几口人？

nǐ shàng jǐ nián jí
(7) 你上几年级？

nǐ bà ba shì lǜ shī ma
(8) 你爸爸是律师吗？

jīn tiān shì jǐ yuè jǐ hào
(9) 今天是几月几号？

jīn tiān xīng qī jǐ
(10) 今天星期几？

jīn nián shì nǎ nián
(11) 今年是哪年？

wǒ jīn nián shí wǔ suì
(a) 我今年十五岁。

wǒ jiào wáng yuè
(b) 我叫王月。

wǒ zhù zài běi jīng
(c) 我住在北京。

wǒ shàng shí yī nián jí
(d) 我上十一年级。

wǒ shì zhōng guó rén
(e) 我是中国人。

wǒ bà ba bú shì lǜ shī
(f) 我爸爸不是律师。

jīn nián shì èr líng líng yī nián
(g) 今年是二〇〇一年。

jīn tiān shì shí yī yuè jiǔ hào
(h) 今天是十一月九号。

wǒ jiā yǒu wǔ kǒu rén
(i) 我家有五口人。

wǒ yǒu xiōng dì jiě mèi
(j) 我有兄弟姐妹。

jīn tiān xīng qī wǔ
(k) 今天星期五。

10 Find the missing words.

lǎo
(1) 老＿＿＿＿＿

yī
(2) 医＿＿＿＿＿

jiā tíng
(3) 家庭＿＿＿＿＿

lǜ
(4) 律＿＿＿＿＿

sī
(5) 司＿＿＿＿＿

bǐ
(6) 笔＿＿＿＿＿

shāng
(7) 商＿＿＿＿＿

dài
(8) 大＿＿＿＿＿

gōng
(9) 工＿＿＿＿＿

yín háng
(10) 银行＿＿＿＿＿

hù
(11) 护＿＿＿＿＿

yǒu
友

jī   fū   rén   jiā
机   夫   人   家

shēng   shì   zhǔ fù   shī
生   士   主妇   师

119

11 Write a sentence for each picture.

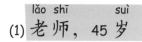

(1) 老师，45 岁
　　lǎo shī　　　　sùi

她是老师，
今年四十五岁。

(2) 司机，30 岁
　　sī jī　　　　sùi

(3) 家庭主妇，35 岁
　　jiā tíng zhǔ fù　　　　sùi

(4) 银行家，38 岁
　　yín háng jiā　　　　sùi

(5) 护士，24 岁
　　hù shì　　　　sùi

(6) 医生，55 岁
　　yī shēng　　　　sùi

(7) 工人，22 岁
　　gōng rén　　　　sùi

(8) 商人，34 岁
　　shāng rén　　　　sùi

12 Translation.

(1) Is he a lawyer ?

(2) My grandpa is a banker.

(3) His mother is a housewife.

(4) The doctor's younger sister is a nurse.

(5) Both his parents are English teachers.

(6) She can speak several languages.

(7) I have been to many countries.

(8) My father wants to learn Chinese.

13 Reading comprehension. Then write a paragraph about yourself.

wǒ jiào hǎi yīng　wǒ jīn nián shí èr suì　shàng bā nián jí　wǒ jiā yǒu sì kǒu rén　bà ba
我叫海英。我今年十二岁，上八年级。我家有四口人：爸爸、
mā ma　dì di hé wǒ　wǒ dì di jīn nián liù suì　shàng xiǎo xué yì nián jí　wǒ dì di chū
妈妈、弟弟和我。我弟弟今年六岁，上小学一年级。我弟弟出
shēng zài fǎ guó　wǒ chū shēng zài yīng guó　wǒ qù guo shì jiè shang hěn duō dì fang　wǒ huì shuō
生在法国，我出生在英国。我去过世界上很多地方。我会说
yīng yǔ　fǎ yǔ hé hàn yǔ　wǒ bà ba　mā ma dōu gōng zuò　wǒ bà ba shì lǜ shī　wǒ
英语、法语和汉语。我爸爸、妈妈都工作。我爸爸是律师，我
mā ma shì yīng yǔ lǎo shī　wǒ men yì jiā rén xiàn zài zhù zài yīng guó
妈妈是英语老师。我们一家人现在住在英国。

Answer the questions.

hǎi yīng jīn nián shàng jǐ nián jí
(1) 海英今年上几年级？

tā huì shuō shén me yǔ yán
(5) 她会说什么语言？

tā shì zhōng xué shēng ma
(2) 她是中学生吗？

tā bà ba gōng zuò ma
(6) 她爸爸工作吗？

tā chū shēng zài nǎr
(3) 她出生在哪儿？

tā mā ma gōng zuò ma
(7) 她妈妈工作吗？

tā yǒu méi yǒu xiōng dì jiě mèi
(4) 她有没有兄弟姐妹？

tā men yì jiā rén xiàn zài zhù zài nǎr
(8) 她们一家人现在住在哪儿？

14 True or false?

zhōng guó dà　lì shǐ cháng
( )(1) 中国大，历史长。

zhōng guó rén shuō fǎ yǔ
( )(2) 中国人说法语。

yīng guó zài fēi zhōu
( )(3) 英国在非洲。

dōng jīng zài rì běn
( )(4) 东京在日本。

yé ye shì bà ba de bà ba
( )(5) 爷爷是爸爸的爸爸。

15 Correct the mistakes.

xiǎng
(1) 想 _____

sī
(6) 司 _____

shī
(2) 师 _____

jī
(7) 机 _____

tíng
(3) 庭 _____

yī
(8) 医 _____

shāng
(4) 商 _____

yǔ
(9) 语 _____

háng
(5) 行 _____

nǎi
(10) 奶 _____

121

生 词

		一	厂	戸	互	至	医	医			
yī medicine	医										
		`	)	丿	师	师	师				
shī teacher; master	师										
		`	二	广	戸	庐	庄	庭	庭		
tíng front; courtyard	庭										
		`	一	三	丰	主					
zhǔ major	主										
		﹂	纟	女	如	妇	妇				
fù woman	妇										
		`	二	广	立	产	产	商	商	商	
shāng businessman	商										
		´	㇕	彳	彳	彳	彳	律	律	律	
lǜ law; rule	律										
		'	㇒	㇏	乍	车	钅	钅	钅	钽	银 银
yín silver	银										
		´	㇒	彳	彳	行	行				
háng profession; business firm	行										
		一	二	丰	夫						
fū husband; man	夫										
		一	十	扌	扩	扩	护	护			
hù protect	护										

122

生 词

		一　十　士								
shì scholar	士									
		刁　刁　司　司　司								
sī take charge of	司									
		一　十　オ　木　杉　机								
jī machine; engine	机									

识字（七）

zhǎng grow; senior; eldest	长	ノ	㇐	长	长						
	长										
kǎ card	卡	丨	上	上	卡	卡					
	卡										
zì self; oneself	自	ノ	亻	竹	白	自	自				
	自										
jǐ oneself	己	㇇	𠃌	己							
	己										
huà draw; paint	画	一	丆	丆	币	雨	画	画	画		
	画										

1   Match the Chinese with the English.

wǒ zhǎng dà le
(1) 我 长 大 了！

(a) She has gone to Japan.

tā lái le
(2) 他 来 了！

(b) Little brother has gone to school.

tā qù rì běn le
(3) 她 去 日 本 了！

(c) I have grown up.

dì di shàng xué le
(4) 弟 弟 上 学 了！

(d) She cannot draw.

tā bú huì huà huàr
(5) 她 不 会 画 画 儿 。

(e) Her grandfather is a painter.

tā yé ye shì huà jiā
(6) 她 爷 爷 是 画 家 。

(f) He has come.

2   Give the meanings of the following phrases.

③ 自
- zì jǐ 自己
- zì xué 自学
- zì lái shuǐ 自来水

3   Give the meanings of each word.

(1)
- tián 田 _____
- nán 男 _____
- huà 画 _____

(2)
- mù 目 _____
- zì 自 _____

(3)
- kǎ 卡 _____
- zhǎng 长 _____

(4)
- suì 岁 _____
- duō 多 _____
- míng 名 _____

第十六课　他做什么工作

1　Find the phrase to match the pinyin.

(1) lǎoshī _____

(2) lùshī _____

(3) fúwùyuán _____

(4) jiātíng zhǔfù _____

(5) sījī _____

(6) hùshi _____

(7) yínhángjiā _____

(8) jīnglǐ _____

(9) mìshū _____

(10) gōngchéngshī _____

(a) 秘书

(b) 家庭主妇

(c) 老师

(d) 服务员

(e) 银行家

(f) 律师

(g) 护士

(h) 工程师

(i) 司机

(j) 经理

2　Find the phrases. Write them out.

大	中	国	家	庭
小	学	工	人	口
姐	生	作	上	海
妹	英	文	学	港
日	语	汉	喜	欢

(1) _____

(2) _____

(3) _____

(4) _____

(5) _____

(6) _____

(7) _____

(8) _____

(9) _____

(10) _____

3 Form as many sentences as you can. Write them out.

wáng péng 王朋	chū shēng zài 出生在	rì yǔ yīng yǔ hé hàn yǔ 日语、英语和汉语。
shǐ lì 史力	zhù zài 住在	dé guó fǎ guó měi guó děng guó jiā 德国、法国、美国等国家。
wáng tiān lì 王天力	qù guo 去过	xiāng gǎng 香港。
mǎ xiǎo yún 马小云	huì shuō 会说	pǔ tōng huà 普通话。
gǔ yuè 古月	xiǎng xué 想学	ào dà lì yà 澳大利亚。
lǐ xiǎo tián 李小田	xǐ huan 喜欢	tā de gōng zuò 他的工作。
	yǒu 有	hǎo jǐ ge bǐ yǒu 好几个笔友。

(1) _____   (4) _____

(2) _____   (5) _____

(3) _____   (6) _____

4 Write the pinyin for the following phrases.

(1) 经理 _____   (6) 家庭主妇 _____   (11) 大夫 _____

(2) 工程师 _____   (7) 司机 _____   (12) 学生 _____

(3) 律师 _____   (8) 护士 _____   (13) 笔友 _____

(4) 服务员 _____   (9) 医生 _____   (14) 朋友 _____

(5) 秘书 _____   (10) 工人 _____   (15) 爷爷 _____

5 Put the words / phrases into sentences.

Example

sī jī   tā bà ba   shì
司机   他爸爸   是。 → 他爸爸是司机。

bù xǐ huan   wǒ mā ma   tā de gōng zuò
(1) 不喜欢   我妈妈   她的工作。 →

xiàn zài   zhù zài   wǒ gē ge   dōng jīng
(2) 现在   住在   我哥哥   东京。 →

qù guo   wǒ yé ye   hěn duō dì fang   shì jiè shang
(3) 去过   我爷爷   很多地方   世界上。 →

xiǎo míng   yǔ yán   huì shuō   hǎo jǐ zhǒng
(4) 小明   语言   会说   好几种。 →

wáng lì   yīng yǔ   bú huì shuō
(5) 王力   英语   不会说。 →

chū shēng zài   wǒ de rì yǔ lǎo shī   fǎ guó
(6) 出生在   我的日语老师   法国。 →

shàng   jiǔ nián jí   jīn nián   wáng yún de mèi mei
(7) 上   九年级   今年   王云的妹妹。 →

shì   tā péng you   dà xué shēng
(8) 是   他朋友   大学生。 →

6 Match the Chinese with the English.

hù shi xiǎo jie tiān tiān hù lǐ wǒ yé ye
(1) 护士小姐天天护理我爷爷。

     (a) Year 2002 was the year of the Horse.

lǐ yī shēng shì wǒ de jiā tíng yī shēng
(2) 李医生是我的家庭医生。

     (b) He is a world famous calligrapher.

tā shì shì jiè yǒu míng de shū fǎ jiā
(3) 他是世界有名的书法家。

     (c) Dr. Li is my family doctor.

èr líng líng èr nián shì mǎ nián
(4) 二〇〇二年是马年。

     (d) The nurse takes care of my grandpa everyday.

tā bà ba shì hǎi yuán tā míng tiān chū hǎi
(5) 他爸爸是海员。他明天出海。

     (e) Grandma is a Northerner.

nǎi nai shì běi fāng rén
(6) 奶奶是北方人。

     (f) His father is a sailor. He is going to the sea tomorrow.

7 Fill in the blanks with the words in the box. Each word can only be used once.

xiǎng xué (a) 想学	xiàn zài (b) 现在	hěn duō (c) 很多	xìng (d) 姓	qù guo (e) 去过
xǐ huan (f) 喜欢	dì fang (g) 地方	jīn nián (h) 今年	yǒu (i) 有	yǔ yán (j) 语言

1

wǒ ___ zhāng, jiào zhāng míng
我___张，叫张明。

wǒ huì shuō hǎo jǐ zhǒng ___ wǒ
我会说好几种___。我

chū shēng zài nán fēi, dàn shì wǒ shì
出生在南非，但是我是

yīng guó rén
英国人。

2

wǒ shì yín háng jiā wǒ ___
我是银行家。我___

wǒ de gōng zuò wǒ ___ yí ge ér
我的工作。我___一个儿

zi hé liǎng ge nǚ ér wǒ de ér zi
子和两个女儿。我的儿子

shì zhōng xué shēng wǒ de liǎng ge nǚ ér
是中学生，我的两个女儿

shì dà xué shēng wǒ ___ shàng hǎi
是大学生。我___上海。

3

wǒ shì fǎ guó rén
我是法国人。

wǒ ___ liù shí bā suì le
我___六十八岁了。

wǒ bù gōng zuò wǒ qù guo shì jiè shang
我不工作。我去过世界上

hěn duō ___ wǒ huì shuō wǔ zhǒng yǔ
很多___。我会说五种语

yán wǒ ___ hàn yǔ
言。我___汉语。

4

wǒ shì lǜ shī wǒ shì měi guó
我是律师。我是美国

rén wǒ ___ zhù zài běi jīng
人。我___住在北京。

wǒ yǒu ___ zhōng guó péng you
我有___中国朋友。

8 Answer the following questions.

nǐ zài nǎr chū shēng
(1) 你在哪儿出生?

nǐ de shēng ri shì jǐ yuè jǐ hào
(2) 你的生日是几月几号?

nǐ jīn nián duō dà le
(3) 你今年多大了?

nǐ shàng jǐ nián jí
(4) 你上几年级?

nǐ bà ba shì gōng chéng shī ma
(5) 你爸爸是工程师吗?

nǐ xiǎng zuò lǜ shī ma
(6) 你想做律师吗?

9 Fill in the blanks with the words in the box.

shén me	ma	nǎr
什么	吗	哪儿
jǐ	nǎ	shuí
几	哪	谁

nǐ bà ba zuò gōng zuò
(1) 你爸爸做 ＿＿＿ 工作?

nǐ mā ma yě gōng zuò
(2) 你妈妈也工作＿＿＿?

tā dì di jīn nián suì le
(3) 他弟弟今年＿＿＿岁了?

tā shì guó rén
(4) 她是＿＿＿国人?

wáng lǎo shī chū shēng zài
(5) 王老师出生在＿＿＿?

lǐ lì yǒu ge xiōng dì jiě mèi
(6) 李力有＿＿＿个兄弟姐妹?

tā jiā yǒu
(7) 他家有＿＿＿?

10 Fill in the blanks with characters.

tā men shì wǒ de hǎo péng you   tā men dōu shì
他们是我的好朋＿＿。他们都是
dà xué shēng   tā men dōu shì rì běn rén   tā men
大＿＿生。他们都是日＿＿人。他们
huì shuō yīng yǔ   dàn shì tā men bú huì shuō hàn yǔ
会说英语,但是他们不＿＿说汉语。
tā men xiǎng xué hàn yǔ   dàn shì tā men méi yǒu lǎo
他们想＿＿汉语,＿＿是他们没有老
shī   tā men xiàn zài zhù zài xiāng gǎng
师。他们现在住＿＿香港。

生 词

		ノ	イ	亻	什	付	佧	估	做	做	做	
zuò make; do	做											
		ノ	刀	月	月	月	肜	那	服			
fú clothes; serve	服											
		ノ	ク	夂	冬	务						
wù affair; business	务											
		丶	口	口	尸	吕	员	员				
yuán member	员											
		一	十	土	吉	吉	吉	壴	壴	壴	喜	喜
xǐ happy; like	喜											
		フ	又	劝	朳	欢	欢					
huān merry	欢											
		ノ	二	千	禾	禾	禾	利	秘	秘		
mì secret	秘											
		フ	马	书	书							
shū book; write; script	书											
		ㄥ	纟	纟	纠	织	经	绎	经			
jīng manage	经											
		一	二	千	王	珇	珇	珇	珒	理	理	
lǐ manage; natural science	理											
		ノ	二	千	禾	禾	利	科	秤	程	程	程
chéng rule; order	程											

识字（八）

		丨	冂	月	月	目					
mù eye	目										
		丶	丷	二	头	头					
tóu head	头										
		丶	丨	口	口	口	尸	足	足		
zú foot	足										
		丿	勹	乌	乌						
wū black; dark	乌										
		乚	少	发	发	发					
fà hair	发										
		丿	亻	白	白	白					
bái white	白										
		一	二	于	牙						
yá tooth	牙										
		丨	丨	业	业	屮	光				
guāng light; smooth	光										

1 Match the words with the pictures.

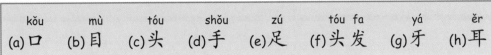

kǒu	mù	tóu	shǒu	zú	tóu fa	yá	ěr
(a)口	(b)目	(c)头	(d)手	(e)足	(f)头发	(g)牙	(h)耳

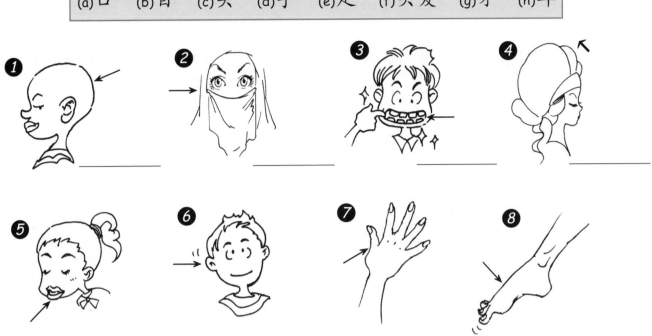

2 Give the meanings of the following phrases.

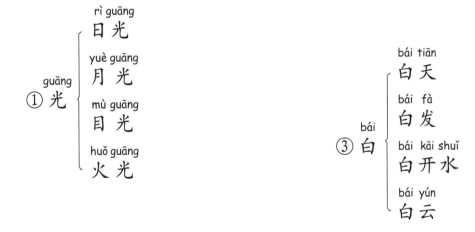

guāng
① 光

rì guāng
日光

yuè guāng
月光

mù guāng
目光

huǒ guāng
火光

bái
③ 白

bái tiān
白天

bái fà
白发

bái kāi shuǐ
白开水

bái yún
白云

tóu
② 头

mù tou
木头

tóu fa
头发

tóu děng
头等

mù
④ 目

mù di
目的

mù dì dì
目的地

第十七课　她在一家日本公司工作

1 Match the words in column A with the ones in column B.

A

(1) yī shēng　dài fu
医生／大夫

(2) hàn yǔ lǎo shī
汉语老师

(3) jīng lǐ
经理

(4) lǜ shī
律师

(5) shāng rén
商人

(6) yín háng jiā
银行家

(7) fú wù yuán
服务员

(8) hù shi
护士

(9) gōng rén
工人

B

(a) lǜ shī háng
律师行

(b) yī yuàn
医院

(c) xué xiào
学校

(d) jiǔ diàn
酒店

(e) gōng sī
公司

(f) yín háng
银行

(g) gōng chǎng
工厂

(h) shū diàn
书店

2 Fill in the blanks with the words in the box.

yī shēng	lǜ shī	lǎo shī	jīng lǐ
医生	律师	老师	经理
gōng chéng shī	yín háng jiā	fú wù yuán	
工 程 师	银行家	服务员	

(1) _____ zài xué xiào gōng zuò
在学校 工作。

(2) _____ zài yī yuàn gōng zuò
在医院 工作。

(3) _____ zài gōng chǎng gōng zuò
在工厂 工作。

(4) _____ zài gōng sī gōng zuò
在公司工作。

(5) _____ zài lǜ shī háng gōng zuò
在律师行 工作。

(6) _____ zài fàn diàn gōng zuò
在饭店 工作。

(7) _____ zài yín háng gōng zuò
在银行 工作。

3 Write the pinyin for the following phrases.

(1) 家庭主妇

(2) 律师行

(3) 服务员

(4) 银行

(5) 学生

(6) 公司

(7) 学校

(8) 酒店

(9) 工厂

(10) 商人

4 Answer the following questions.

(1) nǐ chū shēng zài nǎr
你出生在哪儿？

nǎr
哪儿？

(2) nǐ qù guo nǎr
你去过哪儿？

(3) nǐ bà ba zài nǎr　gōng zuò
你爸爸在哪儿工作？

(4) nǐ mā ma zài nǎr　gōng zuò
你妈妈在哪儿工作？

(5) nǐ men yì jiā rén zhù zài nǎr
你们一家人住在哪儿？

134

5 Circle the correct pinyin.

(1) 丈夫　(a) zhàngfu　(b) zàngfu

(2) 女儿　(a) nǔ'ér　(b) nǚ'ér

(3) 儿子　(a) érzhi　(b) érzi

(4) 先生　(a) xiānshen　(b) xiānsheng

(5) 女士　(a) nǚshì　(b) nǔsì

(6) 太太　(a) tèitei　(b) tàitai

(7) 公司　(a) gōngsī　(b) gōngshī

(8) 一点儿　(a) yìdiǎnr　(b) yìdiǎner

6 Categorize the following words into two groups.

yé ye	mā ma	nǎi nai	mèi mei
爷爷	妈妈	奶奶	妹妹
gē ge	dì di	nǚ shì	xiǎo jie
哥哥	弟弟	女士	小姐
xiān sheng	tài tai	jiě jie	zhàng fu
先生	太太	姐姐	丈夫
nǚ ér	ér zi		
女儿	儿子		

nán
男

nǚ
女

爷爷、_____　　妈妈、_____

_____　　_____

_____　　_____

7 Ask a question for each answer.

(1) A: _____

wǒ jiào lǐ wén
B: 我叫李文。

(2) A: _____?

wǒ chū shēng zài měi guó
B: 我出生在美国。

(3) A: _____?

wǒ jīn nián shí wǔ suì
B: 我今年十五岁。

(4) A: _____?

wǒ jīn nián shàng shí nián jí
B: 我今年上十年级。

(5) A: _____?

wǒ shì zhōng guó rén
B: 我是中国人。

(6) A: _____?

wǒ jiā yǒu sì kǒu rén
B: 我家有四口人。

(7) A: _____?

wǒ bà ba shì lǎo shī
B: 我爸爸是老师。

(8) A: _____?

wǒ mā ma bù gōng zuò
B: 我妈妈不工作。

8 Form as many sentences as you can. Write them out.

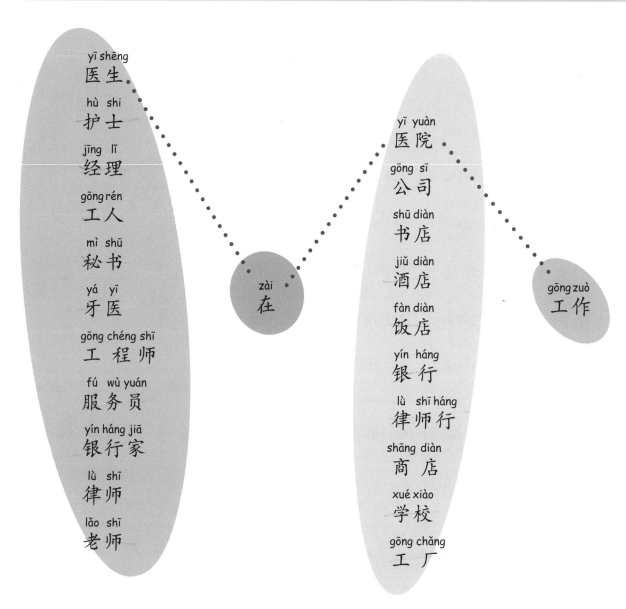

(1) 医生在医院工作。

(2) _____

(3) _____

(4) _____

(5) _____

(6) _____

(7) _____

(8) _____

(9) _____

(10) _____

(11) _____

9 Give the meanings of the following phrases.

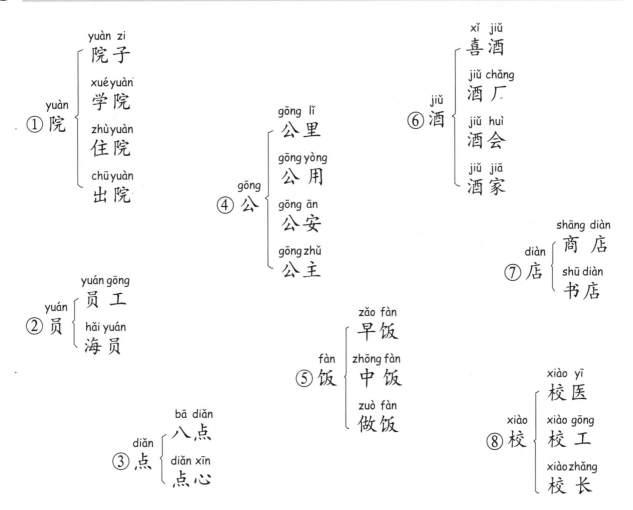

10 Match the Chinese with the English.

wǒ xué guo dé wén
(1) 我学过德文。

(a) Miss Ma is not at home.

mǎ xiǎo jie bú zài jiā
(2) 马小姐不在家。

(b) China is a big country.

wǒ men shì liǎng xiōng mèi
(3) 我们是两兄妹。

(c) Xiao Wang will come immediately.

zhōng guó shì yí ge dà guó
(4) 中国是一个大国。

(d) She is a famous writer.

wǒ gē ge dà wǒ wǔ suì
(5) 我哥哥大我五岁。

(e) I have studied German before.

xiǎo wáng mǎ shàng lái
(6) 小王马上来。

(f) Tian Yun has quite a few friends.

tā shì yí ge yǒu míng de zuò jiā
(7) 她是一个有名的作家。

(g) We are brother and sister.

tián yún yǒu hǎo duō péng you
(8) 田云有好多朋友。

(h) My elder brother is five years older than me.

11 Fill in the blanks with the measure words in the box.

gè	kǒu	jiā
个	口	家

(1) lǐ míng jiā yǒu bā ___ rén
李明家有八___人。

(2) wáng xiān sheng zài yì ___ měi guó gōng sī gōng zuò
王先生在一___美国公司工作。

(3) mǎ lǎo shī de ér zi zài yì ___ jiǔ diàn gōng zuò
马老师的儿子在一___酒店工作。

(4) wáng yuè yǒu yí ___ dì di, liǎng ___ mèi mei
王月有一___弟弟，两___妹妹。

(5) lǐ nǎi nai yǒu liǎng ___ ér zi, sān ___ nǚ ér
李奶奶有两___儿子，三___女儿。

(6) tián lì yǒu liǎng ___ hǎo péng you
田力有两___好朋友。

(7) shǐ yún zài yì ___ yín háng gōng zuò
史云在一___银行工作。

12 Match the Chinese with the English.

(1) měi rén 美人 — (a) headmaster

(2) xué shì 学士 — (b) beauty

(3) xiào zhǎng 校长 — (c) institute; college

(4) guò qù 过去 — (d) bachelor

(5) xué yuàn 学院 — (e) dark clouds

(6) měi hǎo 美好 — (f) in the past

(7) zǐ nǚ 子女 — (g) dentist

(8) wū yún 乌云 — (h) children

(9) yá yī 牙医 — (i) fine; happy

(10) nǚ gōng 女工 — (j) female worker

13 Group the characters according to their radicals.

(1) 广 ___ ___   (4) 王 ___ ___

(2) 禾 ___ ___   (5) 钅 ___ ___

(3) 阝 ___ ___   (6) 纟 ___ ___

tíng	xiàn	cuò	jīng
庭	现	错	经
yuàn	chéng	jí	yín
院	程	级	银
diàn	nà	mì	lǐ
店	那	秘	理

14 Reading comprehension.

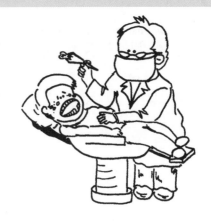

wǒ jiào zhāng guāng míng　wǒ shì yá yī　zài
我叫张光明。我是牙医，在

yì jiā yīng guó yī yuàn gōng zuò　wǒ jiā yǒu sān kǒu rén
一家英国医院工作。我家有三口人：

wǒ　wǒ tài tai hé wǒ ér zi　wǒ tài tai bù gōng
我、我太太和我儿子。我太太不工

zuò　tā shì jiā tíng zhǔ fù　wǒ ér zi jīn nián shí sān
作，她是家庭主妇。我儿子今年十三

suì　shàng zhōng xué èr nián jí　wǒ men qù guo shì
岁，上中学二年级。我们去过世

jiè shang hěn duō dì fang　wǒ men qù guo ōu zhōu　měi
界上很多地方。我们去过欧洲、美

zhōu　yà zhōu hé dà yáng zhōu　dàn shì méi yǒu qù guo
洲、亚洲和大洋洲，但是没有去过

fēi zhōu　wǒ ér zi huì shuō hǎo jǐ zhǒng yǔ yán　tā
非洲。我儿子会说好几种语言。他

huì shuō yīng yǔ　fǎ yǔ　hàn yǔ hé yì diǎnr　rì
会说英语、法语、汉语和一点儿日

yǔ　tā xiǎng qù měi guó shàng dà xué　tā xiǎng xué
语。他想去美国上大学。他想学

fǎ lǜ　tā xiǎng zuò lǜ shī
法律。他想做律师。

True or false?

zhāng guāng míng shì yī shēng
( )(1) 张光明是医生。

zhāng tài tai yě zài yī yuàn
( )(2) 张太太也在医院
gōng zuò
工作。

zhāng guāng míng de ér zi
( )(3) 张光明的儿子
qù guo fēi zhōu
去过非洲。

zhāng guāng míng de ér zi xiǎng
( )(4) 张光明的儿子想
qù zhōng guó shàng dà xué
去中国上大学。

15 Put punctuations where necessary.

wǒ jiào wáng xiǎo míng jīn nián shí èr
我叫王小明今年十二

suì wǒ jiā yǒu bà ba mā ma jiě jie mèi mei
岁我家有爸爸妈妈姐姐妹妹

hé wǒ wǒ shàng zhōng xué wǒ jiě jie shàng
和我我上中学我姐姐上

dà xué wǒ mèi mei yě shàng zhōng xué zài xué
大学我妹妹也上中学在学

xiào wǒ xué yīng yǔ rì yǔ hé hàn yǔ wǒ bà
校我学英语日语和汉语我爸

ba shì dài fu wǒ mā ma shì yīng yǔ lǎo shī
爸是大夫我妈妈是英语老师

wǒ men yì jiā rén dōu zhù zài běi jīng
我们一家人都住在北京

16 Translation.

wǒ yǒu jǐ ge rì běn péng you
(1) 我有几个日本朋友。

tā qù guo hǎo jǐ ge dì fang
(2) 她去过好几个地方。

tā bà ba huì shuō hǎo jǐ zhǒng yǔ yán
(3) 他爸爸会说好几种语言。

hǎo jǐ ge yīng guó rén zài wǒ men xué xiào
(4) 好几个英国人在我们学校
zuò yīng yǔ lǎo shī
做英语老师。

zhè jiā fàn diàn yǒu hǎo jǐ ge nán fú wù
(5) 这家饭店有好几个男服务
yuán
员。

17 Match the Chinese with the English.

(1) wǒ mā ma bù xǐ huan zuò jiā wù
我妈妈不喜欢做家务。

(2) wáng dà lì fū fù dōu zài běi jīng
王大力夫妇都在北京

gōng zuò
工作。

(3) lǐ fāng xiǎng xué yī
李方 想学医。

(4) xiǎo wáng de zhàng ren shì ge yǒu míng de
小王的 丈人是个有名的

yá yī
牙医。

(5) zhāng lǎo shī míng tiān chū yuàn
张老师明天出院。

(6) wǒ xīng qī yī zài lái
我星期一再来。

(a) Both Mr. and Mrs. Wang Dali are working in Beijing.

(b) My mother does not like to do housework.

(c) Teacher Zhang will be discharged from hospital tomorrow.

(d) Li Fang wants to study medicine.

(e) I will come again on Monday.

(f) Xiao Wang's father-in-law is a famous dentist.

18 Translation.

Example

My name is Jane. I'm from England. I can speak English, German, French and a little Chinese.

wǒ jiào   wǒ shì yīng guó rén
我叫 Jane。我是英国人。
wǒ huì shuō yīng yǔ   dé yǔ   fǎ
我会说英语、德语、法
yǔ hé yì diǎnr   hàn yǔ
语和一点儿汉语。

❶
My name is John. I am French, but my wife is Chinese. I can speak French, English and Chinese. My wife and I are living in Beijing at the moment.

❷
My name is Wang Yue. I was born in Shanghai. I am Chinese, but my husband is American. I have been to many places around the world.

❸
My name is David. I am from Germany. My wife is French. I can speak German, French and a little Chinese.

140

19 Reading comprehension.

wáng tài tai shì xiāng gǎng rén　jīn nián sì shí sì suì　tā yǒu yí ge ér zi　liǎng
王太太是香港人，今年四十四岁。她有一个儿子，两

ge nǚ ér　tā de dà nǚ ér jīn nián èr shí yī suì　shàng dà xué sān nián jí　tā zài
个女儿。她的大女儿今年二十一岁，上大学三年级，她在

dà xué xué fǎ yǔ hé dé yǔ　tā de èr nǚ ér jīn nián shí jiǔ suì　shàng dà xué yì nián
大学学法语和德语。她的二女儿今年十九岁，上大学一年

jí　tā xué yī　tā ér zi jīn nián shí wǔ suì　shàng zhōng xué sān nián jí　wáng tài
级，她学医。她儿子今年十五岁，上中学三年级。王太

tai zài yì jiā rì běn gōng sī gōng zuò　tā shì mì shū　tā zhàng fu shì shàng hǎi rén
太在一家日本公司工作，她是秘书。她丈夫是上海人，

zài yì jiā měi guó yín háng gōng zuò　tā men yì jiā xiàn zài zhù zài shàng hǎi
在一家美国银行工作。他们一家现在住在上海。

wáng tài tai
王太太

Answer the questions.

wáng tài tai yǒu jǐ ge zǐ nǚ
(1) 王太太有几个子女？

wáng tài tai de liǎng ge nǚ ér zuò shén me
(2) 王太太的两个女儿做什么？

tā zhàng fu zài nǎr gōng zuò
(3) 她丈夫在哪儿工作？

wáng tài tai zuò shén me gōng zuò　zài nǎr gōng zuò
(4) 王太太做什么工作？在哪儿工作？

20 Write a paragraph about yourself. Follow the guidelines.

jiào shén me míng zi　duō dà le　shàng jǐ nián jí
－叫什么名字？多大了？上几年级？

nǐ jiā yǒu jǐ kǒu rén　yǒu shuí
－你家有几口人？有谁？

zhù zài nǎr　nǎr guó rén
－住在哪儿？哪国人？

bà ba　mā ma zuò shén me gōng zuò　zài nǎr gōng zuò
－爸爸、妈妈做什么工作？在哪儿工作？

nǐ qù guo shén me guó jiā　huì shuō shén me yǔ yán
－你去过什么国家？会说什么语言？

生 词

		丶	八	公	公							
gōng public	公											
		一	ナ	丈								
zhàng a form of address	丈											
		一	十	才	木	杧	杧	杧	栌	栌	校	
xiào school	校											
		丿	仁	屮	生	先	先					
xiān first of all	先											
		了	阝	阝	阝	阝	阰	阰	阰	院		
yuàn courtyard	院											
		丶	丶	氵	汀	汀	沂	沔	沔	酒		
jiǔ alcoholic drink; wine	酒											
		丶	一	广	广	庁	庆	店	店			
diàn shop; store	店											
		一	ナ	大	太							
tài too	太											
		丿	广	广	钅	钌	钌	饬	饭			
fàn cooked rice; meal	饭											
		一	厂									
chǎng factory	厂											
		丶	卜	上	占	占	点	点	点			
diǎn dot; point; o'clock	点											

识字（九）

		一	ナ	ナ	ナ	灰	灰					
huī grey	灰											
		′	″	″	″	彑	免	免	象	象	象	象
xiàng elephant	象											
		′	′	白	白	白	自	鼻	鼻	鼻	畠	鼻 鼻
bí nose	鼻											
		、	ー	亠	市	古	卢	高	高	高	高	
gāo high; tall	高											
		′	′	气	气							
qì gas; air	气											

1 Dismantle the characters into parts.

nán
(1) 男 _____ _____

zhāng
(2) 张 _____ _____

hú
(3) 胡 _____ _____

bí
(4) 鼻 _____ _____ _____

chéng
(5) 程 _____ _____

xiào
(6) 校 _____ _____

yuàn
(7) 院 _____ _____

diàn
(8) 店 _____ _____

2 Give the meanings of the following phrases.

① 象 (xiàng)
- 大象 dà xiàng
- 小象 xiǎo xiàng
- 象牙 xiàng yá

② 气 (qì)
- 天气 tiān qì
- 力气 lì qì
- 和气 hé qì
- 生气 shēng qì
- 小气 xiǎo qì

③ 高 (gāo)
- 身高 shēn gāo
- 高大 gāo dà
- 高山 gāo shān
- 高中 gāo zhōng
- 高级 gāo jí

3 Give the meanings of the radicals. Find a word for each radical.

(1) 饣 _____ _____

(2) 广 _____ _____

(3) 钅 _____ _____

(4) 心 _____ _____

(5) 田 _____ _____

(6) 纟 _____ _____

生词

第十五课
yī shēng	lǎo shī	dōng jīng	jiā tíng zhǔ fù	shāng rén	lù shī
医生	老师	东京	家庭主妇	商人	律师

yín háng jiā	dài fu	hù shi	sī jī
银行家	大夫	护士	司机

zhǎng dà	shēng rì kǎ	zì jǐ	huà
长大	生日卡	自己	画

第十六课
zuò	fú wù yuán	xǐ huan	mì shū	jīng lǐ	gōng chéng shī
做	服务员	喜欢	秘书	经理	工程师

mù	tóu	zú	wū	fà	bái	yá	guāng
目	头	足	乌	发	白	牙	光

第十七课
gōng sī	zhàng fu	xué xiào	xiān sheng	yī yuàn	jiǔ diàn	tài tai
公司	丈夫	学校	先生	医院	酒店	太太

fàn diàn	gōng chǎng	nǚ ér	ér zi	nǚ shì	yì diǎnr
饭店	工厂	女儿	儿子	女士	一点儿

lǜ shī háng
律师行

huī	dà xiàng	bí zi	gè zi	gāo	lì qi
灰	大象	鼻子	个子	高	力气

145

总复习

1. **Jobs and occupations**

yī shēng dài fu	hù shi	yá yī	lǎo shī	lǜ shī
医生／大夫	护士	牙医	老师	律师

gōng chéng shī	shāng rén	jīng lǐ	fú wù yuán	sī jī
工程师	商人	经理	服务员	司机

mì shū	yín háng jiā	gōng rén	jiā tíng zhǔ fù
秘书	银行家	工人	（家庭主妇）

2. **Work places**

yī yuàn	yín háng	lǜ shī háng	xué xiào	gōng sī	jiǔ diàn
医院	银行	律师行	学校	公司	酒店

fàn diàn	gōng chǎng
饭店	工厂

3. **Verbs**

zuò	xǐ huan	huà	zhǎng dà
做	喜欢	画	长大

4. **Adjectives and adverbs**

wū	gāo	bái	guāng	huī	lǎo
乌	高	白	光	灰	老

5. **Parts of the body**

kǒu	mù	tóu	tóu fa	zú	yá	bí zi	gè zi
口	目	头	头发	足	牙	鼻子	（个子）

6. **People**

xiān sheng	tài tai	nǚ shì	zhàng fu	nǚ ér	ér zi
先生	太太	女士	丈夫	女儿	儿子

7. Study the word " 家 " (jiā)

jiā
家

(1) family, home
wǒ jiā yǒu liù kǒu rén
我家有六口人。

wǒ míng tiān qù nǐ jiā
我明天去你家。

(2) measure word
tā zài yì jiā fàn diàn gōng zuò
他在一家饭店工作。

(3) expert
tā shì huà jiā
他是画家。

tā shì yín háng jiā
他是银行家。

8. Study the following sentences

tā mā ma zài yī yuàn gōng zuò
(1) 他妈妈在医院工作。

tā bà ba zài yì jiā lǜ shī háng gōng zuò
(2) 她爸爸在一家律师行工作。

tā zài yì jiā dé guó gōng sī gōng zuò
(3) 他在一家德国公司工作。

wǒ jiě jie xiàn zài zài xiāng gǎng shàng xué
(4) 我姐姐现在在香港上学。

nǐ zài nǎr shàng xué
(5) 你在哪儿上学?

wǒ zài jiā děng nǐ
(6) 我在家等你。

9. Questions and answers

nǐ zuò shén me gōng zuò
(1) 你做什么工作?

wǒ shì yī shēng
我是医生。

nǐ zài nǎr gōng zuò
(2) 你在哪儿工作?

wǒ zài dōng jīng gōng zuò
我在东京工作。

nǐ xǐ huan nǐ de gōng zuò ma
(3) 你喜欢你的工作吗?

bú tài xǐ huan
不太喜欢。

nǐ yǐ hòu xiǎng zuò shén me gōng zuò
(4) 你以后想做什么工作?

wǒ xiǎng zuò lǜ shī
我想做律师。

nǐ yǐ hòu xiǎng zài nǎr gōng zuò
(5) 你以后想在哪儿工作?

jiā ná dà
加拿大。

测验

1 Match the words with the pictures.

kǒu	mù	tóu	shǒu	zú	tóu fa	yá	ěr
(a)口	(b)目	(c)头	(d)手	(e)足	(f)头发	(g)牙	(h)耳

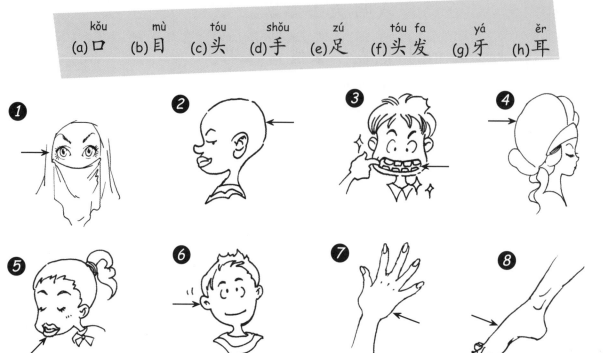

2 Circle the correct pinyin.

(1) 医生   (a) yīshēng   (b) yīsēng

(2) 律师   (a) lǜshī   (b) lǜsī

(3) 做   (a) zòu   (b) zuò

(4) 经理   (a) jīnglǐ   (b) zhīnglǐ

(5) 喜欢   (a) shǐhuan   (b) xǐhuan

(6) 学校   (a) xuéxiào   (b) shuéshào

(7) 公司   (a) gōngshī   (b) gōngsī

(8) 想   (a) xiǎn   (b) xiǎng

3 Match the words in column A with the ones in column B.

A

(1) 医生

(2) 律师

(3) 银行家

(4) 老师

(5) 服务员

(6) 经理

(7) 牙医

(8) 秘书

B

(a) 银行

(b) 学校

(c) 医院

(d) 律师行

(e) 公司

(f) 酒店

(g) 饭店

4 Find the opposites.

小　少　女　去

地　今　很多

(1) 古 →　　　(5) 天 →

(2) 老 →　　　(6) 大 →

(3) 男 →　　　(7) 一点儿 →

(4) 来 →

5 Answer the questions in English.

(1) 你爸爸工作吗?

(2) 你爸爸做什么工作?

(3) 你爸爸在哪儿工作?

(4) 你爸爸喜欢他的工作吗?

(5) 你妈妈做什么工作?

(6) 你以后想做什么工作?

(7) 你以后想在哪儿工作?

6 Translation.

(1) 他爸爸工作，他妈妈也工作。

(2) 她爸爸在西安工作。

(3) 他很喜欢他的工作。

(4) 她在一家美国银行工作。

(5) 他现在没有工作。

(6) He is a family doctor.

(7) She works in a bank.

(8) My father likes his job.

(9) He wants to be a lawyer.

(10) He works in his father's company.

7 Choose the correct translation.

(1) 大夫的律师   (a) doctor's lawyer   (b) lawyer's doctor

(2) 服务员的爸爸   (a) waiter's father   (b) father's waiter

(3) 经理的太太   (a) wife's manager   (b) manager's wife

(4) 她丈夫的老师   (a) her teacher's husband   (b) her husband's teacher

(5) 他哥哥的牙医   (a) his elder brother's dentist   (b) his dentist's elder brother

8 Translation.

(1) the hotel manager   (4) her son's teacher

(2) her husband's secretary   (5) my teacher's mother

(3) his wife's dentist   (6) his mother's job

9 Find the odd one out.

(1) 医生   律师   老师   酒店

(2) 商人   银行   银行家   经理

(3) 医院   学校   公司   牙医

(4) 商店   饭店   书店   校长

他叫李银海,是一个律师,在一家美国律师行工作。

他家有四口人,他太太、两个子女和他。他们是中国人,现在住在上海。他的太太是牙医,在一家医院工作。他女儿今年十二岁,上中学一年级。他儿子今年八岁,上小学三年级。他们都喜欢上学。

Answer the questions.

(1) 李银海做什么工作?

(2) 他在哪儿工作?

(3) 他家有几口人?

(4) 他有几个子女?

(5) 他的女儿今年多大了? 上几年级?

(6) 他的儿子今年几岁了? 上几年级?

(7) 他太太做什么工作?

(8) 他们一家人现在住在哪儿?

第五单元 上学、上班

第十八课 他天天坐校车上学

1 Circle the correct pinyin.

(1) 火车　(a) hǔchē　(b) huǒchē

(2) 汽车　(a) qìchē　(b) qìcē

(3) 地铁　(a) dìtěi　(b) dìtiě

(4) 电车　(a) diàngchē　(b) diànchē

(5) 飞机　(a) fāijī　(b) fēijī

(6) 同学　(a) tónxué　(b) tóngxué

2 Find at least one word for each radical.

(1) 氵　海 _____

(2) 钅　_____

(3) 禾　_____

(4) 冂　_____

(5) 羊　_____

(6) 广　_____

3 Finish the dialogues in Chinese.

(1) A: 你爸爸怎么上班？（开车）
nǐ bà ba zěn me shàng bān　kāi chē

　　B: _____。

(2) A: 你姐姐怎么上学？（坐校车）
nǐ jiě jie zěn me shàng xué　zuò xiào chē

　　B: _____。

(3) A: 你爷爷怎么去东京？（坐飞机）
nǐ yé ye zěn me qù dōng jīng　zuò fēi jī

　　B: _____。

(4) A: 你们怎么去上海？（坐火车）
nǐ men zěn me qù shàng hǎi　zuò huǒ chē

　　B: _____。

(5) A: _____?

　　B: 我哥哥坐电车上学。
wǒ gē ge zuò diàn chē shàng xué

(6) A: _____?

　　B: 李先生坐出租车去医院。
lǐ xiān shēng zuò chū zū chē qù yī yuàn

(7) A: _____?

　　B: 她坐公共汽车去酒店。
tā zuò gōng gòng qì chē qù jiǔ diàn

(8) A: _____?

　　B: 王太太坐地铁去银行。
wáng tài tai zuò dì tiě qù yín háng

4 Fill in the blanks with the words in the box.

shén me	zěn me	nǎr	shuí	jǐ	duō dà
什么	怎么	哪儿	谁	几	多大

nǐ xìng
(1) 你姓 _____ ?

nǐ jiào　　　　　　míng zi
(2) 你叫 _____ 名字?

nǐ jiā yǒu　　　　　　kǒu rén
(3) 你家有 _____ 口人?

nǐ jiā yǒu
(4) 你家有 _____ ?

nǐ jīn nián
(5) 你今年 _____ 了?

nǐ jiā zhù zài
(6) 你家住在 _____ ?

nǐ bà ba zuò　　　　　　gōng zuò
(7) 你爸爸做 _____ 工作?

zài　　　　　　gōng zuò
在 _____ 工作?

nǐ mā ma zuò　　　　　　gōng zuò
(8) 你妈妈做 _____ 工作?

zài　　　　　　gōng zuò
在 _____ 工作?

nǐ　　　　　　shàng xué
(9) 你 _____ 上学?

5 Give the meanings of the following phrases.

kāi
① 开

kāi huì
开会

kāi mén
开门

kāi kǒu
开口

kāi xué
开学

kāi shuǐ
开水

kāi xīn
开心

diàn
② 电

diàn gōng
电工

diàn huà
电话

diàn zǐ
电子

qì
③ 汽

qì shuǐ
汽水

shuǐ qì
水汽

bān
④ 班

bān jí
班级

bān zhǎng
班长

bān chē
班车

bān jī
班机

gōng
⑤ 公

gōng ān
公安

gōng kāi
公开

tóng
⑥ 同

tóng xiào
同校

tóng bān
同班

tóng děng
同等

tóng suì
同岁

6   Match the Chinese with the English.

míngtiān wǒ men kāi xiào huì
(1) 明天我们开校会。

zhè ge shǒu jī shì wǒ gē ge de
(2) 这个手机是我哥哥的。

xiǎo xīn kāi shuǐ
(3) 小心开水！

yín háng jiǔ diǎn kāi mén
(4) 银行九点开门。

míng tiān wǒ men jiǔ diàn kāi zhāng
(5) 明天我们酒店开张。

wáng lì hé wǒ zài tóng yí ge xué xiào shàng xué
(6) 王力和我在同一个学校上学。

wáng xiān sheng míng tiān zuò sān diǎn de bān jī
(7) 王先生明天坐三点的班机

qù yīng guó
去英国。

zhè lǐ méi yǒu gōng yòng diàn huà
(8) 这里没有公用电话。

(a) Our hotel's grand opening is tomorrow.

(b) Be careful with the boiling water.

(c) We are having a school assembly tomorrow.

(d) Tomorrow Mr. Wang is taking the 3 o'clock flight to England.

(e) There is no public telephone here.

(f) This mobile phone is my elder brother's.

(g) The bank opens at nine.

(h) Wang Li and I go to the same school.

7   Reading comprehension.

gāo dà nián jīn nián shí suì   tā bà ba   mā ma dōu shì mǎ lái
高大年今年十岁。他爸爸、妈妈都是马来

xī yà rén   tā men yì jiā wǔ kǒu xiàn zài zhù zài xiāng gǎng   tā hé dì
西亚人。他们一家五口现在住在香港。他和弟

dì   mèi mei tiān tiān dōu zuò xiào chē shàng xué   tā men zài tóng yí ge xué
弟、妹妹天天都坐校车上学。他们在同一个学

xiào shàng xué   tā bà ba shì gōng chéng shī   tā tiān tiān kāi chē shàng
校上学。他爸爸是工程师，他天天开车上

bān   tā mā ma shì lǎo shī   tā zuò gōng gòng qì chē shàng bān
班。他妈妈是老师，她坐公共汽车上班。

True or false?

gāo dà nián shì xiǎo xué shēng
( )(1) 高大年是小学生。

gāo dà nián shì mǎ lái xī yà rén
( )(2) 高大年是马来西亚人。

tā yǒu xiōng dì jiě mèi
( )(3) 他有兄弟姐妹。

tā méi yǒu jiě jie
( )(4) 他没有姐姐。

tā de bà ba zuò dì tiě shàng bān
( )(5) 他的爸爸坐地铁上班。

154

8 Match the Chinese with the English.

shàng xué
(1) 上 学

tóng xué
(2) 同 学

tóng bān
(3) 同 班

xué xiào
(4) 学 校

xué sheng
(5) 学 生

lǎo shī
(6) 老 师

xiào zhǎng
(7) 校 长

xiào chē
(8) 校 车

(a) school

(b) go to school

(c) school bus

(d) teacher

(e) principal

(f) classmate

(g) schoolmate

(h) student

9 Correct the mistakes.

dà xiàng
(1) 大 象   大象

lù shī
(2) 律 师 _____

shāng rén
(3) 商 人 _____

qì chē
(4) 汽 车 _____

kāi chē
(5) 井 车 _____

chū zū chē
(6) 出 相 车 _____

diàn chē
(7) 甩 车 _____

10 Answer the following questions.

nǐ xìng shén me
(1) 你 姓 什么？

nǐ jiào shén me míng zi
(2) 你 叫 什么 名字？

nǐ jīn nián duō dà le
(3) 你 今年 多大 了？

nǐ jīn nián shàng jǐ nián jí
(4) 你 今年 上 几 年级？

nǐ jiā yǒu jǐ kǒu rén
(5) 你 家 有 几 口 人？

nǐ yǒu xiōng dì jiě mèi ma
(6) 你 有 兄弟 姐妹 吗？

nǐ yǒu méi yǒu gē ge
(7) 你 有 没有 哥哥？

nǐ bà ba mā ma dōu gōng zuò ma
(8) 你 爸爸、 妈妈 都 工作 吗？

nǐ bà ba shì lù shī ma
(9) 你 爸爸 是 律师 吗？

nǐ mā ma shì yī shēng ma
(10) 你 妈妈 是 医生 吗？

nǐ bà ba zěn me shàng bān
(11) 你 爸爸 怎么 上 班？

nǐ zěn me shàng xué
(12) 你 怎么 上 学？

nǐ qù guo shì jiè shang shén me dì fang
(13) 你 去过 世界 上 什么 地方？

nǐ huì shuō shén me yǔ yán
(14) 你 会 说 什么 语言？

nǐ xiǎng xué shén me yǔ yán
(15) 你 想 学 什么 语言？

nǐ zuò guò fēi jī ma
(16) 你 坐过 飞机 吗？

155

11 Find the missing words.

chē	jī	qì chē	tiě
(a) 车	(b) 机	(c) 汽车	(d) 铁

gōng gòng
(1) 公共 _____

chū zū
(2) 出租 _____

fēi
(3) 飞 _____

dì
(4) 地 _____

diàn
(5) 电 _____

xiào
(6) 校 _____

huǒ
(7) 火 _____

mǎ
(8) 马 _____

12 Put the words / phrases into sentences.

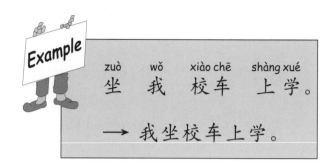

Example

zuò   wǒ   xiào chē   shàng xué
坐　我　校车　上学。

→ 我坐校车上学。

tā   shàng bān   diàn chē   zuò
(1) 他　上班　电车　坐。

kāi chē   shàng bān   wǒ bà ba
(2) 开车　上班　我爸爸。

tā dì di   shàng xué   xiào chē   zuò
(3) 她弟弟　上学　校车　坐。

chū zū chē   shàng bān   zuò   xiǎo wáng
(4) 出租车　上班　坐　小王。

zuò   qù dé guó   mǎ xiǎo lì   fēi jī
(5) 坐　去德国　马小力　飞机。

13 Translation.

dà xiàng de bí zi cháng
(1) 大象的鼻子长。

xiǎo tiān zì jǐ huì huà shēng ri kǎ
(2) 小天自己会画生日卡。

wǒ zuò xiào chē shàng xué
(3) 我坐校车上学。

bà ba kāi chē shàng bān
(4) 爸爸开车上班。

mā ma xīng qī liù zuò fēi jī qù yīng guó
(5) 妈妈星期六坐飞机去英国。

nǎi nai bú huì kāi chē
(6) 奶奶不会开车。

yé ye xǐ huan zuò diàn chē
(7) 爷爷喜欢坐电车。

14 Find the phrases. Write them out.

公	共	汽	车	飞
电	同	天	么	机
地	开	学	校	怎
师	铁	坐	上	班
火	车	出	租	车

(1) _____   (5) _____

(2) _____   (6) _____

(3) _____   (7) _____

(4) _____   (8) _____

生 词

		丶 丿 𠆢 从 丛 坐 坐								
zuò travel by; sit	坐									
		一 𠂇 车 车								
chē vehicle	车									
		丨 𠃌 门 冂 同 同								
tóng same; like	同									
		一 十 廿 共 共 共								
gòng common; general	共									
		丶 丶 氵 汽 汽 汽 汽 汽								
qì vapour; steam	汽									
		一 二 于 开								
kāi drive; open; manage	开									
		一 二 于 王 王 玑 玑 玬 班 班								
bān class; shift	班									
		一 二 千 禾 禾 利 和 租 租 租								
zū rent; hire	租									
		丨 𠃍 冂 日 电								
diàn electricity	电									
		乁 飞 飞								
fēi fly	飞									
		𠂉 𠂊 𠂉 钅 钅 铁 铁 铁 铁 铁								
tiě iron	铁									

生 词

		ノ ⺀ ⺅ 乍 乍 乍 怎 怎 怎									
zěn why; how	怎										

识字（十）

		一	丁	下							
xià below; next; get off	下										
		一	ナ	圡	左	左					
zuǒ left	左										
		一	ナ	才	右	右					
yòu right	右										
		一	二	千	禾	禾	乔	季	季		
jì season	季										
		一	二	三	声	夫	表	春	春	春	
chūn spring	春										
		一	丆	厂	丙	百	百	百	頁	夏	夏
xià summer	夏										
		丿	二	千	禾	禾	禾	秒	秋	秋	
qiū autumn	秋										
		丿	冫	夕	冬	冬					
dōng winter	冬										

1 Finish the following diagrams.

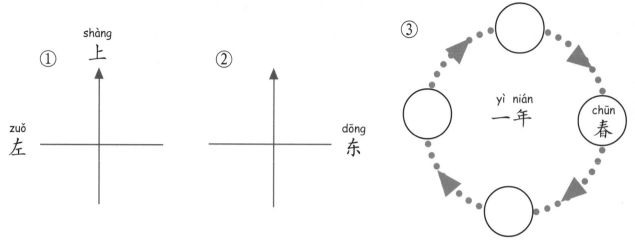

2 Give the meanings of the following phrases.

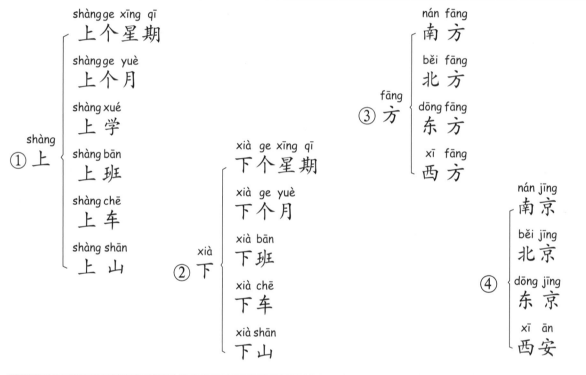

3 Translation.

    tā sān shí suì zuǒ yòu
(1) 他 三 十 岁 左 右。

    tā èr shí wǔ suì shàng xià
(2) 她 二 十 五 岁 上 下。

    wǒ jīn nián xué le hěn duō dōng xi
(3) 我 今 年 学 了 很 多 东 西。

    yì nián yǒu sì jì   chūn   xià   qiū   dōng
(4) 一 年 有 四 季: 春、 夏、 秋、 冬。

    wǒ xǐ huan dōng tiān
(5) 我 喜 欢 冬 天。

160

第十九课　她坐地铁上班

1 Write the pinyin for the following phrases.

(1) 喜欢 _____

(2) 自行车 _____

(3) 长大 _____

(4) 世界 _____

(5) 走路 _____

(6) 骑马 _____

(7) 然后 _____

2 Find the phrases. Write them out.

每	长	大	然	后
骑	天	到	坐	从
走	路	坐	班	船
上	学	自	行	车

(1) _____ (4) _____

(2) _____ (5) _____

(3) _____ (6) _____

3 Match the words in column A with the ones in column B.

A

(1) 走 zǒu

(2) 骑 qí

(3) 坐 zuò

(4) 上 shàng

(5) 去 qù

(6) 开 kāi

(7) 下 xià

B

(a) 班 bān

(b) 路 lù

(c) 北京 běi jīng

(d) 飞机 fēi jī

(e) 汽车 qì chē

(f) 学 xué

(g) 出租车 chū zū chē

(h) 自行车 zì xíng chē

4 Translation.

(1) wǒ míng nián xiǎng qù fǎ guó kàn kan, rán
我明年想去法国看看，然
hòu qù yīng guó hé dé guó
后去英国和德国。

(2) wáng yī shēng xiān zuò huǒ chē, rán hòu zǒu
王医生先坐火车，然后走
lù qù yī yuàn
路去医院。

(3) zhāng lǎo shī měi tiān xiān zuò dì tiě, rán
张老师每天先坐地铁，然
hòu zuò chū zū chē shàng bān
后坐出租车上班。

(4) xiǎo míng zhǎng dà yǐ hòu xiǎng qù měi guó shàng
小明长大以后想去美国上
dà xué, rán hòu qù ōu zhōu gōng zuò
大学，然后去欧洲工作。

161

...p the words according to their
...ls.

_____ (6) 王 _____

(2) 亠 _____ (7) 钅 _____

(3) 足 _____ (8) 舟 _____

(4) 马 _____ (9) 月 _____

(5) 刂 _____ (10) 禾 _____

zū 租	dào 到	tiě 铁	rán 然	qí 骑
bān 班	qī 期	lù 路	chuán 船	měi 每

6 Correct the mistakes.

(1) 海天
    měi tiān
    _____

(2) 骟马
    qí mǎ
    _____

(3) 白仟车
    zì xíng chē
    _____

(4) 走路
    zǒu lù
    _____

(5) 坐般
    zuò chuán
    _____

(6) 然后
    rán hòu
    _____

(7) 气车
    qì chē
    _____

7 Reading comprehension.

wǒ jiào jiā jia
我叫家家，

jīn nián bā suì shàng
今年八岁，上

xiǎo xué sì nián jí
小学四年级。

wǒ jiā yǒu wǔ kǒu
我家有五口

rén   yé ye   nǎi nai   bà ba   mā
人：爷爷、奶奶、爸爸、妈

ma hé wǒ   wǒ yé ye   nǎi nai bú tài
妈和我。我爷爷、奶奶不太

lǎo   liù shí duō suì   tā men bù gōng
老，六十多岁，他们不工

zuò   wǒ bà ba sān shí wǔ suì   shì jīng
作。我爸爸三十五岁，是经

lǐ   wǒ mā ma sān shí èr suì   shì yīng
理。我妈妈三十二岁，是英

yǔ lǎo shī   wǒ měi tiān zuò xiào chē shàng
语老师。我每天坐校车上

xué   wǒ bà ba měi tiān kāi chē shàng
学。我爸爸每天开车上

bān   wǒ mā ma bù xǐ huan zuò chē   tā
班。我妈妈不喜欢坐车，她

měi tiān zǒu lù shàng bān
每天走路上班。

True or false?

jiā jia jīn nián shàng zhōng xué sì nián jí
(　)(1) 家家今年上中学四年级。

tā yé ye   nǎi nai dōu gōng zuò
(　)(2) 她爷爷、奶奶都工作。

tā bà ba shì jīng lǐ
(　)(3) 她爸爸是经理。

tā mā ma shì hàn yǔ lǎo shī
(　)(4) 她妈妈是汉语老师。

tā mā ma měi tiān zuò chē shàng bān
(　)(5) 她妈妈每天坐车上班。

8 Match the Chinese with the English.

mǎ lù
(1) 马路   (a) intersection

shān lù
(2) 山路   (b) from Beijing to Shanghai

lù kǒu
(3) 路口   (c) ask the way

gōng lù
(4) 公路   (d) from yesterday to today

wèn lù
(5) 问路   (e) mountain road

fēi xíng yuán
(6) 飞行员   (f) pilot

cóng běi jīng dào
(7) 从北京到   (g) road; street

shàng hǎi
上海   (h) highway

cóng zuó tiān dào
(8) 从昨天到

jīn tiān
今天

9 Translation.

(1) He was born in Beijing, but he grew up in Hong Kong.

(2) He takes the bus to school everyday.

(3) They attend the same school.

(4) From Monday to Friday, she takes the taxi to school.

(5) His younger brother likes riding horses.

(6) Can you ride a bicycle?

10 Fill in the blanks with the words in the box.

zěn me	shén me	jǐ	shuí	nǎ
怎么	什么	几	谁	哪
nǎr	duō dà	ma	ne	
哪儿	多大	吗	呢	

nǐ jiā yǒu   kǒu rén
(1) 你家有_____口人？

shì tā gē ge
(2) _____是他哥哥？

tā xìng
(3) 他姓_____？

xiǎo míng shì   guó rén
(4) 小明是_____国人？

wáng lǎo shī zhù zài
(5) 王老师住在_____？

nǐ de bǐ yǒu jīn nián   le
(6) 你的笔友今年_____了？

nǐ mèi mei jīn nián   suì le
(7) 你妹妹今年_____岁了？

nǐ mā ma hǎo
(8) 你妈妈好_____？

wǒ xìng shǐ   nǐ
(9) 我姓史。你_____？

tā huì shuō   yǔ yán
(10) 她会说_____语言？

nǐ bà ba zuò   gōng zuò
(11) 你爸爸做_____工作？

nǐ měi tiān   shàng xué
(12) 你每天_____上学？

11 Reading comprehension.

lǐ yīng tián shì yī shēng tā de
李英田是医生。她的
nán péng you jiào qí guǎng ān   yě shì
男朋友叫齐广安，也是
yī shēng tā men zài tóng yì jiā yī yuàn
医生。他们在同一家医院
gōng zuò lǐ yīng tián shì shàng hǎi rén
工作。李英田是上海人，
qí guǎng ān shì běi jīng rén lǐ yīng tián
齐广安是北京人。李英田
měi xīng qī gōng zuò sì tiān tā zuò gōng
每星期工作四天。她坐公
gòng qì chē shàng bān qí guǎng ān měi
共汽车上班。齐广安每
xīng qī gōng zuò liù tiān tā xiān zuò
星期工作六天。他先坐
chuán rán hòu zuò dì tiě shàng bān
船，然后坐地铁上班。

qí guǎng ān
齐广安

lǐ yīng tián
李英田

Answer the questions.

lǐ yīng tián zài nǎr   gōng zuò
(1) 李英田在哪儿工作？
qí guǎng ān shì shuí
(2) 齐广安是谁？
lǐ yīng tián měi xīng qī gōng zuò jǐ tiān
(3) 李英田每星期工作几天？
tā zěn me shàng bān
(4) 她怎么上班？
qí guǎng ān zěn me shàng bān
(5) 齐广安怎么上班？

12 Interview your partner with the following questions.

nǐ xìng shén me   jiào shén me míng zi
(1) 你姓什么？叫什么名字？
nǐ chū shēng zài nǎr   duō dà le
(2) 你出生在哪儿？多大了？
shàng jǐ nián jí
上几年级？
nǐ shì nǎ guó rén
(3) 你是哪国人？
nǐ jiā lǐ yǒu jǐ kǒu rén   yǒu shuí
(4) 你家里有几口人？有谁？
nǐ qù guo shén me guó jiā
(5) 你去过什么国家？

nǐ huì shuō shén me yǔ yán
(6) 你会说什么语言？
nǐ bà ba zuò shén me gōng zuò
(7) 你爸爸做什么工作？
zài nǎr   gōng zuò
在哪儿工作？
nǐ mā ma gōng zuò ma
(8) 你妈妈工作吗？
nǐ bà ba   mā ma zěn me shàng bān
(9) 你爸爸、妈妈怎么上班？
nǐ zěn me shàng xué
(10) 你怎么上学？

164

生 词

		丿 厂 厂 厂 斤 斤 后 后							
hòu behind; back	后								
		丿 一 仁 与 每 每 每							
měi every	每								
		丁 马 马 马 马 马 骄 骄 骑 骑 骑							
qí ride	骑								
		丿 彳 彳 彳 行 行							
xíng go; travel	行								
		丿 人 从 从							
cóng from	从								
		一 工 工 互 至 至 到 到							
dào arrive; until	到								
		一 十 土 卡 卡 走 走							
zǒu walk	走								
		丶 口 口 口 口 尸 尸 足 趵 跠 趵 路 路							
lù road; journey	路								
		丿 厂 力 月 角 角 舟 舟 船 船							
chuán boat; ship	船								
		丿 夕 夕 夕 夕 外 狀 狀 然 然 然							
rán right	然								

识字（十一）

		` ⺖ ⺀ 写 写										
xiě write	写											
		⺍ ⺀ 三 毛										
máo writing brush	毛											
		一 十 卄 艹 艹 艹 苙 苙 苹 苹 菜										
cài vegetable; dish	菜											
		ノ ⺂ 午 仩 竹 竹										
zhú bamboo	竹											
		ノ ⺂ 亇 ⺮ 竹 竹 竹 竻 竻 筚 筷 筷										
kuài chopsticks	筷											

166

1 Match the words with the pictures.

dà zì
(a) 大字   máo bǐ
(b) 毛笔   guó huà
(c) 国画

zhú kuài
(d) 竹筷   zhōng guó fàn
(e) 中国饭

①   ②   ③   ④   ⑤

3 Give the meanings of the following phrases.

hàn zì
汉字

wén zì
文字

① zì   míng zì
字   名字

shēng zì
生字

máo bǐ zì
毛笔字

xiě zì
写字

xiě zuò
写作

② xiě   dà xiě
写   大写

xiǎo xiě
小写

máo bǐ
毛笔

bǐ jiān
笔尖

③ bǐ   bǐ míng
笔   笔名

bǐ yǒu
笔友

2 Dismantle the characters into parts.

guó
(1) 国 __口__ __玉__   cài
(5) 菜 ____ ____

xiě
(2) 写 ____ ____   kuài
(6) 筷 ____ ____

zì
(3) 字 ____ ____   tiě
(7) 铁 ____ ____

bǐ
(4) 笔 ____ ____

zhōng guó cài
中国菜

fǎ guó cài
法国菜

④ cài   bái cài
菜   白菜

zuò cài
做菜

第二十课　我早上七点半上学

1 Write the time in Chinese.

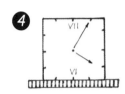

(1) 现在两点。　　(4) _____

(2) _____　(5) _____

(3) _____　(6) _____

2 Finish the dialogues in Chinese.

nǐ bà ba jǐ diǎn shàng bān
(1) A: 你爸爸几点上班？ (9:00)

B: _____。

nǐ mā ma jǐ diǎn shàng bān
(2) A: 你妈妈几点上班？ (8:30)

B: _____。

nǐ gē ge jǐ diǎn shàng xué
(3) A: 你哥哥几点上学？ (7:55)

B: _____。

nǐ yé ye jǐ diǎn qù yín háng
(4) A: 你爷爷几点去银行？ (3:15)

B: _____。

wáng xiǎo jiě jǐ diǎn qù gōng sī
(5) A: 王小姐几点去公司？ (10:20)

B: _____。

3 Write the pinyin for the following words.

(1) 菜 _____　(5) 半 _____　(9) 慢 _____

(2) 零 _____　(6) 表 _____　(10) 写 _____

(3) 分 _____　(7) 点 _____　(11) 筷 _____

(4) 刻 _____　(8) 快 _____　(12) 竹 _____

168

4 Match the Chinese with the English.

yí bàn
(1) 一半   (a) right hand

bàn tiān
(2) 半天   (b) half

yòu shǒu
(3) 右手   (c) festival

bàn nián
(4) 半年   (d) half a day

zuó shǒu
(5) 左手   (e) Miss World

kuài chē
(6) 快车   (f) half a month

bàn ge yuè
(7) 半个月   (g) express train

màn chē
(8) 慢车   (h) left hand

jié rì
(9) 节日   (i) half a year

shì jié xiǎo jiě
(10) 世界小姐   (j) slow train

5 Finish the following sentences.

xiàn zài
(1) 现在 ____九点____ 。(9:00)

xiàn zài
(2) 现在 _____ 。(8:05)

xiàn zài
(3) 现在 _____ 。(10:15)

xiàn zài
(4) 现在 _____ 。(12:45)

xiàn zài
(5) 现在 _____ 。(3:30)

6 Finish the following dialogues in Chinese.

❶

3:10

nǐ jǐ diǎn lái wǒ jiā
A: 你几点来我家?

B: _____ 。

❷

12:00

nǐ jǐ diǎn qù fàn diàn
A: 你几点去饭店?

B: _____ 。

❸

7:30

nǐ jǐ diǎn shàng xué
A: 你几点上学?

B: _____ 。

7 Finish the following dialogues in Chinese.

nǐ zuò jǐ diǎn de chuán qù shàng hǎi
(1) A: 你坐几点的船去上海？ (8:15)   B : _____

nǐ zuò jǐ diǎn de huǒ chē qù běi jīng
(2) A: 你坐几点的火车去北京？ (10:15)   B : _____

nǐ zuò jǐ diǎn de fēi jī qù měi guó
(3) A: 你坐几点的飞机去美国？ (6:40)   B : _____

nǐ zuò jǐ diǎn de qì chē qù xué xiào
(4) A: 你坐几点的汽车去学校？ (7:45)   B : _____

nǐ zuò jǐ diǎn de huǒ chē lái wǒ jiā
(5) A: 你坐几点的火车来我家？ (12:08)   B : _____

8 Make new sentences based on the information given.

Example 8:00

zhāng yī shēng
张医生

zuò dì tiě   shàng bān
坐地铁 / 上班

张医生八点上班。

她每天坐地铁上班。

7:45

wáng fēi
① 王飞

zuò xiào chē   shàng xué
坐校车 / 上学

lǐ xiān shēng
② 李先生

kāi chē   shàng bān
开车 / 上班

8:15

mǎ xiǎo jiě
③ 马小姐

zuò fēi jī   qù yīng guó
坐飞机 / 去英国

9:30

zhāng jīng lǐ
④ 张经理

zuò huǒ chē   qù běi jīng
坐火车 / 去北京

9 Finish the dialogues in Chinese.

tā shì zhōng xué shēng hái shi dà xué shēng
A: 她是中学生还是大学生？

B: 她是中学生。

1

tā shì zhōng xué shēng hái shi dà xué shēng

zuò huǒ chē kuài hái shi qí zì xíng chē kuài
A: 坐火车快还是骑自行车快？

B: _____

2

tā shì rì běn rén hái shi zhōng guó rén
A: 她是日本人还是中国人？

B: _____

3

tā shì hù shi hái shi lǎo shī
A: 她是护士还是老师？

B: _____

4

nǐ zuò kuài chē qù běi jīng hái shi zuò màn chē qù
A: 你坐快车去北京还是坐慢车去？

B: _____

5

tā zǒu lù shàng xué hái shi qí chē shàng xué
A: 他走路上学还是骑车上学？

B: _____

10 Reading comprehension.

wǒ yǒu yí ge gē ge tā jīn nián shí jiǔ suì tā xiàn zài zài yīng guó yí ge yǒu
我有一个哥哥,他今年十九岁。他现在在英国一个有
míng de dà xué lǐ shàng yì nián jí tā xué fǎ lǜ hé zhōngwén míng nián tā men quán
名的大学里上一年级。他学法律和中文。明年他们全
bān tóng xué dōu huì qù zhōng guó de běi jīng dà xué xué zhōngwén tā yǐ hòu xiǎng qù zhōng
班同学都会去中国的北京大学学中文。他以后想去中
guó zuò lǜ shī
国做律师。

True or false?

tā gē ge zài měi guó shàng dà xué
( )(1) 他哥哥在美国上大学。

tā gē ge xué fǎ yǔ hé zhōngwén
( )(2) 他哥哥学法语和中文。

míng nián tā gē ge hé quán bān tóng xué qù zhōng guó
( )(3) 明年他哥哥和全班同学去中国。

tā gē ge yǐ hòu xiǎng qù zhōng guó gōng zuò
( )(4) 他哥哥以后想去中国工作。

11 Correct the mistakes.

xiě
(1) 写 _____

dōng
(8) 冬 _____

kè
(2) 刻 _____

cháng
(9) 长 _____

bàn
(3) 羊 _____

qí
(10) 骑 _____

biǎo
(4) 表 _____

chuán
(11) 舩 _____

màn
(5) 慢 _____

dào
(12) 到 _____

fēn
(6) 分 _____

zuǒ
(13) 左 _____

xiān
(7) 旡 _____

chūn
(14) 春 _____

12 Translation.

(1) What time is it by your watch?

(2) I will take the 8 o'clock flight to Shanghai.

(3) Are you a student or a teacher?

(4) My father first takes the bus and then the train to work.

(5) Mr. Wang will take the express train to Beijing.

生 词

	丶 丷 丷 兰 半										
bàn half	半										
	一 厂 厂 币 示 示 雨 雫 雫 零 零										
líng zero	零										
	丿 八 分 分										
fēn minute	分										
	丶 一 亠 亥 亥 亥 刻 刻										
kè a quarter (of an hour)	刻										
	一 二 丰 丰 声 耒 表 表										
biǎo meter; watch	表										
	丶 丷 忄 忄 忙 快 快										
kuài quick; fast	快										
	丶 丷 忄 忄 忄 忆 忆 忆 惧 慢 慢 慢										
màn slow	慢										

识字（十二）

		一 十 艹 节 节
jié festival; knot; section	节	
		ㄥ ㄠ ㄠ 纟 纠 纠 纠 纠 给 给
gěi give; for	给	
		ㄥ ㄠ ㄠ 纟 纟 红 红
hóng red	红	
		㇀ ㄅ 勹 匀 包
bāo packet; bag	包	
		㇇ 了 孑 孑 孑 孑 孩 孩 孩
hái child	孩	
		㇒ ㇒ ㇒ 竻 竻 竻 竺 竺 笑 笑
xiào smile; laugh	笑	

1 Give the meanings of the following phrases.

① 孩 (hái)
- hái zi 孩子
- xiǎo hái 小孩
- nán hái 男孩
- nǚ hái 女孩

② 包 (bāo)
- bāo zi 包子
- shū bāo 书包
- hóng bāo 红包

③ 笑 (xiào)
- hǎo xiào 好笑
- kě xiào 可笑
- dà xiào 大笑
- shuō xiào hua 说笑话

④ 节 (jié)
- chūn jié 春节
- zhōng qiū jié 中秋节
- jié rì 节日
- jì jié 季节

2 Translation.

(1) cóng shàng dào xià 从 上 到 下

(2) cóng zuǒ dào yòu 从左到右

(3) cóng xiǎo dào dà 从 小 到 大

(4) cóng gǔ dào jīn 从古到今

(5) cóng běi jīng dào shàng hǎi 从北京到上海

3 Give the meanings of the following phrases.

(1) chūn jié 春节 _____

(2) hóng bāo 红 包 _____

(3) hái zi 孩子 _____

(4) máo bǐ 毛笔 _____

(5) zhōng guó huà 中 国 画 _____

(6) xiě zì 写字 _____

(7) chūn tiān 春天 _____

(8) dōng tiān 冬天 _____

(9) xià tiān 夏天 _____

(10) qiū tiān 秋天 _____

第二十一课 汽车比自行车快

1 Write the time in Chinese.

①
zǎo shang
早上

④
xià wǔ
下午

②
zǎo shang
早上

⑤
xià wǔ
下午

③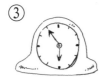
xià wǔ
下午

⑥
wǎn shang
晚上

(1) 现在是早上六点。_____

(2) _____

(3) _____

(4) _____

(5) _____

(6) _____

2 Answer the questions based on the calendar.

二○○一年						一月
日	一	二	三	四	五	六
	1	2	3	4	5	6
7	8	9	10/今天	11	12	13
14	15	16	17	18	19	20

jīn tiān shì jǐ yuè jǐ hào   xīng qī jǐ
(1) 今天是几月几号? 星期几?

zuó tiān shì jǐ yuè jǐ hào
(2) 昨天是几月几号?

míng tiān xīng qī jǐ
(3) 明天星期几?

jīn nián shì nǎ nián
(4) 今年是哪年?

qù nián shì yī jiǔ jiǔ jiǔ nián ma
(5) 去年是一九九九年吗?

shàng ge yuè shì jǐ yuè
(6) 上个月是几月?

yī yuè èr hào shì xīng qī jǐ
(7) 一月二号是星期几?

3 Write the pinyin for the following phrases.

(1) 上午_____

(2) 晚上_____

(3) 吃早饭_____

(4) 放学_____

(5) 回家_____

(6) 看书_____

(7) 更快_____

(8) 最慢了_____

(9) 下班_____

4 True or false ?

( )(1) qí zì xíng chē bǐ zǒu lù kuài
骑自行车比走路快。

( )(2) yīng guó bǐ dé guó xiǎo
英国比德国小。

( )(3) fǎ guó bǐ měi guó dà
法国比美国大。

( )(4) zhōng guó de lì shǐ bǐ měi guó de cháng
中国的历史比美国的长。

( )(5) zhōng guó de rén kǒu bǐ jiā ná dà de duō
中国的人口比加拿大的多。

( )(6) shàng hǎi de rén kǒu bǐ xiāng gǎng de duō
上海的人口比香港的多。

( )(7) zuò huǒ chē bǐ zuò fēi jī kuài
坐火车比坐飞机快。

( )(8) zǒu lù bǐ zuò chū zū chē màn
走路比坐出租车慢。

5 Give the meanings of the following radicals. Find at least one word for each radical.

(1) 日 _____

(2) 王 _____

(3) 方 _____

(4) 门 _____

(5) 雷 _____

(6) 禾 _____

(7) 月 _____

6 Match the Chinese with the English.

(1) shǒu biǎo
手表   (a) tonight

(2) biǎo gē
表哥   (b) good night

(3) diàn biǎo
电表   (c) watch

(4) shuǐ biǎo
水表   (d) good-looking

(5) jīn wǎn
今晚   (e) cousin

(6) wǎn ān
晚安   (f) electricity metre

(7) hǎo kàn
好看   (g) return to the country

(8) huí guó
回国   (h) water metre

7 Correct the mistakes.

(1) chī fàn
吃饭 _____

(2) shàng wǔ
上牛 _____

(3) wǎn shang
晚上 _____

(4) kàn shū
看书 _____

(5) nán fāng
南方 _____

(6) máo bǐ
毛笔 _____

(7) xiě zì
写字 _____

(8) gèng kuài
更快 _____

(9) fàng xué
欨学 _____

8 Put the hands on the clocks.

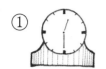 ①
 ⑤

 ②
 ⑥

 ③
 ⑦

 ④
 ⑧

xiàn zài shí èr diǎn bàn
(1) 现在十二点半。

xiàn zài qī diǎn yí kè
(2) 现在七点一刻。

xiàn zài sān diǎn èr shí fēn
(3) 现在三点二十分。

xiàn zài qī diǎn sān kè
(4) 现在七点三刻。

xiàn zài bā diǎn wǔ shí fēn
(5) 现在八点五十分。

xiàn zài shí diǎn èr shí wǔ fēn
(6) 现在十点二十五分。

xiàn zài shí yī diǎn bàn
(7) 现在十一点半。

xiàn zài jiǔ diǎn líng wǔ fēn
(8) 现在九点零五分。

9 Reading comprehension.

liǎng ge xīng qī
两个星期

hòu   wǒ jiě jie qù
后，我姐姐去

měi guó shàng dà xué
美国上大学。

tā qù xué fǎ lù
她去学法律，

tā yǐ hòu xiǎng zuò lǜ shī   wǒ men quán jiā zài
她以后想做律师。我们全家在

měi men guó zhù guo sì nián   wǒ men xiàn zài zhù zài
美国住过四年，我们现在住在

xiāng gǎng   wǒ hé jiě jie dōu hěn xǐ huān měi guó
香港。我和姐姐都很喜欢美国，

wǒ yǐ hòu yě xiǎng qù měi guó shàng dà xué
我以后也想去美国上大学。

Answer the questions.

tā jiě jie nǎ tiān qù měi guó
(1) 她姐姐哪天去美国？

tā jiě jie xiǎng zài dà xué lǐ xué shén me
(2) 她姐姐想在大学里学什么？

tā jiě jie yǐ hòu xiǎng zuò shén me
(3) 她姐姐以后想做什么？

tā men yì jiā zài měi guó zhù guo ma
(4) 他们一家在美国住过吗？

tā men yì jiā xiàn zài zhù zài nǎr
(5) 他们一家现在住在哪儿？

10 Find the opposites.

kuài
(1) 快 →

lái
(4) 来 →

nán
(2) 男 →

shàng bān
(5) 上班 →

lǎo
(3) 老 →

shàng xué
(6) 上学 →

fàng xué   nǚ   shào
(a) 放学   (b) 女   (c) 少

qù   xià bān   màn
(d) 去   (e) 下班   (f) 慢

11 Match the question with the answer.

nǐ zuò jǐ diǎn de bān jī qù měi guó
(1) 你坐几点的班机去美国？

méi yǒu qù guo běi jīng　dàn shì qù guo shàng hǎi
(a) 没有去过北京，但是去过上海。

nǐ nǎ tiān cóng yīng guó huí lai
(2) 你哪天从英国回来？

zuò jiǔ diǎn wǔ shí fēn de bān jī
(b) 坐九点五十分的班机。

nǐ bà ba jǐ diǎn xià bān
(3) 你爸爸几点下班？

wǒ gē ge zuì gāo
(c) 我哥哥最高。

nǐ jiā shuí zuì gāo
(4) 你家谁最高？

wǒ xǐ huan kàn xiǎo rén shū
(d) 我喜欢看小人书。

nǐ qù guo běi jīng ma
(5) 你去过北京吗？

sān diǎn bàn fàng xué huí jiā
(e) 三点半放学回家。

nǐ mā ma shì lǎo shī hái shi hù shi
(6) 你妈妈是老师还是护士？

tā wǔ diǎn xià bān
(f) 他五点下班。

nǐ xǐ huan kàn shén me shū
(7) 你喜欢看什么书？

xià ge yuè jiǔ hào
(g) 下个月九号。

nǐ jǐ diǎn fàng xué huí jiā
(8) 你几点放学回家？

tā shì hàn yǔ lǎo shī
(h) 她是汉语老师。

12 Translation.

hòu tiān shì wǒ de shēng ri
(1) 后天是我的生日。

wǒ mā ma zuò de cài hěn hǎo chī
(2) 我妈妈做的菜很好吃。

wǒ dì di bú huì xiě máo bǐ zì
(3) 我弟弟不会写毛笔字。

bà ba bǐ wǒ gāo
(4) 爸爸比我高。

tā de shū bāo bǐ wǒ de hǎo kàn
(5) 他的书包比我的好看。

xià gè yuè liù hào shì zhōng qiū jié
(6) 下个月六号是中秋节。

wǒ zuì xǐ huan chūn tiān
(7) 我最喜欢春天。

13 Answer the questions in English.

shì jiè shang nǎ ge dì fang zuì gāo
(1) 世界上哪个地方最高？

shì jiè shang nǎ ge guó jiā de rén kǒu zuì duō
(2) 世界上哪个国家的人口最多？

shì jiè shang nǎ ge guó jiā zuì dà
(3) 世界上哪个国家最大？

nǎ zhǒng fēi jī zuì kuài
(4) 哪种飞机最快？

yì nián lǐ nǎ yì tiān zuì cháng
(5) 一年里哪一天最长？

shì jiè shang nǎ zhǒng huǒ chē zuì kuài
(6) 世界上哪种火车最快？

shì jiè shang nǎ ge hǎi yáng zuì dà
(7) 世界上哪个海洋最大？

14 Answer the questions according to the timetable.

	Departure	Arrival
shàng hǎi běi jīng 上 海 → 北 京	8:00	22:05
běi jīng xī ān 北 京 → 西 安	5:30	21:30
shàng hǎi nán jīng 上 海 → 南 京	12:15	14:15
nán jīng běi jīng 南 京 → 北 京	5:45	20:45

cóng shàng hǎi qù běi jīng   nǐ zuò jǐ diǎn

(1) A: 从 上 海去北 京，你 坐 几点

de huǒ chē   nǐ jǐ diǎn dào běi jīng

的火车？你几点到北京？

B: 坐早上八点的火车。晚上

十点零五分到北京。

cóng běi jīng qù xī ān   nǐ zuò jǐ diǎn

(2) A: 从北京去西安，你坐几点

de huǒ chē   nǐ jǐ diǎn dào xī ān

的火车？你几点到西安？

B: _____

cóng shànghǎi qù nán jīng   nǐ zuò jǐ diǎn

(3) A: 从 上海去南 京，你坐几点

de huǒ chē   nǐ jǐ diǎn dào nán jīng

的火车？你几点到南京？

B: _____

cóng nán jīng qù běi jīng   nǐ zuò jǐ diǎn

(4) A: 从南京去北京，你坐几点

de huǒ chē   nǐ jǐ diǎn dào běi jīng

的火车？你几点到北京？

B: _____

15 Ask questions.

Example

měi guó
→ 美 国

你坐几点的飞机去美国？

①
yīng guó...

1 → shàng hǎi
上 海

_____ ?

2 → yīng guó
英 国

_____ ?

16 Make comparative sentences. Follow the example.

Example

骑自行车比走路快。

坐出租车更快。

坐地铁最快了。

1

妹妹　　二姐　　大姐　　妈妈

二姐比妹妹高。

_____

_____

17 Reading comprehension.

zhè ge xīng qī liù
这个星期六
xiǎo hóng hé tā jiā rén
小红和她家人
zuò fēi jī qù běi jīng　　tā men xiǎng qù kàn
坐飞机去北京。他们想去看
kan tiān ān mén　　yě xiǎng qù kàn kan yǒu míng
看天安门，也想去看看有名
de běi jīng dà xué　　běi jīng dà xué yǒu
的北京大学。北京大学有 100
nián de lì shǐ　　dà xué lǐ de xué sheng dōu
年的历史，大学里的学生都
shì lái zì quán guó zuì hǎo de xué sheng
是来自全国最好的学生。

True or false ?

xiǎo hóng yì jiā rén xià ge xīng
( )(1) 小红一家人下个星
qī liù qù běi jīng
期六去北京。

tā men zuò huǒ chē qù běi jīng
( )(2) 他们坐火车去北京。

tiān ān mén zài běi jīng
( )(3) 天安门在北京。

běi jīng dà xué hěn yǒu míng
( )(4) 北京大学很有名。

běi jīng dà xué de xué sheng dōu
( )(5) 北京大学的学生都
shì běi jīng rén
是北京人。

181

生 词

		一 ├ ╘ 比								
bǐ compare	比										
		ノ 亠 ⸗ 午								
wǔ noon	午										
		丨 刀 月 日 日′ 旷 旷 旷 晄 晚								
wǎn evening; late	晚										
		丶 口 口 口′ 吃 吃								
chī eat	吃										
		丶 亠 亍 方 方′ 劝 放								
fàng let go	放										
		丨 冂 冋 冋 回 回								
huí return	回										
		一 二 三 手 看 看 看 看								
kàn see; look; watch	看										
		一 ㇆ 一 币 百 更 更								
gèng ever more	更										
		丨 冂 曰 日 旦 早 杲 杲 杲 最 最 最								
zuì most	最										

生词

第十八课

tiān tiān	zuò xiào chē	tóng xué	gōng gòng qì chē	kāi chē	shàng bān
天天	坐校车	同学	公共汽车	开车	上班

chū zū qì chē	diàn chē	huǒ chē	fēi jī	dì tiě	zěn me
出租（汽）车	电车	火车	飞机	地铁	怎么

xià	zuǒ	yòu	yì nián sì jì	chūn	xià	qiū	dōng
下	左	右	一年四季	春	夏	秋	冬

第十九课

yǐ hòu	měi tiān＝tiān tiān	qí mǎ	qí zì xíng chē
以后	每天＝天天	骑马	骑自行车

cóng	dào	zǒu lù	chuán	xiān	rán hòu
从……到……		走路	船	先……然后……	

xiě	máo bǐ	cài	zhú kuài
写	毛笔	菜	竹筷

第二十课

zǎo shang	qī diǎn bàn	sì diǎn	jǐ diǎn	liǎng diǎn líng wǔ fēn	shí yī diǎn yí kè
早上	七点半	四点	几点	两点零五分	十一点一刻

shí yī diǎn sān kè	biǎo	kuài chē	hái shi	màn chē
十一点三刻	表	快车	还是	慢车

chūn jié	gěi	hóng bāo	hái zi	kāi kǒu	xiào
春节	给	红包	孩子	开口	笑

第二十一课

bǐ	shàng wǔ	zhōng wǔ	xià wǔ	wǎn shang	chī zǎo fàn
比	上午	中午	下午	晚上	吃早饭

chī wǔ zhōng fàn	chī wǎn fàn	fàng xué	huí jiā	xià bān	quán jiā
吃午／中饭	吃晚饭	放学	回家	下班	全家

kàn shū	gèng kuài	zuì kuài
看书	更快	最快

总复习

1. Modes of transport

汽车　公共汽车　电车　火车　飞机　出租（汽）车

qì chē　gōng gòng qì chē　diàn chē　huǒ chē　fēi jī　chū zū　qì　chē

地铁　船　自行车　校车

dì tiě　chuán　zì xíng chē　xiào chē

2. Means of travel

坐车　骑自行车　走路　开车　坐船　坐飞机　坐火车

zuò chē　qí zì xíng chē　zǒu lù　kāi chē　zuò chuán　zuò fēi jī　zuò huǒ chē

坐公共汽车　坐出租车　坐校车　坐地铁　骑马

zuò gōng gòng qì chē　zuò chū zū chē　zuò xiào chē　zuò dì tiě　qí mǎ

3. Time words

点　分　刻　半　零　早上　上午　中午　下午　晚上

diǎn　fēn　kè　bàn　líng　zǎo shang　shàng wǔ　zhōng wǔ　xià wǔ　wǎn shang

每天＝天天　后天　以后

měi tiān　tiān tiān　hòu tiān　yǐ hòu

4. Verbs

坐车　开车　骑车　走路　吃饭　放学　回家

zuò chē　kāi chē　qí chē　zǒu lù　chī fàn　fàng xué　huí jiā

上／下班　看书　比　写字　用　给　开口　笑

shàng　xià bān　kàn shū　bǐ　xiě zì　yòng　gěi　kāi kǒu　xiào

5. Conjunctions

(1) 从……到……　从星期一到星期五我每天早上七点上学。

cóng……dào……　cóng xīng qī yī dào xīng qī wǔ wǒ měi tiān zǎo shang qī diǎn shàng xué

(2) 先……，然后……　我每天先走路，然后坐校车上学。

xiān……rán hòu……　wǒ měi tiān xiān zǒu lù，rán hòu zuò xiào chē shàng xué

184

6. Adjectives and adverbs

kuài	màn	wǎn	hóng	gèng	zuì
快	慢	晚	红	更	最

7. Directions

dōng	nán	xī	běi	shàng	xià	zuǒ	yòu
东	南	西	北	上	下	左	右

8. Seasons

jì jié　chūn　xià　qiū　dōng
季节: 春　夏　秋　冬

9. Festivals

jié rì　chūn jié
节日：春节

10. Grammar

qù běi jīng de huǒ chē sān diǎn kāi
(1) 去北京的火车三点开。

wǒ zuò bā diǎn de fēi jī qù dōngjīng
(2) 我坐八点的飞机去东京。

qí chē bǐ zǒu lù kuài
(3) 骑车比走路快。

gē ge bǐ jiě jie gèng gāo
(4) 哥哥比姐姐更高。

wáng xiǎo jie zuì hǎo kàn le
(5) 王小姐最好看了。

11. Questions and answers

(1) nǐ měi tiān zěn me shàng xué
你每天怎么上学？
wǒ zuò xiào chē shàng xué
我坐校车上学。

(2) nǐ bà ba měi tiān zěn me shàng bān
你爸爸每天怎么上班？
tā kāi chē shàng bān
他开车上班。

(3) jīn tiān nǐ xiǎng zěn me qù xué xiào
今天你想怎么去学校？
wǒ xiǎng zuò chū zū chē qù xué xiào
我想坐出租车去学校。

(4) nǐ de biǎo jǐ diǎn le xiàn zài jǐ diǎn le
你的表几点了？（现在几点了？）
shí yī diǎn yí kè
十一点一刻。

(5) nǐ míng tiān jǐ diǎn lái wǒ jiā
你明天几点来我家？
jiǔ diǎn
九点。

(6) nǐ míng tiān zuò jǐ diǎn de fēi jī qù shàng hǎi
你明天坐几点的飞机去上海？
zuò xià wǔ sì diǎn èr shí fēn de fēi jī
坐下午四点二十分的飞机。

(7) nǐ huì qí zì xíng chē ma
你会骑自行车吗？
huì
会。

(8) nǐ jīn nián shàng qī nián jí hái shi bā nián jí
你今年上七年级还是八年级？
wǒ shàng qī nián jí
我上七年级。

(9) jīn tiān shì bā hào hái shi jiǔ hào
今天是八号还是九号？
jiǔ hào
九号。

(10) nǐ xǐ huan chūn tiān hái shi dōng tiān
你喜欢春天还是冬天？
wǒ xǐ huan dōng tiān
我喜欢冬天。

测验

1 Finish the following diagrams.

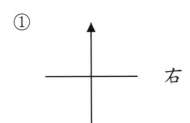 右   西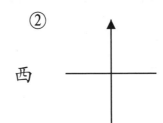

2 Find the odd one out.

(1) 飞机   火车   汽车   开车

(2) 分   上   刻   半

(3) 快   慢   晚   表

(4) 自行车   人力车   出租车   走路

(5) 在   来   去   到

(6) 春   笑   夏   秋

3 Fill in the blanks with the words in the box.

(1) 他每天_____电车上班。

(2) 我今天_____飞机去北京。

(3) 她明天_____自行车去公司。

(4) 我弟弟非常喜欢_____马。

(5) 他爸爸每天先_____船，然后_____地铁上班。

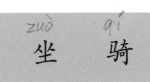

187

4 Fill in the blanks with the words in the box.

> 呢　吗　什么　几　多大　谁　哪　哪儿　怎么

(1) 你家人好_____?

(2) 我很好，你_____?

(3) 你姓_____?

(4) 他叫_____名字?

(5) 你的汉语老师住在_____?

(6) 她是_____?

(7) 你是_____国人?

(8) 你家有_____口人?

(9) 你每天_____上学?

(10) 你有_____个兄弟姐妹?

(11) 你妈妈会说汉语_____?

(12) 你哥哥_____了?（二十六岁）

(13) 你去过_____国家?

(14) 你家有_____?

(15) 你爸爸做_____工作?

(16) 你妈妈在_____工作?

(17) 你每天_____点上学?

(18) 你在_____个学校上学?

(19) 你妹妹今年_____岁了?（六岁）

(20) 你上_____年级?

(21) 现在_____点了?

(22) 你坐_____点的火车去南京?

5 Answer the following questions.

(1) 你每天几点上学？

(2) 你怎么上学？

(3) 你几点放学回家？

(4) 你喜欢你的学校吗？

(5) 你爸爸、妈妈工作吗？

(6) 他们怎么上班？

(7) 你妈妈会开车吗？

(8) 你坐过船吗？

(9) 你会骑自行车吗？

(10) 你骑过马吗？

(11) 你的表现在几点了？

(12) 你喜欢看英文书还是中文书？

6 Translation.

(1) I am taller than my younger brother.

(2) My elder brother is even taller.

(3) My father is the tallest.

(4) Trains are faster than cars.

(5) He is the tallest in the class.

(6) From 6:00 am to 7:00 am , I eat breakfast.

(7) My father first takes the train, and then walks to work everyday.

7 Translation.

(1) 去北京的飞机

(2) the express train to Shanghai

(3) 来香港的船

(4) the slow train to Nanjing

(5) 骑自行车的小孩儿

(6) the boy who can ride a bicycle

(7) 喜欢看书的同学

(8) the students who are going to America

8 Reading comprehension.

小红和哥哥都是小学生,在同一个小学上学。小红今年八岁,上小学三年级。哥哥今年十岁,上小学五年级。他们每天早上七点半先走路,然后坐校车上学。小红很喜欢写毛笔字,她每天都写毛笔字。哥哥最喜欢骑马,他每个星期六上午都去骑马。他们都喜欢看书。

Answer the questions.

(1) 小红今年几岁了?

(2) 小红的哥哥今年上几年级?

(3) 他们两个人每天几点上学?

(4) 他们怎么上学?

(5) 小红喜欢做什么?

(6) 她哥哥喜欢不喜欢骑马?

(7) 他们在同一个学校上学吗?

(8) 谁喜欢看书?

词汇表

A

ān	安	safe
ào	澳	inlet of the sea; bay
àodàlìyà	澳大利亚	Australia

B

bā	八	eight
bāhào	八号	the 8th
bā	巴	hope earnestly
bāxī	巴西	Brazil
bàba	爸爸	dad; father
bái	白	white
bān	班	class; shift
bàn	半	half
bāo	包	packet; bag
běi	北	north
běijīng	北京	Beijing
běiměizhōu	北美洲	Continent of North America
běn	本	root; origin
bí	鼻	nose
bízi	鼻子	nose
bǐ	笔	pen
bǐyǒu	笔友	penpal
bǐ	比	compare
biǎo	表	meter; watch
bù	不	not; no
búcuò	不错	not bad

C

cài	菜	vegetable; dish
cháng	长	long
chǎng	厂	factory
chē	车	vehicle
chéng	程	rule; order
chī	吃	eat
chīfàn	吃饭	eat; have a meal
chī zǎofàn	吃早饭	eat breakfast
chī wǔ/zhōngfàn	吃午／中饭	eat lunch
chī wǎnfàn	吃晚饭	eat dinner
chū	出	out; exit
chūshēng	出生	be born
chūzhū(qì)chē	出租（汽）车	taxi
chuán	船	boat; ship
chūn	春	spring
chūnjié	春节	the Chinese New Year
cóng	从	from
cóng...dǎo...	从……到……	from... to...
cuò	错	mistake; bad

D

dà	大	big
dà dìdi	大弟弟	big younger brother
dàgē	大哥	eldest brother
dàxiàng	大象	elephant
dàxuéshēng	大学生	university student
dàyángzhōu	大洋洲	Australasia; Oceania
dàifu	大夫	doctor
dàn	但	but; yet
dànshì	但是	but
dào	到	arrive; until
de	的	of; 's
dé	德	morals; virtue
déguó	德国	Germany
déyǔ	德语	German
děng	等	etc.; rank; wait
dìdi	弟弟	younger brother
dì	地	earth; fields; ground
dìfang	地方	place
dìtiě	地铁	underground
diǎn	点	dot; point; o'clock
diàn	电	electricity
diànchē	电车	tram
diàn	店	shop; store
dōng	东	east
dōngjīng	东京	Tokyo
dōng	冬	winter
dōu	都	all; both
duō	多	more; many
duō dà	多大	how old

E

ér	儿	child; son; suffix
érzi	儿子	son
ěr	耳	ear
èr	二	two
èrgē	二哥	second eldest brother

F

fǎ	法	law; method
fǎguó	法国	France
fǎyǔ	法语	French
fà	发	hair
fàn	饭	cooked rice; meal
fàndiàn	饭店	restaurant; hotel
fāng	方	square; direction
fāngyán	方言	dialect
fàng	放	let go
fàngxué	放学	finish school

fēi	飞	fly		hěnduō	很多	many
fēijī	飞机	plane		hěnhǎo	很好	very good; very well
fēi	非	wrong; not; no		hóng	红	red
fēizhōu	非洲	Africa		hóngbāo	红包	red packet
fēn	分	minute		hòu	后	behind; back
fū	夫	husband; man		hú	胡	surname
fù	妇	woman		hù	护	protect
fú	服	clothes; serve		hùshi	护士	nurse
fúwù	服务	service		huà	画	draw; paint
fúwùyuán	服务员	attendant		huà	话	word; talk
				huān	欢	merry
				huī	灰	grey
	G			huí	回	return
				huíjiā	回家	go home
gǎng	港	harbour		huì	会	can; meeting; party
gāo	高	high; tall		huǒ	火	fire
gēge	哥哥	elder brother		huǒchē	火车	train
gè	个	measure word (general)				
gèzi	个子	height; build				
gěi	给	give; for			**J**	
gèng	更	even more				
gèng kuài	更快	quicker		jī	机	machine; engine
gōng	工	work		jí	级	grade
gōngchǎng	工厂	factory		jǐ	几	how many; several
gōngchéngshī	工程师	engineer		jǐ diǎn	几点	what time
gōngzuò	工作	work		jǐ hào	几号	what date
gōng	公	public		jǐ kǒu rén	几口人	how many members in the family?
gōnggòng	公共	public				
gōnggòng qìchē	公共汽车	public bus		jǐ suì	几岁	how old
gōngsī	公司	company		jǐ yuè	几月	which month
gōng	弓	bow		jǐ	己	oneself
gòng	共	common; general		jì	季	season
gǔ	古	ancient		jiā	加	add
guāng	光	light; smooth		jiānádà	加拿大	Canada
guǎng	广	broad		jiā	家	family; home
guǎngdōng	广东	Guangdong, a province in China		jiātíng	家庭	family
				jiātíng zhǔfù	家庭主妇	housewife
guǎngdōnghuà	广东话	Cantonese		jiān	尖	tip; pointed; sharp
guó	国	country; kingdom		jiàn	见	see
guójiā	国家	country		jiào	叫	call
guò	过	pass; cross over; particle		jié	节	festival; knot; section
				jiějie	姐姐	elder sister
				jiè	界	boundary; scope
	H			jīn	今	today
				jīnnián	今年	this year
hái	还	also; fairly		jīntiān	今天	today
hái kěyǐ	还可以	OK; pretty good		jīnglǐ	经理	manager
háishi	还是	or		jīng	京	capital
hái	孩	child		jīng	经	manage
háizi	孩子	child; children		jiǔ	酒	alcoholic drink; wine
hǎi	海	sea		jiǔdiàn	酒店	hotel
hàn	汉	the Han nationality		jiǔ	九	nine
hànyǔ	汉语	Chinese				
háng	行	profession; business firm				
hǎo	好	good; well			**K**	
hǎo jǐ zhǒng	好几种	several kinds of				
hào	号	number; date		kǎ	卡	card
hé	和	and		kāi	开	drive; open; manage
hěn	很	very; quite		kāichē	开车	drive a car

kāikǒu	开口	open one mouth
kàn	看	see; look; watch
kànshū	看书	read a book
kě	可	can; may
kěshì	可是	but
kěyǐ	可以	can; pretty good
kè	刻	a quarter (of an hour)
kǒu	口	measure word; mouth
kuài	快	quick; fast
kuàichē	快车	express train or bus
kuài	筷	chopsticks

L

lái	来	come
lǎo	老	old
lǎoshī	老师	teacher
le	了	particle
lǐ	里	inside
lǐ	理	manage; natural science
lǐ	李	plum; surname
lì	力	power; strength
lìqi	力气	physical strength
lì	历	experience; calendar
lìshǐ	历史	history
lì	利	sharp; advantage; benefit
liǎng	两	two
liǎngdiǎn líng wǔfēn	两点零五分	five past two
liǎng ge dìdi	两个弟弟	two younger brothers
líng	零	zero
liù	六	six
lù	路	road; journey
lǜ	律	law; rule
lǜshī	律师	lawyer
lǜshīháng	律师行	law firm

M

mǎ	马	horse; surname
mǎláixīyà	马来西亚	Malaysia
ma	吗	particle
māma	妈妈	mum; mother
màn	慢	slow
mànchē	慢车	slow train
máo	毛	hair; wool
máobǐ	毛笔	writing brush
méi	没	no
méiyǒu	没有	not have; there is not
měi	美	beautiful
měiguó	美国	U.S.A.
měi	每	every
měitiān	每天	every day
mèimei	妹妹	younger sister
men	们	plural suffix
mén	门	door
mì	秘	secret
mìshū	秘书	secretary

míng	明	bright; clear
míngtiān	明天	tomorrow
míng	名	name
míngzi	名字	(given) name
mù	木	tree; wood
mù	目	eye

N

ná	拿	take
nà	那	that
nǎ	哪	which; what
nǎ guó rén	哪国人	what nationality
nǎi	奶	milk; grandmother
nǎinai	奶奶	grandmother
nán	南	south
nánfēi	南非	South Africa
nán měizhōu	南美洲	Continent of South America
nán	男	male
nǎr	哪儿	where
ne	呢	particle
nǐ	你	you
nǐhǎo	你好	hello
nǐhǎo ma	你好吗	how are you
nǐ ne	你呢	how about you
nǐzǎo	你早	good morning
nián	年	year
niánjí	年级	grade; year
nín	您	you (respectfully)
nínhǎo	您好	hello
nínzǎo	您早	good morning
nǚ	女	female
nǚshì	女士	Ms.; lady
nǚ'ér	女儿	daughter

O

ōu	欧	Europe; surname
ōuzhōu	欧洲	Europe

P

péng	朋	friend
péngyou	朋友	friend
pǔ	普	general; universal
pǔtōnghuà	普通话	Putonghua

Q

qī	七	seven
qīdiǎn bàn	七点半	half past seven
qī kǒu rén	七口人	seven members in the family
qī	期	a period of time
qí	骑	ride

qímǎ	骑马	ride a horse
qí zìxíngchē	骑自行车	ride a bicycle
qí	齐	in order; together
qì	汽	vapour; steam
qìchē	汽车	car; motor vehicle
qì	气	gas; air
qīn	亲	parent; relative
qīnpéng hǎoyǒu	亲朋好友	close friends
qiū	秋	autumn
qù	去	go
qù guo	去过	have been to
quán	全	whole
quánjiā	全家	the whole family

R

rán	然	right
ránhòu	然后	then; after that
rén	人	person; people
rénkǒu	人口	population
rì	日	sun; day
rìběn	日本	Japan
rìběnrén	日本人	Japanese
rìyǔ	日语	Japanese

S

sān	三	three
shān	山	mountain
shānlǐ	山里	in the mountains
shāng	商	trade; business
shāngrén	商人	businessman
shàng	上	up; previous; attend
shàngbān	上班	go to work
shànghǎi	上海	Shanghai
shàng wǔniánjí	上五年级	in Grade 5
shàngwǔ	上午	morning
shào	少	young
shēn	身	body
shēnxīn	身心	body and mind
shénme	什么	what
shēng	生	bear; grow
shēngrikǎ	生日卡	birthday card
shī	师	teacher; master
shí	十	ten
shíyī diǎn sānkè	十一点三刻	eleven forty-five
shíyī diǎn yíkè	十一点一刻	a quarter past eleven
shíyuè	十月	October
shí'èr suì	十二岁	twelve years old
shǐ	史	history
shì	世	lifetime; world
shìjiè	世界	world
shìjièshang	世界上	in the world
shì	士	scholar
shì	是	be
shǒu	手	hand

shū	书	book; write; script
shuí	谁	who
shuǐ	水	water
shuō	说	speak; talk; say
sī	司	take charge of
sījī	司机	driver
sì	四	four
sì diǎn	四点	four o'clock
suì	岁	year of age

T

tā	他	he; him
tā	她	she; her
tāmen	他们	they; them
tài	太	too
tàitai	太太	Mrs.; madame
tiān	天	sky; day
tiāntiān	天天	every day
tián	田	field
tiě	铁	iron
tíng	庭	front; courtyard
tōng	通	open; through
tóng	同	same; like
tóngxué	同学	schoolmate
tóu	头	head
tǔ	土	soil

W

wǎn	晚	evening; late
wǎnshang	晚上	evening
wáng	王	king; surname
wén	文	word; literature
wèn	问	ask
wǒ	我	I; me
wǒde	我的	my; mine
wǒmen	我们	we; us
wū	乌	black; dark
wú	吴	surname
wǔ	五	five
wǔ	午	noon
wù	务	affair; business

X

xī	西	west
xī'ān	西安	Xi'an
xǐ	喜	happy; like
xǐhuan	喜欢	like; be fond of
xià	下	below; next; get off
xiàbān	下班	go off work
xiàwǔ	下午	in the afternoon
xià	夏	summer
xiān	先	first of all
xiānsheng	先生	Mr.; husband; teacher

194

xiān..., ránhòu...	先……，然后……	first..., then...
xiàn	现	present
xiànzài	现在	now
xiāng	香	fragrant
xiānggǎng	香港	Hong Kong
xiǎng	想	think; want to; would like to
xiàng	象	elephant
xiǎo	小	small; little
xiǎo dìdi	小弟弟	little younger brother
xiǎoxuéshēng	小学生	primary school student
xiào	校	school
xiàochē	校车	school bus
xiào	笑	smile; laugh
xiě	写	write
xiè	谢	thank
xièxie	谢谢	thanks
xīn	心	heart
xīng	星	star
xīngqī	星期	week
xīngqīyī	星期一	Monday
xīngqījǐ	星期几	what day of the week
xīngqīrì / tiān	星期日／天	Sunday
xíng	行	go; travel
xìng	姓	surname
xiōng	兄	elder brother
xiōngdì jiěmèi	兄弟姐妹	brothers and sisters
xué	学	study
xuésheng	学生	student
xuéxiào	学校	school

Y

yá	牙	tooth
yà	亚	second; Asia
yàzhōu	亚洲	Asia
yán	言	speech; say
yáng	洋	ocean
yé	爷	grandfather
yéye	爷爷	grandfather
yě	也	also; as well
yī	一	one
yìdiǎnr	一点儿	a little bit
yí ge gē ge	一个哥哥	one elder brother
yìjiārén	一家人	one family
yìnián sìjì	一年四季	throughout the year
yìqí	一齐	together
yī	医	medicine
yīshēng	医生	doctor
yīyuàn	医院	hospital
yǐ	以	use; take
yǐhòu	以后	after
yín	银	silver
yínháng	银行	bank
yínhángjiā	银行家	banker
yīng	英	hero
yīngguó	英国	Britain
yīngguórén	英国人	the British

yīngyǔ	英语	English
yòng	用	use
yǒu	有	have; there is
yǒu	友	friend
yòu	右	right
yǔ	语	language
yǔyán	语言	language
yuán	员	member
yuàn	院	courtyard
yuè	月	the moon; month
yún	云	cloud

Z

zài	再	again
zàijiàn	再见	good-bye
zài	在	in; on
zǎo	早	early; morning
zǎoshang	早上	early morning
zěn	怎	why; how
zěnme	怎么	how
zhāng	张	surname; measure word
zhǎng	长	grow; senior; eldest
zhǎngdà	长大	grow up
zhàng	丈	a form of address
zhàngfu	丈夫	husband
zhè	这	this
zhōng	中	middle; centre
zhōngguó	中国	China
zhōngguórén	中国人	Chinese
zhōngwén	中文	the Chinese language
zhōngwǔ	中午	noon
zhōngxuéshēng	中学生	secondary school student
zhǒng	种	type; race; seed
zhōu	洲	continent
zhú	竹	bamboo
zhúkuài	竹筷	bamboo chopsticks
zhǔ	主	major
zhù	住	live; reside
zǐ	子	son
zì	自	self; oneself
zìjǐ	自己	oneself
zìxíngchē	自行车	bicycle
zì	字	character; word
zǒu	走	walk
zǒulù	走路	walk
zū	租	rent; hire
zú	足	foot
zuì	最	most
zuìkuài	最快	the fastest
zuó	昨	yesterday
zuótiān	昨天	yesterday
zuò	坐	travel by; sit
zuò xiàochē	坐校车	take the school bus
zuǒ	左	left
zuò	做	make; do
zuò	作	do; work

195